97

Morris Kaufman became interested and involved in the education and training of young people when he was Chief Training Adviser of the Rubber and Plastics Industry Training Board. He is currently Chairman of Youthaid. As Chairman of the Governors of the Polytechnic of North London he appreciates the unity between education and training.

Sheila Marsh is head of the support unit to the GLC's Greater London Training Board. She previously worked at the Hotel and Catering Industry Training Board.

Anna Pollert is currently researching youth unemployment and training in the West Midlands. She has written on women and work and racism and the Youth Training Scheme.

Eric Robinson is the Director of Lancashire Polytechnic and has been a Vice President of the Socialist Education Association for almost 20 years. He was formerly a teacher of mathematics and has been a member of many national committees including the NUT executive, Council for National Academic Awards, the Equal Opportunities Commission, the Burnham Committee and UNESCO.

Clare Short has been MP for Birmingham Ladywood since June 1983. Since January 1985 she has been a junior front-bench spokesperson on employment for the Labour Party. Between 1979 and 1983 she was Director of Youthaid, and she was Director of the Unemployment Unit until 1984. Her contribution to this book is written in a personal capacity and is not necessarily the view of the Labour Party or other members of the front-bench team.

Challenging the MSC

On Jobs, Training and Education

Edited by Caroline Benn and
John Fairley

Pluto  Press

London   Sydney   Dover New Hampshire

First published in 1986 by Pluto Press Limited,
The Works, 105a Torriano Avenue, London NW5 2RX
and Pluto Press Australia Limited, PO Box 199, Leichhardt,
New South Wales 2040, Australia. Also Pluto Press,
51 Washington Street, Dover, New Hampshire 03820 USA

Copyright © Caroline Benn, Clyde Chitty, John Eversley, John Fairley,
Dan Finn, Leisha Fullick, Andy Green, Mark Jackson, Morris Kaufman,
Sheila Marsh, Anna Pollert, Eric Robinson and Clare Short, 1986

7   6   5   4   3   2   1

90   89   88   87   86

Phototypeset by AKM Associates (UK) Limited,
Ajmal House, Hayes Road, Southall, London
Printed in Great Britain by Guernsey Press Co. Ltd.
Guernsey, C.I.

British Library Cataloguing in Publication Data
Challenging the MSC on jobs, training and education.
   1. Great Britain, *Manpower Services Commission*
   I. Benn, Caroline   II. Fairley, John
   331.12'042   HD5915.A6

ISBN 0 7453 0095 2

Contents

Acknowledgements

The authors would like to thank Archie Fairley, Alec Gordon and Narendra Makanji for their help.

Introduction: Towards an Alternative Policy for Jobs, Training and Education

Caroline Benn and John Fairley

The Manpower Services Commission started in 1974 as a small public agency. Since then successive governments have turned it into a huge organization whose activities are changing the nature of British society – in particular jobs, training and education.

Those contributing to this book believe that the MSC's activities are now so potentially disastrous that Britain's social wellbeing and economic recovery require a complete break with its present policy. Most believe as well that the crisis in training and education – but particularly in jobs – is so great that we also need a policy of social transformation far more radical than any yet devised.

It is hard for those new to the MSC to understand why this apparently inoffensive section of the civil service has become so controversial – apart from its colossal growth. To read that the MSC has become bureaucratic or inefficient is one thing, but to hear repeatedly that the MSC has now become a new instrument of state power that is being grossly misused, requires more explanation.

The MSC didn't start out deserving its new street name: the Ministry of Social Control. It was a Conservative act of parliament, true; but apart from its sexist title, uncontroversial. Its task was straightforward: to plan jobs for the future, particularly in public industries. Initially indeed, the TUC had a lot of influence on the MSC's shape.

The MSC had cross-party support, as had policy from 1964 giving major sectors of industry – like engineering or catering – their own training boards (ITBs). It made sense to have a single government agency to co-ordinate their activity and see that work in the new technologies was encouraged and people trained for it. Contrary to propaganda from the political Right during the 1960s and 1970s about progressive reforms going too far – particularly in education, the real truth was that Britain lagged behind all comparable countries in both its education and training systems.

Today it lags even further – in part because of the MSC's failure to do what it was supposed to do.

The charges

Thus the first charge is that the MSC didn't plan new jobs and get the much-needed new skill training launched throughout British industry. Indeed, as these essays show, genuine skills training has been decimated by MSC activity through destruction of the training boards, closure of the skills centres, and the progressive eradication of apprenticeships. Apart from a brief period which started in 1975, the MSC had no links with job creation.

Almost every essay in this book documents this failure, which is serious enough, but nothing like as serious as the next: that the MSC has changed its whole nature as an organization and betrayed its original brief by turning its attention to job destruction. The whole reason for the MSC's existence was – and is – to manage employment and help in the process of structured change. Yet today almost all its work is bound up with managing unemployment, including changing the boundaries between employment and unemployment.

The swift rise in unemployment during the last decade was not the MSC's fault – it was the fault of an inevitably malfunctioning world capitalism, made worse by the inadequate economic policies of successive governments. But all the more reason why the MSC's original role was so essential. Yet instead of sticking to this brief, the MSC surreptitiously dropped it, changed its direction and adopted a quite different objective: that of preparing a nation to accept job losses and worklessness as permanent features of our social landscape.

Such an unpopular objective required a sustained strategy of deceit for, of course, the MSC's 'turnaround' was never publicly proclaimed. It was accomplished, as several chapters show, by the mechanism of starting – and then cancelling – one job creation and training 'scheme' after another in relatively rapid succession over a few crucial years. Changes were touted as 'improvements' when, in fact, with each successive reshaping of a scheme, the pay, conditions, standards and choice for those receiving MSC 'help' became progressively less favourable.

A veneer of credibility, however, has been preserved. As this book shows, a few of the MSC programmes do involve genuine education and training, or assistance for entrepreneurial activity, particularly for the professional middle class. But such shop-front activity is very small-scale compared to the two programmes that dominate the MSC's £2 billion budget and account for most of its staffing: the Youth Training Scheme (YTS) and the Community Programme (CP). These are what the MSC is really about – not about 'high tech' industries, high-skills training for young people and adults, or extension of comprehensive education for the majority, but about 'work schemes' for the working class – especially its poorest section.

Although in public view the old objectives of jobs, training and education were and are still being claimed, fewer and fewer adults or young people are getting jobs after MSC schemes, and most are being trained in no real skills at all. Most are getting nothing in the way of education either, despite highly publicized paper planning, including the Task Group Report. Indeed, throughout education the 'new vocationalism' is narrowing educational experience and denying choice to the majority. Ever larger areas of the curriculum in schools and colleges are being redirected to limited commercial ends and leading to losses of significant academic freedoms for staff and students alike. MSC activity in education is also being used as a stick to enforce lower wages and poorer working conditions on teachers and lecturers, particularly in further education.

The 'new training philosophy' of MSC schemes is being used to break people, especially working-class young people, into a life of low wages and long periods of poor employment – because this is all employers have to offer them in a market economy. Employers take part because they are able to substitute MSC-paid 'trainees' for waged workers, and so realize large savings on labour costs.

Although MSC schemes often offer welcome comradeship and a temporary relief from worklessness, those experiencing them know they are more often than not being put to work in menial employment and paid a rock-bottom 'allowance' or 'wage' that gets lower every year, since neither is pegged to inflation. They also know that the 'training' or 'work' is temporary, despite the promise 'hidden' in much MSC propaganda about YTS and the CP that they will ensure people will be better placed to get work afterwards.

Although lack of genuine skills training and denial of equal educational choice cause some disillusion, most of those with no choice but MSC schemes never had any education or training in times past. Deception in these two areas is nothing like as deeply felt as the failure of YTS and the CP to lead to permanent, real work. For everyone once had jobs.

As these chapters show, there is widespread hostility associated with YTS – and increasingly the Community Programme – on the grounds of pay received for contribution made. Regardless of whether people get training or jobs, and certainly in the case of the vast majority who fail to get both, young and old feel their labour has been exploited. They have created wealth for employers, but none has been returned to them. Despite tireless MSC propaganda, this near-universal reaction pervades the popular perception of MSC activity and in the long term possibly forms the most powerful charge of all.

These charges against the MSC cannot be divorced from the policies directing its work. The MSC is part of the Department of Employment and was created to provide a public service under the control of elected governments. Labour governments from 1974 to 1979, thrown off any socialist course by successive crises, and as unsure about what policy to pursue with the MSC as with everything else, alternated between using the MSC as a training agency and using it to cover up unemployment. The MSC's change in role began during this period of Labour's embarrassment at rising unemployment when MSC palliatives were a cheap way of concealing the reality; and the Youth Opportunities Programme, the precursor of YTS, was started by Labour in 1978 at the request of the TUC.

Conservatives had no embarrassment or hesitation once they had decided to keep the MSC in 1981. They used it single-mindedly in the service of monetarism. They wanted to reorganize the labour market to suit employers. From that point onwards the MSC's destructive role became more prominent, its faults more extreme, and deception a way of life.

Conservatives continue to claim to be concerned to provide jobs for school leavers, but leaving everything to 'the market' has meant progressively – and largely secretly – planning to close down work for everyone under 18. By 1986 YTS meant keeping young people for two years, after which they are on the dole or in work that would have been available anyway – but with this major difference: their pay, conditions, prospects, training and education are all inferior compared to the standards previous generations have enjoyed or those they could enjoy today were society organized differently.

As the unemployment crisis escalates, the Community Programme is being misused in the same way: turned from a scheme to meet community needs by providing permanent jobs doing work that society requires, into a 'recycling' process for long-term unemployed doing the often menial jobs employers want done at the pitiful 'rates' employers are being permitted to get away with paying.

Conservatives' misuse of MSC schemes as instruments to attack the poor – consciously intended to lower wages and worsen conditions of work as well as to enforce acceptance of unemployment or intermittent work as a fact of life – is a travesty of the MSC's original brief.

Misusing the MSC to attack labour goes hand in hand with reinforcement of race and sex discrimination in jobs, training and education – despite much-publicized policies proclaiming 'equality of opportunity' as an MSC 'goal'. The chapters on race and sex inequality are perhaps the most damning of all, testimony to the destructive effects of a national policy which enshrines employers' needs above all others, and thus also enshrines employers' prejudices and backward practices.

An ideology leaving everything to market forces not only makes employers the only ones who can 'give' people jobs – and whose voice is allowed to count – but makes private employers count first among the equals. They, and the many private managing agencies the MSC has created to provide them with trainees, often pocket cash given for training and put the 'trainees' to do their dirtiest short-term jobs. Again, it is 'understood' behind the scenes that 'training places' are provided to cut employers' labour costs rather than to meet any long-term social needs or skill requirements.

Privatization of its own public services – like the skillcentres – is another MSC abuse, for such services were always intended to be open to the whole community as a community service. Now they are being given over to private owners for their own use and profit making. In addition, the government has handed over large sections of education and training to unaccountable private agencies – many in it for the profit they can make at trainees' expense. The disappearance of public accountability for the standards of so much education and training – particularly for young people – is a national dereliction of public duty that will take years to correct.

The MSC: facing judgement in its own right

The MSC is no longer the service to the whole community it was intended to be when parliament set it up, but an organization serving the interests of a small group of largely white, middle-class males: the nation's employers. As a result, it has developed not only its own policy but very specific ways of working. It has to be judged in its own right, as well as in the light of its use, or misuse, by governments.

The MSC has not only grown in size but in range of activities. At the start its role was meant to be strictly limited – only concerned with broad trends, forecasting and providing general national guidelines. Gradually, however, it has invaded and taken over much of the work of other departments and national agencies, pushing beyond its assigned territory – virtually to subordinate the national Careers Service, for example. Its YTS controls entry to employment for school leavers. Its Jobcentre staff regulate entry to adult employment. It has invaded deeply the Department of Education, displacing traditional supervision for curriculum and examinations by pushing its own directives into schools and colleges.

Today the MSC's command comprises a huge network of regional and local offices and an army of enforcement personnel. Its dictatorial methods have drawn fire from critics across the political spectrum. In education, for example, the MSC departed from all accepted democratic conventions by announcing it was commandeering a quarter of all further education in England and Wales, and, earlier, inserting new vocational sectors into schools. Both major changes were announced without warning – with negotiation on the fundamental principles not possible, and no attempt made to consult representatives of those who will experience the changes or who must carry them out. To ensure compliance with its directives and policies the MSC uses public funding as its own personal blackmail. MSC policies have curtailed many generally accepted freedoms – again making it the target of libertarian critics from left, right and centre. This includes directives forbidding discussion of social and political issues in certain schemes. Not only are education, training and work to be recast, but so too, it appears, is the way in which people think about these activities.

The humanities and social studies are being progressively squeezed into an ever smaller space. Components of vocational or training schemes ensuring the development of the skills of critical enquiry – particularly those associated with high-level general education – are being reduced or atomized under the banner of the 'new vocationalism'. Under that of the 'new training' philosophy trainees are being policed for thought as well as behaviour, backed by DHSS enforcement of benefit withdrawal.

Social engineering on this scale has rarely been attempted in Britain and has been made possible by ignoring the forms of democratic accountability normally practised by governments. The MSC is supposed to be under the same kind of democratic control as any other part of the civil service, its legal position exactly comparable to the Health and Safety Executive. It is hard to imagine the latter dictating policy over so wide an area in the way the MSC has become used to doing.

It could be said that creating a 'Commission' to run Manpower Services is part of the problem, for it could have made the MSC see itself mistakenly as a quango – that is, an organization intended to act independently of representative government and provided with accountability machinery to do so. The MSC acts on its own alright, but it has no accountability machinery. It is run entirely from the top down. All its boards – both national and local area boards – are created by appointment from overseeing bodies.

There is no mechanism for representative elections, nor for election from those working in the MSC or participating in its schemes. Nothing comes from the bottom up as in properly constituted democratic activity. Even if there were representative reconstitution, boards are often so ill served with information, time or power that their overseeing function is totally impossible to perform.

Meanwhile, those at the receiving end have few rights and little say. Nor has the electorate power to change matters locally. Only the slimmest tie to elected democracy exists, and that is at the very top through the occasional parliamentary select committee review which requires government ministers to answer questions about the MSC. Even this disappears when the minister in question is a member of the House of Lords, as was the case when Lord Young was appointed a minister.

As many chapters show, the MSC's dynamic is also a centralizing one. Its commands come not only from the top down, but from the centre outwards. Its objectives for work, education and unemployment require only that MSC orders are carried out. There is no need for feedback or discussion.

It is an irony that in order to promote a 'free' economy so much denial of freedom and such dictatorial methods – beyond precedent in recent history – are having to be used. No wonder many Conservatives believe Conservatives have now become their own worst caricature of socialism: the party of a bureaucratic and centralized state, riding roughshod over individuals in pursuit of a doctrinaire objective.

Disturbing as the methods are, it is the doctrine that is the heart of the fault. For an ideology that 'leaves everything to the market' requires coercive methods in the end. It may start by claiming that its methods will create jobs, new technology will be wisely used, people will be rewarded for effort and society will prosper. But the policy does not work. The more it fails the greater the temptation to rely on the iron hand of the MSC.

The MSC can rely on a glossy publicity and press department to provide the velvet glove. No expense is spared in MSC promotions and Saatchi and Saatchi – who 'marketed' Mrs Thatcher – were paid over £1 million to 'sell' YTS alone. One of their advertisements showed bowler-hatted businessmen lying down in the City of London, with the caption, "A Scheme to Put Business Back on its Feet".

At least this was honest about those people MSC activity is intended to benefit: the same business community which owns most of the mass media. Not surprisingly, the media has acted as a tame conduit for all MSC output – not like in the 1960s and 1970s when it found room for endless, savaging reports on every aspect of progressive reform, be it comprehensive schools or industrial democracy. When it comes to the far more extreme changes and highly controversial methods in use today, there is a startling absence of sustained critical comment.

The public at large is thus unaware of the MSC's secret and undemocratic decision-making, its dictatorial imposition of directives on local authorities and voluntary organizations, and the irrational way in which its policy fluctuates – opening schemes or centres one year and shutting them the next – making continuity and long-term planning virtually impossible.

The public may have heard a little about the MSC's failures to maintain safe conditions on its schemes – a succession of deaths is hard to hide entirely – but it knows next to nothing of many schemes with faulty quality monitoring or absent evaluation; or of the large amounts of money being poured into employers' and managing agents' pockets with scant accountability required.

By any of the criteria of democratic debate these essays point to a major national scandal, yet with a few exceptions, the media let it pass, and consequently protect the slipshod arrangements that all too often pass for 'quality' courses of education and training in so many little sweatshops or battery hen training houses. No investigative journalism there.

What the public is allowed to hear about are the good things: the small percentage of young people who still get real training, and occasionally rigorous general education through specific MSC programmes (for which selection and resulting inequality are far worse than anything the 11-plus ever imposed). There have been a few good adult training programmes too, especially in the early days. But the evidence in this book suggests that not only are there more excellent training and education advances outside the MSC, but that within it quality appears by chance rather than design, the outcome of commitment by dedicated teachers, trainers and workers advancing new practices in spite of – rather than because of – MSC directives. Often good practice is achieved only because teachers and trainees are willing to risk their jobs by deliberately ignoring the MSC's restrictive objectives.

Blame the victims

However, the media's complicity is much deeper than mere failure to provide the proper critical commentary that democracy requires. For at least a decade they have actively colluded with successive governments in placing the blame on the victims themselves. This is a strategy to convince the public that the problem is located not in the system but in the people, especially those experiencing the most difficulty. The problem is people's 'failure' to have the 'right' qualifications or approach, or the defects in the institutions and organizations they have fashioned for their use.

The fault was with the trade unions, so propaganda went, for being greedy and self-defeating in asking for living wages or safe working environments (as agitators were once blamed for nine-teenth-century poverty); or it was with the schools (but only comprehensive ones) for failing to give the right academic qualifications, or contradictorily, giving academic education rather than vocational 'relevance'; or the trouble was in colleges (in the further education sector, never the universities) for being 'out of date'. If you were a woman or black, you particularly 'lacked' expertise that would make you employable. If you were young, your aspirations or independence created attitudes that were a 'problem' to employers who might otherwise give you work. And always: only employers had the right or knowledge to define employability.

The MSC could help, so continued the propaganda, seeming in the process to promise everyone jobs through a high-tech paradise to be provided by market forces, if only people would submit to the discipline of Conservative strategy for remoulding work and education and training through the MSC. But the policy has been a failure. British industry is not investing adequately in new technology, and even if it were, high-tech development will not create work for more than a small number of people, since, arguably, it destroys more jobs than it creates. Nor will work be provided by the MSC's massive expenditure of public money, because this expenditure is not for the purpose of creating real jobs, but for the opposite purpose of alleviating unemployment through 'schemes'. At the very kindest we might say it was trying to ease the patient's symptoms rather than cure the illness.

Neither YTS nor the CP creates a single job for participants; they simply redistribute the burden of unemployment through schemes of temporary 'work' and 'training'. In many cases MSC schemes have taken over real jobs and turned them into poorly paid 'work experience' instead. This is happening now throughout the public and private sectors. Conditions of labour are being systematically worsened and the clock turned back to Victorian values.

We have to go a long way back in history to find comparable social 'reform' – where something was being done for those without work in ways that were so highly favoured by the establishment but so completely unacceptable to those supposed to benefit. One such time was the 1830s when 'workhouses' were started by the enlightened ruling class – many with the best intentions – to deal with the dislocation of the first industrial revolution.

Workhouses were repudiated by the poor from the start. Dickens set out their iniquities in *Oliver Twist* a bare three years after parliament had passed the legislation and many chapters in this book – as well as many anti-MSC cartoons – turn automatically to Dickensian imagery when recording today's popular verdict on MSC work schemes. The comfortably off Victorians found hatred of their benevolent projects hard to understand; the poor should be grateful that so much was 'being done for them'. Unless you have a radical perspective, it is easy to fall into this same trap today.

Matters did not improve for the majority in Victorian times until they organized themselves – and fought for change; and later for democratic rights. That is why the next charge against the MSC is so serious: that through its activity many of these hard-won improvements and rights are being eroded just as society returns to the age of an ever-widening gap between rich and poor.

Particularly significant is the way in which two MSC partners – government and employers – have repeatedly sanctioned MSC developments which sharply reduce the effectiveness of the third: the trade unions. Thus the main lifeline of those caught in MSC schemes is being frayed at a time when so many are reaching for help. This includes those who work for the MSC, many of whom suffer insecurity, low pay and incredible overwork; while others – like many in the Careers Service – feel they are being manipulated to act as gatekeepers to a system they no longer accept but cannot alter.

Although new forms of union organization have not yet materialized to tap most of it, resistance to all MSC activity is widespread and growing. Fear of unrest reinforces the government's original wish to make MSC work schemes compulsory, although employers and the TUC persuaded the government otherwise because of fear of even greater unrest if it did.

Agitators often get the blame for opposition, as in the widespread schoolchildren's strike of 1985. However, anyone close to events knows outsiders are not required to stir up feeling against MSC schemes. No group is more knowledgeable about YTS, for example, than those about to experience it, unless it is those who just have. The miracle is that there has not been more unrest.

The government has relied on indirect coercion: the withholding of supplementary benefit, 21-hour rules against sustained studying in full-time education, the cutting of youth housing benefits – all cruel and petty deprivations, to force young people on to MSC schemes. Had either government or employers, or TUC or opposition parties for that matter, been quite sure that what was being offered was really the wonderful opportunity propaganda claimed, there would have been no need for discussion, either way, of how to get places filled.

Despite all pressure, thousands refuse YTS or leave it midway. Many new forms of activity to initiate change are taking place – from informal discussion inside schemes (despite bans on such discussion) to the National Enquiry into Training, set up in 1983 by Trades Councils, Labour local councils and voluntary pressure groups. Much of this new thinking has been initiated outside traditional left or political groupings as well as below the top levels of TUC and Labour Party machinery – as if, somehow, people experiencing the old problems all over again are having to organize all over again, from the bottom up.

Education and Training

Every chapter in this book contains evidence of the MSC as an increasingly sinister corporate creature, and of the negative ways in which it is being used: to smash apprenticeship training, undermine the Industrial Training Board tradition of planning, corrupt comprehensive education, harness the curriculum to commerce, deskill thousands of workers, push trade unions to the margin of debate, exclude many women and most blacks and Asians from the best jobs, depress wages, and redefine poverty downwards – while protecting the privileges of all elites and diverting ever-increasing public funding to private education, private training and private employers.

To many the answer might seem obvious: scrap the MSC and you have got rid of the problem. But it is not that simple. The MSC may be greater than the sum of its parts, but there can be no alternative without changes in policy affecting the parts as well.

Different commentators differ in their weighting of the blame for present difficulties between government, employers and TUC, but most cite government policy as central. In many cases that includes the policies of all governments in the last decade. It was Labour's muddled 'SDP consensus' course of the 1970s that weakened social resistance and allowed the virulent Conservatism of the 1980s to get its hold.

In education and training it was the Great Debate of 1976 that marked the significant shift from support for continued comprehensive reform towards emphasis on schooling's 'relevance' to industry – not in terms of a radical and genuinely comprehensive extension of high-quality education and training for all alike, so long neglected by the Left – but in terms of more attention to 'needs' as employers saw them. This allowed Conservatives to instal 'employer need' as the dominant criterion of their own training and education policy and thus to go much further than the mere reinstatement of differentiation and selection in schools' and colleges' organization, curriculum and exams, or mere increases in subsidies and legal protection for private education at the expense of the public services.

It was not enough merely to halt the forward march of a high-standard general education for all – going on for two decades in the name of comprehensive change, even though it had not got very far. There also had to be a significant drive backwards, to undermine existing change and forestall any radical future policy. Several chapters point to the alarm in high places at the way increased educational opportunities in the 1960s and 1970s had raised people's general level of understanding and consequently their expectations. A market-led society, no longer able to meet expectations, required the decision by Conservatives to control curriculum centrally in order to dampen social aspiration. In the words of one DES official, making sure education enabled people 'to know their place once more'.[1]

Hierarchy and apartheid having been forcefully reinstated as desirable goals, new policy could appear to be as 'innovative' as it liked, for any change would only reinforce – even validate – the divisive structures. The 'new vocationalism' and the 'new training philosophy' both kill two birds with one ideological stone: they protect ruling elites' positions while at the same time dismantling the majority's gains and rearranging their education and training 'anew'. Deeply characteristic of each is that – with the exception of the proliferation of business and technological courses for further and higher education and attempts to limit study of the humanities (the changes the new political Right object to) – the educational institutions, examination paths, curriculum and professional training of Britain's ruling elites, academic or social, are not being much disturbed by government policy. Most changes in fact strengthen their positions, and they are the last to experience cuts.

All the change, all the radical rearrangement (including rationalization of institutions and qualifications) are being directed at the majority's education and training alone. Several authors are critical of the failure of progressive education to stake out its territory and prevent the formation of a vocational corral, for again this has not only opened the way to development of reactionary policies but has enabled the government to commandeer and misuse 'progressive rhetoric' and methods to promote them. Schemes like YTS, the Technical and Vocational Education Initiative (TVEI) in schools, or the Certificate of Prevocational Education in colleges (CPVE) are promoted under the camouflage of 'experiential' and 'negotiated' learning, choice, quality control, equality, profiling and 'transferable' skills, while what is being experienced is often loss of quality, denial of choice, social control, narrowing of the curriculum, reinforcement of inequality and the raising of many new exam barriers within the assessment system. Of course there are advances being made, and we should spotlight their continuing development, as do several contributors to this volume. But far too much of the new vocationalism and the new training seem to involve the writing in of content and process for commerce, while writing out the general skills of critical analysis and conceptual understanding.

John White sums it up well, 'The great mass of the population are thought to need education that fits them for certain kinds of jobs and gives them no deeper understanding of society as a whole than their particular role requires, while those who belong to the ruling elite are held to need a more rounded education'.[2] By a sleight of hand the rigorous comprehensive education once intended for everyone becomes the property of the elite, while the majority's watchword continues to be limitation, extending particularly to 'deeper' understanding'. Literally and figuratively, education should see to it that not too many people 'get ideas'. It could be dangerous.

The division between academic-rich and academic-poor is not new, of course; nor is institutional and course apartheid. What is new is the justification of a limited education for the majority, and the capping of ideas, in the name of the needs of their future work roles. Extension capitalizing on fear of unemployment's effects rather than out of any wish to extend comprehensive training and education to all lies behind the great sea change which has taken place since 1983. In that year only a minority stayed on after 16 for education or training; today the majority do.

This momentous extension has taken full advantage of a national consensus that comes but once in every few generations, the last one being embodied in the 1944 Education Act, when all sides agreed about the need for 'secondary education for all after 11'. This time it is the need for 'education and training for all after 16' that is agreed.

But what kind of education and training? What kind of system? There is no consensus on this, and several contributors to this book are rightly critical of the failure of progressive education to stake out the territory of comprehensive reform from 13-plus to 19 years, and to set the principles for an integrated training and education in a new unified system. With no criteria to guide the great sea change, Conservatives have been free to reorganize it for narrow market-led purposes, using much the same methods as a Labour government chose in 1945: a 'separate but equal' segregation of the majority in a tertiary modern sector guarded by a 16-plus (which actually starts at 13-plus) matching the earlier creation of a secondary modern sector guarded by an 11-plus (which actually started at 7-plus).

There is even the same revived attempt at a segregated 'technical' layer, and in time, the process of financial support for grammar schools after the 1944 Act (making them free for all who were selected for them) will be matched by educational maintenance allowances for all full-time students over 16 (making more staying on for full-time academic education possible). This may well be a positive step but if the past is any guide, by itself it will do little for equality. It is no substitute for the comprehensive reorganization of institutions, curriculum and assessment of the 16–19 system.

Challenging the 16-plus

Considering the fact that the Labour Party itself never accepted the Labour government policy of 1945 and had forced its leadership to change by 1955 to a comprehensive policy which eventually won wide agreement across society, it is surprising that so few are mounting any of the same principled opposition to similar government policy today. Indeed, it is more common to hear disavowal of past overconcentration on reorganization and failure to deal with curriculum and assessment change, as if the point was not that all three must take place simultaneously, and that what was wrong in the past, particularly in comprehensive reform after 1964, was that only one was attempted.

None of these tasks is being attempted now either, although we can often hear leisurely discussions of what some future opposition government will or should do in the way of tertiary reform, many taking part not appearing to notice that tertiary reform has already taken place under our noses. It escapes us because it was entirely in a backwards direction and we are used to changes taking society forward. It escapes us too because the Left has also been more concerned with how the academic elite are educated than, for example, with comprehensive vocational development for all.

After decades of struggle to end the '11-plus process' within education, it is not only back, it is stronger. In 1945 it was merely a case of our challenging the assumption that future capacity – and present educational choice – should not be determined by present academic attainment; today, not only does this have to be challenged all over again, but so too does the barrier to present choice determined by assumed future work roles. In dealing with this point where work and learning meet, we come to the heart of what educational injustice has always been about, even if never explicitly stated: learning determined not just by attainment levels at the time of leaving compulsory education but by a person's assumed future relationship to work; and work determined by sex, race, social background and financial circumstances. Challenging society's allocation of work roles is thus at the heart of today's resistance to the selective process.

In challenging the 16-plus, the Left also has its own conflicts to resolve. Several of the chapters in this book show an apparent difference of view between, on the one hand, those who believe that the working class can best control its own entry into adulthood, and later its own social and economic development, by the work process and skills training for it, and, on the other, those who argue that such control only comes through mastery of the dominant culture, and change only through gaining the capabilities provided by mainstream general education.

The conflict is only apparent, however, for implicit in all the authors' writing is the assumption that both high-level training and high-level education are required for adequate control, and that the purpose of the integration of education and training – the object of change – must be to give experience of both to everyone as of right, regardless of the route chosen initially. This requires disowning the false debate which has become embedded in labour movement thinking – as in the Labour Party's Clause 4, which speaks of 'workers by hand or brain'. All work involves both hand and brain; and needs both education and training, not one or the other.

There needs to be a recognition of the legitimacy of education through the training process and through work, and at the same time acknowledgement of the central importance of a high-quality general education for everyone, regardless of the work they want to do or the training they undertake. Working out this synthesis is what the Left should be doing, not spending its energy colluding with a conservative consensus to argue the merits of a new grading system for A level, an examination less than one in five are even permitted to enter.

These essays do not set out the new synthesis in any detail but suggest that any attempt to develop education apart from training, or vice versa, would widen the chasm between them, postpone the majority's educational rights indefinitely, and continue to support the misuse of training as a substitute for work.

Training policy at present has practically nothing to do with real skills training. Young people in most cases are being fobbed off with largely meaningless 'skills' which they could learn in a day, perhaps in two weeks. Certification is often bogus, YTS instructors even on occasion falsifying reports on young people's training experience. Government propaganda is patronizing and insulting – as with David Young's assertion that a YTS certificate is worth more than an A-level pass – when most trainees and workers know that under present policy they only find work when training allowances and wages come to reflect the 'real state' of the depressed market.

Training content is employer-determined and employers' perspectives are even transported into schools and colleges. Education within training schemes – particularly general education – will never be developed until it is part of the mainstream process of comprehensive curriculum development.

Our policy has to be on our terms, not theirs. Education and training require democratic organization honouring people's right to choose the education they want, regardless of the choice of work that may be available. It carries with it the right to high-level training for all jobs. It presupposes a system organized to accommodate this choice, and provision for groups and individuals to negotiate their programmes with providers – along with reorganization bringing all providers and institutions into a new public network. From universities to workshops, all involved in the education and training of adults over 16 would be required to enlarge and diversify their activities. Mere provision of 'access' – with providers given rights to reject – is ineffective. The obligation society must accept is to guarantee the experience of education and training of choice, without discrimination of any kind.

Developing a policy of equal rights to equal education and training would provide a catalyst for new forms of employment by itself. But unless work is simultaneously planned and created, and its forms, purpose and future widely discussed, major transformational possibilities are not possible. Both processes have to be developed together.

The MSC has shifted the ideological focus far to the right and outwitted the labour movement for the time being. It can only be shifted forward again when that movement rediscovers its own ideology and begins creating policy that matches the Right's policy point for point. This requires a broadening of perspective that recognizes the backwardness and elitism of Britain's education and training system and finds the will to forge alliances with women, ethnic minorities, young people, disabled people and the older age groups, as well as with people outside Britain.

Training and jobs: turning society around

Present training policy is inadequate to meet present needs, let alone transform society and reconstruct the job market in the light of new technologies that could be put to work to meet new as well as existing social needs. The MSC's destruction of the planning function associated with the ITBs was an act of national vandalism that has crippled economic recovery and long-term planning for jobs and training.

Voluntarism continues to fail. Despite billions poured into their pockets, many employers show they are no more capable of investing in the skills of their own workforces than they are of investing in old or new technology. Conservatives themselves must sometimes wonder whether in fact British industry is even ready for capitalism, when so much of it operates so feudally. Thus several contributors to this volume recommend a revival of the training board tradition – though not necessarily its form – as well as a strong policy requiring all employers to undertake, and contribute to, training directed in the public, and their own, interest. Leaving training to employer preferences and market forces is as doomed as trusting education to the MSC.

Employment is also much too important to be left to employers. Everything to do with job planning, as well as education and training, should be brought back into the public domain, and through the process of democratic development, made subject to local as well as national planning, funding and accountability. Employers can have their say along with everyone else, but their present dominance leaves no role for employees, trade unions, parents or young people themselves. Social reconstruction requires everyone.

There is widespread belief that a 'market economy' policy is failing society at large and that the ideology of monetarism is heartless. Yet everything continues to run by it. Most chapters imply that this will go on until an equally strong ideological counterthrust takes place. Where can rescue come from but from the only area of policy not yet tried: a genuine socialist alternative?

One reason that this is still so far from sight is the ambiguous position of the labour movement in relation to the TUC's role as one of the MSC's three equal partners. Much of the material in this book illustrates the deep conflict which the MSC has brought to the labour movement, weakening its response at the very moment it is most needed.

The judgement of TUC leaders has been dented by their acceptance of assurances from the other two partners – the CBI and government – that MSC activities would not be used to cut wages, destroy jobs, and substitute training for real work – when in plain view of millions, this is what it has been used for. The TUC responds by covering one eye and blaming government ministers for mishandling MSC policy. The other eye cannot see that it is the MSC itself that is being used by ministers to attack trade union rights, workers' pay and conditions and security of work, as well as local government and public services. It is the MSC that is intimately implicated in the narrowing of education and the perpetuation of sex and race discrimination in training and in work. Today the MSC is affecting a very large area of activity in Britain and is in full command of a drive to detach workers from loyalty to unions and train them in obedience to employers' interests and a new state ideology.

The labour movement has no coherent response. Instead it deals with all policy decisions on an ad hoc basis. The TUC, for example, leaves unions to decide policy on the MSC on an individual basis, even in respect of common issues faced by all unions involved with MSC activity. There is no collective agreement on strategy: some unions resolutely fight MSC proposals that harm their members, others rush to identify with MSC activities in the hope of temporary spin-off for members, and some do both at once. Important connections between activities have not been made; and the organization of trainees and those working for and in MSC activity has never been discussed as an across-the-board issue of urgency.

With collectivity absent, the labour movement has crippled itself and allowed the MSC to feed on sectionalism in a divide and rule policy. As a result, many unions are failing to develop their own wider political and social activity and understanding; and nothing shows this more clearly than their ineffectiveness in dealing with racism and sexism inside the workplace, including in MSC schemes.

In desperation many trade unionists and MSC workers have called for a boycott of all MSC activities by the TUC. This only leads TUC leaders to defend the MSC and put more blame on Tory ministers. The more the TUC fails to confront the issues, the more it is confronted by its own dilemma, for the same Tory ministers tell those who do confront the issues, or the MSC's anti-union activity, that all MSC policy developments have the blessing of the TUC. The TUC thus loses more credibility with its own grassroots or with those in schemes, and golden opportunities to organize against and within the MSC are lost.

There is little hope of persuading the majority of those experiencing the MSC to change their minds about what is happening to them or of dissuading the many radical, community, political and trade union groups to stop meeting, organizing, and planning alternative ways forward – and to observe a boycott. A boycott is also of little use to the hundreds of thousands now dependent on the MSC itself.

A boycott is not the answer; opposition is, and no body is better placed to undertake it than the TUC. Until it stands up to government and employers within the MSC itself, it will be difficult to shape alternative policies which have popular credibility. All authors agree that the creation of an alternative policy is the key.

Alternative policy presents difficulties to a Labour Party leadership tied to the TUC position. Beyond the skeletal commitments – to policies like enforced day release – of the TUC/Labour Party Plan for Training, the Party has failed to agree on a credible and popular policy on many issues, which distinguishes itself sufficiently from the now-overtaken policies of its past, and from those in other parties today. The Labour Party's own policy-making is divided into compartments on education, training, jobs, youth and industrial planning – again without the necessary connections being made; and further fragmented by origin: one policy from the Party Conference, another from front-bench spokespersons.

At present there is no 'matching' Left policy present in the popular mind on most issues. At best in many trades councils or in parliament there is talk about 'improvements' to YTS and/or the need for 'more' community places. If the government attempts to dodge its own disastrous policies by drawing labour movement leaders into 'co-operative responsibility' for future failure, matters will be even worse.

The labour movement's crying need is for its own clear alternative socialist policies – to be widely canvassed and understood – on every aspect of education, training and job creation.

We need a policy based on our own criteria, arising from our own principles and linked to our own analysis. A good deal of difficulty, therefore, can be traced to a loss of ideological activity, including the traditional socialist work of future, or utopian, imagination. Our greatest asset was once our vision of how things might be. This loss of social vision is reflected constantly, and leads to plans for a better future being entirely monopolized by Conservatives commercial images.

Opposition parties dutifully oppose from day to day and can sometimes be quite sharp in comment, but none is able or willing to match widespread doctrinal support for a destructive retreat to the past with energetic support for policies of our own for constructive social, economic and political advance. For Liberals or Social Democrats it is of little importance if ideological coherence is absent: they operate in an ad hoc way and can always count on respectful silence from the media if their policies do not work out. For socialists, however, lack of concerted ideological activity is not just debilitating, it is wholly self-destructive. As our traditional cement melts, the Left threatens to fall apart, even come to blows. Advance is possible only with a return to popular ideological understanding of the forces at work, and the development of our own future imagination.

These essays represent a wide range of socialist and radical opinion. We do not peddle any line, but rather concentrate upon the cement required to build that understanding and vision. Social reconstruction based on a shared experience of what is wrong, has to proceed from the forms of resistance that work best, the innovations in organization that are possible and the development of jobs, education and training that meets individual and social needs.

Millions now share experience of the MSC and can respond to a new policy that seeks to mobilize their knowledge and understanding in a popular campaign for alternatives. All chapters show how much room there is within MSC activity for successful challenge, and how possible it is today to involve a wide range of opinion, well beyond traditional labour activities by providing a forum for debate, community by community, designed to turn society around. There is a clear path for the Left out of its own imposed self-isolation of the 1970s, if it will be taken.

Loss of jobs, side by side with a massive array of needs waiting to be met, is a worldwide phenomenon. So too is the irony of so many individual nations, advanced as well as advancing, taking no interest in training during full employment but obsessed with it only as jobs disappear. In Britain the problems are more severe than in most other industrial nations and they will remain so until the MSC or whatever takes its place, turns aside completely from its present validation of worklessness and is redirected to the serious business of social advance through jobs, training and education.

New jobs have to come from enterprise and new enterprise has to be tied to the needs of people for their own social advance – here and throughout the world. It must provide the goods and services required for food, housing, health, education, social care, environmental protection, recreation, transport, free communications and cultural development – and the democratic structures to develop activity in all these areas.

Unemployment is socially immoral not because people are left on the scrapheap, though that is criminal enough, but because people's lives could be helped and their conditions improved if needed services and products were made available through the training, education and work of those at present doing nothing or being kept in costly MSC custody. MSC schemes fetter genuine enterprise which can only be developed by attention to the social and material conditions in which people live, learn, train and work. The British establishment fears genuine social enterprise, for if truly let loose, it would indeed take society in a different direction from the goal which state Conservatism has set.

Summary

Certain common themes emerge in these chapters. The first is that a new national initiative far beyond any so far discussed by any political party is required to plan the work which society requires to meet its needs. The new drive should focus on employment creation, operating through locally accountable structures which return power, authority and funding – now handed over to the MSC – back to the democratic process.

The second is that this process should be opened up to widespread participation in order to discuss the nature of work and to plan the kind of work society needs and how it should be organized. It should involve a fundamental challenge to the prevailing practices of work allocation according to hidden social assumptions about the 'type of work' appropriate to individuals on account of their sex, race or social origins.

The third is that education and training need to be integrated – in recognition of the fact that the best preparation for any job is a high level of general education and that all jobs should involve high-quality training. This process also requires the development of a new national training policy based on a new understanding that we – the Left included – cannot divide people into those who use their hands at work against those who use their brains. All work involves both hand and brain; all individuals have a right to education and training that acknowledges both parts of themselves.

The fourth is that education and training must be available – comprehensively, and in new ways, locations and forms – to all adults throughout life, regardless of their sex, race, age, social origins or level of previous attainment. These changes require major acts of legislation that bring all education and training back into proper oversight within the public domain, enabling society's resources to be redistributed equitably between groups and regions.

Our policy's objectives are to raise educational and training standards and to develop the critical understanding required to engage in the long-postponed debate about society's survival and future development, both here and in the rest of the world.

Lastly, to make these advances through education and training and work, people must have a new right to be sustained in decent living conditions, with a high given level of public services, throughout their lives. The basis of the initiative must be the right to useful work that is personally fulfilling.

Conclusion

It is not just jobs to be created. As these essays make clear, with jobs must go the education and training each job requires. This is an integral part of the process of developing people socially and of developing work itself. Education and training have to grow with the creation of work, to include education through the work process and training through education about the social consequences of all jobs; and taking account of people's full responsibilities and life situations.

At the same time, the whole nature of work needs to be the subject of a full-scale debate in public – the real Great Debate so long postponed. Above all, we have to challenge assumptions about the allocation of work roles, since no progress is possible without this – except for the rich, the educational elite and certain groups of highly skilled white men.

For almost everyone else the path is at best uncertain, at worst downwards. That is why one crucial part of social reconstruction is the understanding and agreement that everyone needs maintenance or pay at acceptable levels in order to enjoy and exercise equal rights and freedom of choice in education and training, as well as to control the conditions of their own lives and acquire the power and knowledge to make changes through the democratic process.

None of these basic requirements for social or democratic advance exist in Britain. Yet these essays suggest that they would enjoy wide popular support from most sections of the community.

The political Right is in retreat, but that is not enough. Bad ideas are not defeated by continuing to say how bad they are; only by good ideas. A radical, popular and transforming alternative policy on jobs, training and education has to take us well behind the lines of current consensus discussion and well beyond even the most radical proposals of the past. Even then, society will almost certainly look back and say it wasn't radical enough.

1. P. Broadfoot (ed.), *Curriculum, Certification and Control*, Falmer Press, Lewes, 1984.
2. John White, *The Aims of Education Restated*, Routledge & Kegan Paul, London, 1982.

1. A Seat at the Table?

Mark Jackson

The Manpower Services Commission is the brainchild of the TUC, which explains a lot. Its creation is seen by the TUC establishment as a great historical achievement to be preserved at virtually any cost. For the Commission embodies the aspirations of the movement's top bureaucracy to a formal share in the central structure of the state and recognition as part of the establishment of officialdom. It is the biggest and most influential of the governmental 'arms-length' agencies, semi-autonomous bodies which have a separate corporate existence outside the Whitehall machine and carry out public service activities for which they are responsible to ministers. In many ways these agencies are like the nationalized industries, except that they earn little or no revenue from their operations and can therefore only do what the government is prepared to pay for.

The Commission's job is to advise the government on national manpower policies and to execute them under ministerial authority. It runs the state employment services; carries out government training and temporary work programmes; supports training in industry, and more recently, vocational courses in schools and colleges. It also monitors the labour market and conducts research on manpower matters.

To carry out these activities, the Commission employs around 20,000 staff and has an annual budget running near to £2 billion. In theory, they are under the control of the ten commissioners appointed by the Employment Secretary to run the organization. It is at this highest level that the TUC is represented, nominating three of the commissioners, with the CBI having the same number, local government choosing two, and a college teacher representing professional education interests. The remaining commissioner is the chairperson, a full-time paid official who is appointed by the Employment Secretary and is the organization's chief executive.

Constitutionally, the commissioners are free to make their own decisions and to carry them out, subject only to the willingness of the government to provide the money. The Employment Secretary has a reserve right to issue formal directions to the commissioners, but has never been forced to use it, since the commissioners have always, when it has come to the crunch, done what he wants.

And, in practice, the staff and their director, most of them career civil servants, take more notice from day to day of ministers and the civil service department than of their own titular masters. The MSC slots into the civil service structure as a part of 'the DE (Department of Employment) group' which includes other agencies such as the Health and Safety Executive. Although the chairperson, on a three-year contract, is not a civil servant, much of the time he acts as the voice of his officials or of ministers to the lay commissioners, presenting them with proposals from the staff or demands from the government. The whole thing works fairly smoothly when the chairperson is a skilled consensus man who understands that the commissioners will agree to practically anything as long as they think they can manage to sell it to the interests they represent. It took the Thatcher government to demonstrate that even that proviso can easily be overridden; and that the commissioners – certainly the TUC representatives – will in the end acquiesce in the implementation of policies they say are completely unacceptable rather than give up their seats on the Commission. Behind the show of autonomy and corporatism, and despite the Commission's fondness for buzzwords like participation, consultation, open government, partnership, and accountability, the MSC has proved itself to be a pliant and convenient instrument which ministers can use to carry out questionable or oppressive policies and to confuse and split any resistance to them.

This is not, of course, anything like the dream of real corporative power, shared only with the employers, which had sustained the TUC's long years of lobbying for a central manpower agency. Nor, despite the attractions of conspiracy theory, was it in the mind of the Tory government which set up the MSC.

Early in 1973, the Edward Heath government – which was to be toppled before the end of the year by a successful miners' strike – decided to give way to demands from employers for a modification of the grant-and-levy system under which they were made to contribute to the cost of training in their own industrial sectors. It was not a question of the Tories trying to demolish, Thatcher-style, the achievement of an earlier Labour administration. The 1964 Industrial Training Act, which brought the state back into the regulation of training after more than a century and a half of *laissez-faire*, had also been the work of a Conservative government, Harold Macmillan's. In 1964 the TUC had argued for a strong central control of manpower activities despite divided views within the movement. While Frank Cousins, the transport workers' leader, wanted a central structure which could bring some hope of training for the mass of unskilled workers, many of the craft union leaderships suspected it might weaken the traditional arrangements under which they controlled apprenticeship in their own industries. They wanted no more than to take their seats on the separate industrial training boards to be set up under the act for each industry – or rather, for 27 industries, leaving half the nation's workforce outside the system.

The Macmillan government, intent on getting employers in each industry to foot the bill, was just as reluctant to see any transfer of responsibility to the centre. Although Cousins had persuaded the majority of the TUC general council to back his demand for 'a strong central authority to draw its strength both from its statutory responsibilities and from public money which it would make available in grants', all that the government would concede, at the last moment, was a Central Training Council with an advisory role, few resources, and no power.

In agreeing in 1973 to relieve employers of the obligation to pay for the training of staff other than their own, the Heath Government accepted that it was creating a gap which the state itself would have to fill and that some kind of central training organization would be required. Initially the government's plan had been to create simply a national training agency which would co-ordinate the work of the industrial training boards and take over the government's own existing vocational training scheme, which was to be expanded into a mass Training Opportunities Scheme (TOPS). The agency would be independent and not part of the civil service, and would be run by full-time training and educational professionals. It would become the employer of the staff serving the training boards.

That, indeed, was more or less what the TUC had been calling for nine years earlier; but now it was aiming higher. What the TUC wanted now was nothing less than a full-scale Manpower Board with the combined responsibility for manpower planning, employment services and job creation, as well as training. At the last minute it convinced the CBI that the whole thing could be run effectively by the two bodies working together. Whatever rank and file unionists and individual employers might think, the central bureaucracies at Congress House and at the CBI headquarters in Tothill Street had a lot in common and should have no difficulty in sharing power.

Confronted by this line-up, the Heath government agreed that the Training Services Agency (TSA), and the Employment Services Agency (ESA) which had been set up to run the job placement activities of the Department of Employment should be, not independent agencies, but the executive arms of a Manpower Services Commission which would be responsible to the Secretary of State. The government was still very wary of creating a powerful new empire outside its own control, and made it plain that it saw the Commission primarily as a policy planning and co-ordinating body, through which the operational agencies would report – not as a super-agency which would take over from them.

The Manpower Services Commission came into existence on 1 February 1974, a few months after Harold Wilson's return to Downing Street for his second term. Its first chairperson was Sir Dennis Barnes, formerly permanent secretary at the Department of Employment, whose career had taken off in the years of the first postwar Labour government. Barnes, very much the laid-back Whitehall mandarin, had not seemed at first a very exciting choice either to the TUC or the CBI – 'a bit cynical' was their description, which suggests that he did not echo their clichés as enthusiastically as they might have liked. But chatting with Barnes in an anteroom while they were waiting to discuss the approaching launch of the new body with the Employment Secretary, John Hare, the TUC's General Secretary Vic Feather found that the Whitehall luminary's thinking was surprisingly close to his own. When the two went in to see the minister, they presented a common front.

During Barnes's three years in the job the Commission could claim to be providing a model of institutional modesty. Its total staff was 40, compared with the 13,000 in the ESA and the TSA's 3,000. Its first full year's report stressed that they were statutory bodies in their own right, and talked of 'urging' or 'requesting' them to undertake various measures. It spent in that first year only a quarter of a million on its own activities, the two agencies accounting for the rest of the £125 million budget. It was clear that the Commission recognized that for the moment it was little more than a holding company for the operational agencies.

But there were already signs that the men and their officials who met once a month in the modest offices off Piccadilly wanted more. Labour's election manifesto had promised to turn the MSC into 'a powerful body responsible for the development and execution of a comprehensive manpower policy'. Michael Foot, later to become Labour's leader, but now enjoying ministerial office after long years of leading the backbench Left, was the Employment Secretary. In a submission to him the Commission argued that honouring that pledge meant making them the central authority responsible for 'managing and co-ordinating the executive instruments of manpower policy' and for influencing through its advice other national policy on related matters. Although the Commission was careful to avoid stirring up a premature row in its own backyard by making any threat to the independence of the two agencies, it gave some other hints of its imperial ambitions. It suggested that it ought to take over the manpower intelligence network of the DE, turning the department's regional directors into the Commission's representatives on the ground. And it staked out new ground by asking that it should be given responsibility for the work creation programmes begun by the department, and for sheltered employment for the disabled. And, almost in passing, it put in a claim to take over the central oversight of the local authority careers service.

The Commission's shopping basket might have seemed unexciting, involving little more than the transfer of a few hundred civil servants to its payroll. But the items were carefully chosen. They were the basis for the empire which the Commission was to build over the next ten years.

The takeover of the regional directors and their staff gave the MSC the skeleton field network which would be used to absorb and integrate the staff and activities of the two operating agencies. The work creation programmes run directly by the Commission would be the big growth area as unemployment mounted and new measures proliferated and overran training. The Careers Service, loosely overseen by a small and notoriously ineffective branch of the DE, was run by the local education authorities: the MSC's hopes of taking it over were to be shelved when the incoming

Thatcher government cut back the MSC budget and forced it to close down even its own patchy occupational guidance service.

But in making their pass at the Careers Service, which worked mainly inside the schools and colleges and was very much part of education, the MSC's establishment provided a momentary glimpse of the scope of its ambitions. In the years that followed, it repeatedly denied any designs on the education service, while its actions and policies steadily positioned it for the moment when it would be given the authority to intervene directly in the work of the schools and colleges. The threat to give the MSC the Careers Service was revived in the 1980s by Peter Morrison, a junior employment minister with the delicacy of an adolescent buffalo, to dragoon Careers officers into making YTS recruitment their overriding priority. Thus Barnes, the Whitehall professional, had identified the road to influence and empire, ready for the time when the way would be open. That time came in 1976 together with the ideal man to lead the MSC's advance into its golden era.

It was the arrival of mass unemployment and within it the horrendous rocketing of youth unemployment which provided the context for the MSC's crash expansion. When the Commission was set up, the unemployment rate for the under-24s was less than 3 per cent and still under 5 per cent in 1975: now, a year later, it was nearly three times that. The Callaghan government was in a panicky fix: its ideology and its allegiancies precluded any radical response to the crisis in manufacturing capitalism which was destroying the jobs; but it needed desperately to be seen to be trying to do something for, at least, the youngest of the workless.

It was at this point that Barnes handed over the chair to Richard O'Brien, who was everything the beleaguered government could have wished. It had not in fact chosen him: he was nominated by the CBI. O'Brien had some experience as a senior civil servant, but his main background after wartime service as an aide to Field Marshall Montgomery (the youthful O'Brien had accepted the surrender of a large part of the German army on Monty's behalf) had been in big manufacturing companies. If it was the employers who put him forward, it was the TUC who quickly learned to love him and became his principal support. A personnel director who spoke the language of social responsibility and reform, O'Brien patently believed it: an active churchman, he did not quarrel with suggestions that he was a Christian socialist of sorts. But he was also careful to add quickly that the primary reason he wanted progressive and humane industrial relations and training policies was that they were essential to efficient management. As a bonus, he had once worked as a professional youth club leader, and was at home with voluntary agencies and the educational service whose co-operation was to play an essential role in his plans.

The most important of O'Brien's qualities, apart from his clear and agile intellect, was his very real and obvious integrity. Even those who did not believe in the reality of his promises – over such matters as the quality of youth training programmes, or opportunities for grassroots participation in the running of schemes – rarely doubted that he honestly believed them himself. It made him the perfect front man for policies of expediency which, however limited or cosmetic, were based on some real attempt to ameliorate the problems of the unemployed or to bring about some genuine improvement in the training system. In the end, however, under another government which did not rate even the appearance of integrity very highly, his honesty was to undo him.

O'Brien was, of course, a natural manager of consensus. In his book it meant rather more than persuading people to go along with whatever the government wanted. There were occasions when he told ministers that their wishes were unacceptable to the commissioners – as when Albert Booth, the declared leftwinger who was Callaghan's Employment Secretary, wanted to deny the dole to youngsters who refused to go on the Youth Opportunities Programme or other training schemes. More important perhaps, O'Brien consistently published forecasts from the MSC's own sources which showed that government's own estimates of unemployment were unduly optimistic and questioned its claim that its industrial strategy and its efforts to keep down wages were in themselves the answer to the problem. On the other hand, O'Brien's repeated public assurances that the MSC would use the huge resources and responsibility, which the government was ready to provide for new kinds of emergency programmes, to keep the unemployed off the streets, to create a new style of democratic and decentralized public service, rarely materialized.

The biggest and most controversial of these schemes was the Youth Opportunities Programme (YOP). In 1976 Shirley Williams, then Education Secretary and a leading apologist for the Cabinet's monetarist policies, had started to talk about the possibility of a government-funded scheme to offer all the under-18s a guarantee of some kind of education or training if they could not find a job. The scheme would be run primarily by the education service and the youth agencies, with the participation of employers, and be the responsibility of the Department of Education and Science. The MSC moved quickly. Its supporters within the government poured scorn on the notion that the DES could organize and run a broad mass programme of this kind effectively, let alone move with the required urgency. Publicly, they argued that the DES had no constitutional power to instruct local authorities in such matters, or to ensure that any money provided to them through the department would actually be spent on the scheme. O'Brien gave one of the MSC's shrewdest and most ambitious officials, a young civil service high flier who was running the Commission's planning division, the go-ahead to prepare an alternative plan. By the spring of 1977 Geoffrey Holland had, using a small committee drawn from the interests represented on the Commission, produced a detailed scheme under which the MSC would fund a mass programme to provide work experience and/or training and related education for unemployed school leavers.

In both the Holland report and in the subsequent consultations, and in speeches delivered almost daily by O'Brien and Holland (whose talent for visionary eloquence matched that of his boss), great emphasis was laid on the need for local communities to play a leading role in managing the scheme. At the same time they made it plain that, however desirable it might be to provide a variety of opportunities including college-based courses and voluntary agency projects, they considered work experience the next best thing to an actual job for the majority of leavers. That meant handing most youngsters over to employers as free labour, and there was never really much chance that those employers would accept control over the scheme by their local community bodies.

In the event, YOP was run by 26 MSC area offices, with a lay area board in each to oversee policy: each area was several times the size of a local education authority and a long way from the scale which permits local control. Congress House found this convenient: its hierarchy pointed out that the movement could not spare enough full-time officials to man more than that number of boards, and that it was unthinkable to entrust such responsibility to lay union members.

The Thatcher victory in 1979 brought the first check to the MSC's growth with a demand for immediate cuts in spending and staff. They forced the MSC to drop its occupational guidance service (a thin network of careers advisors in Jobcentres), to cut the Skillcentre chain, and to start turning PER, its management and professional recruitment service, into a commercial agency. The Commission had forecast in its first report that its expenditure, including that of the two agencies, would rise to nearly £300 million (at constant prices) by 1979/80. The 1980 report estimated that the Commission had spent, in that first year of Thatcher, a little under £700 million. A third of that was the cost of the Youth Opportunities Programme, and another £70 million or so went on the Job Creation Programme and its successor, the Special Temporary Employment Programme, first of a series of schemes to provide spells of makeshift work for some of the long-term unemployed.

Out of a staff now numbering close to 25,900 – fewer in total than the previous year because of the Thatcher cuts – 1,250 were in the Special Programmes Division. That Division, and the MSC's own management, were the only areas of continuing staff growth. The two agencies lost their separate existence in 1978, but their structures were kept as new divisions run from the massive new Commission headquarters in Sheffield.

While special programmes went on expanding, after 1980 some of the most important training programmes started to contract. The training agency had been told when YOP began that it must no longer take the under-19s into the Training Opportunities Programme, which immediately fell from its peak of nearly 100,000 trainees to 75,000. In the next three years the abolition of most of the training boards, the ending of financial support to group training associations, and finally the ending of the grants to employers which had shored up the dying apprenticeship system, further reduced the work of the Training Services Division. The introduction of the Youth Training Scheme (YTS) was the occasion for the merging of the division with special programmes to form a new Training Division whose priority was running the YTS.

The new division was well resourced with more than £900 million in 1984–5 to spend on the YTS and the Community Programme for the adult unemployed, and another £235 million for TOPS – more than the total MSC budget of only three years earlier. The MSC budget by now totalled more than £2 billion, and would go up by another £110 million when, in 1986, the Tories fully implemented their plan to give the MSC control over a large part of further education funding. Only in terms of its own manpower were the Commission's original resource expectations disappointed. There, the Tories' determination to go on reducing jobs in the public sector meant that the MSC had to give up all hope of ever reaching the peak of 30,000 staff it had expected to have by 1983-4. Of the Commission's 20,000 employees in 1985, more than a quarter were engaged in running the special programmes.

O'Brien went in early 1981 at the end of his three-year term. Everyone had expected he would be reappointed, but he ran foul of Norman Tebbit, the new Thatcherite Employment Secretary. The MSC chairperson sealed his fate at a British Association for Commercial and Industrial Education conference where Tebbit was making his first public speech in his new job. O'Brien, weighing his words carefully, told the audience he was convinced that Tebbit's aim of reforming the training system would not work without a statutory framework: voluntarism, which the Tories were hoping would replace the dismantled training board system, had been proved over the years to be insufficient because employers would simply not pay for the training the country needed. O'Brien was replaced by a man nobody had ever heard of, a banker named David Young from Margaret Thatcher's Finchley constituency who was a close friend of Sir Keith Joseph, Thatcher's intellectual guru and later her Education Secretary. Young himself had no pretensions to intellectual distinction, but impeccable credentials as a Tory hatchet man: he had drawn up the plans for the 'liberalization' of British Telecom as a prelude to selling it off. His only claim to head the world's biggest national training organization was his chairing of British ORT (Organization for Rehabilitation and Training), a body which raised funds for an international voluntary agency which provided training mainly in the Third World.

ORT had been founded in the nineteenth century to teach desperately poor Russian Jews a trade (and perhaps to divert them from meddling in revolutionary politics). Its approach was firmly grounded in the overriding need of illiterate immigrants to equip themselves with the means of earning a living, and in the schools it ran in France as well as in the underdeveloped countries, general education and broad learning came very much second. ORT people tended to talk a lot about motivating 'non-academic' pupils by their concentration on vocational instruction. It was this approach that Young now tried to introduce into the British education systems through the MSC.

The commissioners found themselves confronted in rapid succession with proposals to cut social education, such as it was, out of the new Youth Training Scheme; to bring back open selection within the secondary schools by teaching 'non-academic' youngsters a trade from the age of 14; to cut back the Skillcentre network dramatically in preparation for its commercialization; and to take over control of a large part of the courses in local authority colleges. In presenting these demands to the commissioners, Young barely maintained the fiction that he was simply passing on government decisions: few doubted that he was their principal architect. Only in the case of the attempt to ban YTS social education did he bother, faced by a contemptuously hostile response from the more progressive employers, to distance himself from the idea, implying that Peter Morrison, the junior minister, was entirely to blame. In putting forward the Technical and Vocational Education Initiative (TVEI), Young showed no such coyness: he told Len Murray, then the TUC's General Secretary, that he was only trying to give the education service a badly needed short sharp shock. Murray, he claims, retorted approvingly that one such shock would not be enough.

Young thought he could coerce the local authorities, who were angered, Labour and Tory alike, at the brutalistic announcement of the scheme without any prior warning or consultation, by threatening to set up the MSC's own technical schools if the authorities did not play ball. It was always an empty threat: Young was after changing the whole school system by example, and he knew that the MSC had neither the expertise nor the credibility to achieve this without the willing co-operation of the professionals. In the end he had to hand over the planning and the supervision of the new scheme to a group dominated by educationists, who did what they could to limit its threat to comprehensive education.

More damaging, perhaps, than any of the specific measures which Young introduced was his encouragement to ministers like Morrison to behave as though the MSC were an extension of their own private offices. Young passed on unchanged to his field staff instructions from ministers to cut back the sort of YTS schemes they disliked: when commissioners and area board members protested that they were being bypassed, Young told them that as the Commission's 'accounting officer' he had the unchallengable final say, and that he agreed with the ministers. At a more risible level, Morrison was even allowed to dictate the way in which MSC staff signed their letters.

Young disappeared from the scene to join the Cabinet, of which he had long been virtually an undercover member, just at the point where he had got the Commission into a real mess. The MSC had, since the mid 1970s exercised an increasing backdoor influence over further education through its sponsorship of courses in the colleges for programmes like TOPS and the schemes for the young unemployed. In early 1984 Young and his Cabinet friends decided the time was ripe for the MSC to take an open hand in running the college system. Encouraged by the success of the fait accompli tactic used to force the TVEI on the local authorities, they sprung the decision without warning in a White Paper which simply announced that the government was in future going to hand over to the MSC part of the further education money it had always supplied to the authorities through the annual rate support grant. The idea was that the MSC would distribute the money to local authorities who ran their colleges the way the MSC told them to. What Young and the others did not understand was that, while the authorities had been prepared to accept under protest the additional money offered them for the TVEI, they would react very differently to a plan to take some of their existing cash out of their control. The Labour-controlled Association of Metropolitan Authorities refused even to discuss the idea; and the Tory-dominated Association of County Councils was prepared to talk only about how the scheme could be run in a way which returned the money to them without too many strings.

The professional education groups and the local government bureaucrats, whatever their feelings about the power battle and the constitutional issues involved, thought the whole government strategy wildly impracticable and likely to bring chaos down on the further education system. The TUC commissioner, for once, came down uncompromisingly on the side of the education service, a stand which diverted attention from other proposals in the white paper which were potentially even more destructive, but in whose development the TUC had acquiesced. The education service commissioner, Wilson Longden (a Tory further education man chosen by Sir Keith against the protests of the further education bodies) rounded on the government for its high-handed tactics.

But even so, when the Employment Secretary wrote telling the Commissioners that he expected them to implement the decision, they all came into line. Longden and the TUC members later said they thought they had no choice because the minister was using his power of direction; but the Department of Employment categorically denied that a directive was ever issued.

The MSC officials started working out plans to set up a big new bureaucracy to plan and control college courses. The local authorities hardened their resistance, but Young went around saying he was not worried because enough individual authorities would cave in eventually to enable the plan to go ahead. His optimism was never put to the test. In the autumn of 1984, after Young's sudden departure from the MSC to the House of Lords and the Cabinet, Bryan Nicholson, an unpretentious Tory industrialist from Surrey who had no personal links with the Thatcher set, was appointed in his place.

If Young was the archetypal Thatcherite wheeler-dealer, Nicholson was from the cream of modern progressive manufacturing management. Without the intellectual brilliance or visionary appeal of O'Brien, he was nevertheless a highly able and patient man who wanted to see the training system improved quickly and get the YTS living up to the promises which had been made. Unlike Young he did not feel committed to the Thatcher crusade to bring down youth wages; and he did not care much for the bully-boy tactics of his predecessor.

Once again, the MSC had a skilled consensus practitioner at its head, who set about securing the trust and co-operation of the groups represented on the Commission. He patched up an armed truce with the local authorities by agreeing to let them have their diverted further education money back without strings for the first year; and got them to join a working party which within a few months drew up an agreement for a more permanent arrangement under which the MSC would have a very limited role in the planning of the colleges' work. Nicholson also embarked almost immediately on the development of a two-year version of the YTS, while endearing himself to the TUC by persuading the government to sanction a general review of the funding of training, a proposal which ministers had explicitly rejected in the white paper a year earlier. Within a few months of his arrival the new chairperson was being praised fulsomely by some of those who had been urging that the Labour movement should finally disown the monster it had spawned. TUC commissioners who had feared that they could not hold the line much longer in the face of growing anger at the blatant use of the MSC as an instrument of reaction started to breathe more easily. Nicholson was the man who could restore the Commission's respectability in good time for the next election and the possible return of a Labour government.

And moreover, it was clear that he was a man of sound instincts. There had been no nonsense about letting outsiders join in the shaping of the new two-year YTS: it had all been decided in private by the people who really mattered: the TUC, the CBI and the MSC top brass.

2. The MSC and Special Measures for Unemployment

Clare Short

Many of us who are deeply critical of the Conservative government's special measures for the unemployed and of its training policy have reached the conclusion that the Manpower Services Commission (MSC) is a thoroughly reactionary arm of the state which must be abolished at the first possible opportunity. In my own view this is a mistaken analysis. It is not the nature of the MSC itself which is objectionable, but the policies which it has been operating. The MSC is after all simply an arm of the Department of Employment (DE). Its budget and overall policy is determined by ministers and announced to parliament in the usual way. The only difference between the MSC and any other section of the DE is that it operates through a Commission which is made up of representatives of the TUC and CBI and education interests.

It is arguable that by remaining a member of the Commission the TUC has given an appearance of TUC support for government policy which has misled the trade union movement and weakened its response to measures that attack its fundamental interests. This is my own view. But representatives of the TUC would argue that by being there they have managed to moderate some of the government's most reactionary proposals. There is a case to be made for both viewpoints. But no-one in the TUC would argue that they are able to control the MSC or develop the programmes and policies which they would have chosen, given a free hand. It is a confusion to believe that present government policy is an inevitable outcome of the structure of the MSC itself. There is room for argument about whether in future there should be a Commission made up of employers and trade union interests which plays a part in the development of policy on training. But whatever the conclusion reached, it will tell us nothing about the kind of training system and special measures for the unemployed that we should construct in the future.

My views are based on a very close study of the development of special measures for the unemployed from 1979 to 1983. I believe that the government has used the Youth Opportunities Programme (YOP), the Youth Training Scheme (YTS) and the Community Programme (CP) for a number of ulterior purposes. I think it is important that we should examine in detail what they have been up to so that future developments in youth training and special measures for the unemployed will not build on the dubious foundations that have been laid down.

The MSC was established by the Heath government in 1973. In those days hiving off was the fashionable remedy for what was seen as over-large, over-centralized government departments. There was bipartisan agreement on the need for the MSC as there had previously been for the Tory legislation setting up the Industrial Training Boards (ITBs) in 1964. The MSC also had the support of the TUC and CBI.

The role conferred on the MSC was that of co-ordinating public employment and training policy. Important as this remit is, the MSC caused little controversy until the present government set about the destruction of the traditional training system and made major cutbacks in the Jobcentre network. It was the inclusion in the MSC brief of responsibility for co-ordinating short-term responses to unemployment which brought the MSC into the political limelight and led to a massive growth in its size and budget.

These developments began under the 1974–9 Labour government. Following the oil price increases of 1974, unemployment rose to the then unprecedented and embarrassing level of 1.7 million before it fell to the 1.3 million level that the Thatcher government inherited in 1979. The government responded by launching the Job Creation Programme which provided money for worthwhile community projects which would create employment for unemployed young people and adults. They also supported additional special programmes for young people such as short courses in Skillcentres and work experience placements.

The government remained acutely embarrassed by the high levels of youth unemployment. At that time about one in ten school leavers was failing to find work. This contrasted with the experience of the postwar period when school leavers had been snapped up into jobs and had an unemployment level consistently lower than the general one.

Under pressure from the TUC, the Labour government set up a MSC committee chaired by a then unknown civil servant called Geoffrey Holland. It was asked to examine whether it would be possible to give a guarantee to every unemployed school leaver of a place on a training course or a work experience programme. The Holland Committee reviewed the nature of existing schemes and recommended that they should all be drawn into one programme which would be known as the Youth Opportunities Programme (YOP). It also proposed that a guarantee of a place on the programme should be given to every unemployed school leaver.

The government accepted this recommendation and YOP was born in 1978. It was authoritatively rumoured at the time that a battle raged in Cabinet before the decision was made between the Department of Education and Science (DES) and the DE about which of them should be given the money to provide for the young unemployed. We are told that DE won because it could guarantee to produce places very quickly on the ground. The DES could promise much less because it would have to make grants to local education authorities and simply exhort them to deliver.

In the light of subsequent developments, it is important to be clear about the thinking that underpinned the launch of YOP. Considerable research was commissioned before the programme was launched. It was concluded that the rise in youth unemployment was due to two temporary factors: economic recession and a bulge in the number of school leavers. It was also recognized that young people tended to compete for jobs with married women returning to the labour market. It was intended that YOP should be a temporary programme lasting five years which would keep the young unemployed busy, overcome their problem that 'without a job you can't get experience and without experience you can't get a job' and sharpen up their competitive edge in the labour market. The implication of this was that they would compete better against married women.

The early YOP was small by present-day standards and fairly popular with young people. The early allowance was worth £40 at current prices. About one in eight school leavers entered the programme and 80 per cent got jobs on leaving.

At the same time a smaller programme for the adult unemployed was launched. It provided 25,000 places in projects of benefit to the community. It was really a continuation of the old Job Creation

Programme. The wage rate paid was equivalent to over £100 per week at current prices. Priority was given to the long-term unemployed, but any unemployed adult could take a place on the programme.

The 1979 election campaign was fought on the Tory slogan 'Labour isn't working'. The Tory leadership dismissed the special programmes of which the Labour government was quite proud and insisted that what people wanted was real jobs. The Tories won the election, partly no doubt because unemployment was too high, partly because Labour had imposed cuts in public expenditure programmes, and partly because the election followed the Callaghan–Healey attempt to impose a 5 per cent pay norm which led on to the 'winter of discontent'.

James Prior became the new Secretary of State for Employment. The introduction of monetarist economic policies led to a sharp rise in unemployment and growing criticism of YOP. As youth unemployment rose, more and more young people entered the programme and less and less got jobs at the end. Increasingly YOP was dismissed as a cheap labour scheme which simply exploited the young unemployed. The MSC commissioned research and found that large numbers of YOP jobs would have existed anyway. Not only were young people being exploited as cheap labour, but the vast bulk of them were on work experience placements which would otherwise have provided permanent jobs for young people.

As YOP became increasingly unpopular, there was a growing demand that it should be replaced by a proper training programme for the young. The TUC had campaigned for years for an expansion of training opportunities for the 40 per cent of young people who got few qualifications at school and little or no training on entry to work. In the good old days of full employment they entered the labour market without qualifications, worked in low-paid, unskilled jobs and retired in poverty on the state pension. International comparisons showed that Britain was providing less training for young people than most other OECD countries. There was a widespread consensus on the grounds of both social justice and economic efficiency that the old YOP should be replaced by a new programme which would provide training for this deprived group of young people.

In 1981–2 the Thatcher government moved in to take a much firmer control of the MSC. They had been embarrassed by various

MSC activities, in particular the publication of figures projecting further rises in unemployment. In addition, Thatcherism required a major restructuring of the labour market. The old consensus which was operating at the MSC was getting in the way. Mr Prior was despatched to Northern Ireland. He had made it clear that he would not welcome the move but when the time came he accepted the public humiliation. Norman Tebbit became Secretary of State for Employment. Shortly afterwards it was made clear to Richard O'Brien that despite his willingness to serve a further term as chairperson of the MSC, his services were not required. A then little known Thatcherite called David Young (now Lord Young and a member of the Cabinet) was appointed chairperson. The new regime intended to take full control of the MSC. Well-informed sources said that Tebbit was willing to abolish the MSC and run its services directly from the DE if the TUC resisted the changes he wanted.

Shortly after this Mr Tebbit produced the white paper which promised a new Youth Training Scheme to replace YOP. It suggested that young people would be gaining such a lot from the new scheme that they should accept a payment of £15 a week. Because this was considerably less than they were entitled to on supplementary benefit, it was proposed that the scheme should be compulsory.

All these developments caused enormous concern at the MSC. The government agreed to allow the MSC to set up a committee or task group to examine the details of the government's proposals. Tebbit agreed to look at any new scheme they might come up with provided it could operate within the £1 billion the government had made available. Much was made by the government of its generosity in finding £1 billion for youth training. In fact, the cost of keeping vast numbers of school leavers on benefits, plus the money that could be claimed from the EEC for youth training meant that the real cost of the programme was very small indeed.

The MSC Task Group proposed an alternative to Tebbit's compulsory scheme. They were forced of course to suggest a lower allowance for trainees than they had had under YOP, but it was widely agreed that this would be better than a compulsory £15 scheme. The promise of the Task Group was great. All school leavers whether employed or unemployed were to be guaranteed training. Steps were to be taken to ensure that young women and young black people were given equal opportunities. Everyone was to be guaranteed high-quality training both on and off the job. Mr Tebbit accepted the Task Group and the TUC were jubilant.

But the YTS which was implemented looked much more like the old YOP than the dreamed-of high-quality training scheme. The guarantee of training for those in work was quietly forgotten. First-year apprenticeships were converted to YTS. Soon it became clear that the scheme was being used to destroy the old apprentice-ship tradition which was under strain as a result of the recession. The race and sex discrimination of the old labour market continued to operate in YTS. The allowance got lower and lower. Very few trainees were unionized and the trade union movement started to realize that it was losing control of the youth labour market. The YTS allowance set the standard for acceptable wage levels for young people. The quality of training was low and trade unions no longer controlled access to training or its quality.

The scheme has also been used to undermine the further education sector. Private training agencies were established which offered YTS simply for profit. They undercut the values and standards of FE and provided schemes at a price that FE could not afford. On top of this the trainers employed by such agencies were themselves untrained, low-paid and employed on short-term contracts.

Mr Tebbit's plans for the development of YTS were very clever. He took over the arguments for an expansion of training opportu-nities for the young, but in fact brought in a scheme which massaged the unemployment figures, gave a pretence of government concern for the young unemployed, reduced youth wages, their attachment to trade unions, and also weakened union control over the training of young people.

A very similar exercise was conducted on the adult labour market with the introduction of the Community Programme (CP) which replaced the Community Enterprise Programme in 1982. In the name of an expansion of provision to help the long-term unemployed, the government cut the wages paid on the scheme from nearly £100 to an average of £65. The government used exactly the same tactic that they had used with YTS. They threatened to introduce a scheme which would pay participants their benefit plus £15–20. The TUC insisted that any such scheme must pay the rate for the job. The compromise that was reached meant that the TUC would accept an average wage of £65. This was achieved by offering part-time jobs to people who were seeking full-time work. Thus the adult unemployed began to accept part-time jobs paying as little as £45 per week. They too had lowered their expectations of the acceptable minimum a job could offer.

At the same time public sector services were constantly cut back. The only money that was available was for MSC schemes. As public services were cut back, more and more projects caring for the elderly, improving community buildings and restoring the environment were funded through the MSC. But the jobs provided were temporary and very low paid. The adult labour market was being restructured in exactly the same way as the youth labour market. Unionization was weakened and low-paid, insecure jobs became acceptable alternatives to unemployment.

When the CP was first introduced there was a fierce opposition led by the voluntary sector. TUC support eventually undermined trade union opposition to the cut in wages that was involved. It is a measure of the success of the government strategy that a year or so later defenders of the long-term unemployed were calling for an expansion of the programme. The government were happy to comply since it costs little more than unemployment benefit. At the same time it exerts a downward pressure on wage levels, undermines public sector services and cuts the unemployment figures. The recent increase in vacancy levels is largely due to the expansion of the CP announced in the 1985 budget.

In parallel with these developments came a restructuring of the training system, the abolition of the ITBs, cutbacks in the Skillcentres and a requirement that they should operate at a profit, a move by the MSC to take control of the training provided in FE and a cutback in the Jobcentre network. In schools we got the introduction of the Technical and Vocational Initiative which was intended to encourage the development of vocational education for the many but has actually preserved the full benefits of a broad-based education for the few.

The philosophy underpinning all of these developments was the same: a belief in increased inequality and the domination of market forces. Training should be provided by and controlled by employers. The public training system which provided training for workers as a right was to be eliminated. Trade union controls over training and wage levels must be weakened. Workers must be encouraged to accept lower wages and more insecure conditions.

The opposition of the labour movement to all these developments was muted. This was partly because the Labour leadership felt responsible for the early development of special measures and unable to turn round and attack its own creation. It was also because the TUC helped to run the MSC and therefore defended MSC programmes. Labour's front-bench spokespeople were briefed by the TUC and therefore engaged in nothing more than mild criticism of the Tebbit–Young development.

Towards an alternative

We have spent very little time discussing what an incoming Labour government should do with the MSC empire. What discussion there has been has tended to focus on the reorganization of government departments. Many people have argued that the MSC should be abolished and a Department of Education and Training established. But this tells us very little about what to do with YTS and the Community Programme. I suspect that a better starting point is for us to ask what should replace the programmes on the ground and than decide what machinery would best deliver what we have in mind.

Labour has a clear commitment to provide a two-year education or training opportunity for everyone between the ages of 16 and 18. This includes a promise to provide a grant of £28 per week (increased with inflation) to everyone who continues in full-time education. This commitment means that young people will have considerably more choice than they have at present. The need for an income will no longer drive them onto YTS or the dole. We know already that traditional sixth-form courses suit only a small proportion of the age group. We must build therefore on recent developments in providing a wider range of courses and better advice on the alternatives available. There should be more access courses for those who are unsure of the direction they want to take. Ideally this would lead into a wide range of academic and vocational courses built around the needs and interests of the age group.

We must also reform and rationalize the vast range of certification currently on offer. Ideally we should work towards a coherent system of recognized qualifications which would enable young people to gain credits from whatever course they take so that they can move either immediately or at some time in the future into further study or skill training or into work. We must look to a future in which all of us move in and out of work and education and training throughout our lives. Our system of certification will have to be modified considerably to accommodate this.

It is likely that increased opportunities to study will diminish the numbers seeking to enter work at 16. But our secondary school system will have to be transformed before we reach the situation when there are no longer large numbers of young people who reject further education as an option at 16. Even when the transformation comes about it should remain possible for young people to seek to enter work at 16 and think perhaps of returning to college later in their lives.

This brings us to the question of what should replace YTS. I suspect that one of the major flaws in both YOP and YTS has arisen from the mixture of objectives behind both programmes. YTS is talked of as a training programme but its overwhelming aim is to remove young people from the dole queue and to provide something akin to the real jobs for which they yearn. I believe that we should cease to muddle these objectives. Employers should be encouraged to recruit young people in proportion to the numbers they intend to employ on a permanent basis. A government allowance should be made available to subsidize their wages and to contribute towards the cost of training. But all employers should be expected to top up this allowance to an established minimum. Beyond this it would be for collective bargaining to establish what their wages should be.

If this approach is adopted, we will be left with two problems. In the early days, it is unlikely that there will be as many jobs as young people seeking places. It is to be hoped that in time our economic policies will generate sufficient jobs to provide two alternatives for 16-and 17-year-olds, a real job with training or a college-based course. We will however need additional programmes in the meantime. The second problem arises in the fields of retailing, catering, distribution and other similar sectors which have tradi-tionally employed large numbers of young people but been notoriously bad at training and had a high labour turnover. It is also in these sectors that some of the most exploitative and least satisfactory YOP and YTS has flourished. I suggest that this problem could be overcome by the establishment of training agencies which would replace existing managing agencies and cease to operate for profit. Such agencies could be based in colleges, voluntary organizations or perhaps Careers Offices. They would be expected to place young people into permanent jobs in these sectors and to supervise their placements, provide training and assist young people to find a new employer if their placement proves unsatisfactory. Such employers should be expected to top up the trainees' allowance just like large employers. There would be an established minimum and it would be for young people to join trade unions and bargain in the usual way to obtain better wages.

The final element of the scheme would be provided by the voluntary sector. Voluntary organizations could be invited to join the scheme either on the same basis as small employers or as training agencies. The difference in their situation would be that they would not be expected to top up wages from their own resources. Government money would have to be made available to provide such trainees with the minimum wage guaranteed to others. This would constitute the residual make-work part of the scheme. The jobs provided would be approved by trade unions as now. But we would hope that in time such make-work schemes would decline in size. The voluntary sector would then participate in the training of young people either because of a proven track record on training or because there were real jobs to be done, or perhaps because the schemes had shown themselves particularly able in providing for groups with special needs.

The great advantage of such a scheme to replace YTS is that we would move back to real jobs and to real training. Employers would again be required to pay for their labour and normal collective bargaining would be restored to the youth labour market. Strict monitoring of equal opportunities for young women, young black people and the disabled should be made a condition for participation in the scheme. No employer should be allowed to recruit young people without participating in the scheme. Thus every young worker would be guaranteed training.

The question that then arises is what machinery should be used to deliver local schemes. It is impossible to answer this question fully without considering how our national training system is to be structured. But whatever form the national machinery takes, local colleges are clearly going to play a central role. Given also that local government will have a major economic role under the alternative economic strategy (AES), it seems obvious that the local supervisory body should be a local authority committee with co-opted representatives from trade unions, employers, colleges and voluntary organizations. The local delivery and supervision of all provision for 16–18-year-olds should thus be restored to local education authorities.

The starting point in relation to the Community Programme should be a concern to minimize temporary work schemes and abolish them as soon as possible. Jobs that need to be done should be permanent jobs. It is unsatisfactory in the extreme to offer those who have been without work for a very long time a temporary job which will return them to the dole queue in a year. This does not mean however that we will not need special job creation programmes for the long-term unemployed. It is impossible that a change in economic policy will create 4 million jobs immediately. And without special provision the normal operation of the labour market would have the long-term unemployed last in the queue for the new jobs.

The Community Programme should be abolished and replaced by a scheme that makes funds available to public sector employers and the voluntary sector to provide jobs for the long-term unemployed. All such jobs should pay the trade union negotiated rate for the job and offer prospects for promotion in the normal way. The reason for special funding would be to encourage the creation of jobs in labour-intensive areas – home helps, youth workers, care assistants for the elderly, environmental work, improvements to community buildings and all the other sectors which have been shown through the development of MSC schemes to be badly neglected. But instead of special schemes for the unemployed threatening the jobs that already exist by providing cheap alternatives, they would simply enlarge the number of posts available. The second reason for a special fund would be to ensure that priority was given to the long-term unemployed and to impose equal opportunity conditions on all who participate. It should also be an element of the scheme that induction training would be provided to help those who had been demoralized by long-term unemployment to regain confidence in their ability to take on such jobs.

Such a scheme would have enormous potential to create vast numbers of useful permanent jobs in the public and voluntary sector. My hope would be, to take one example, that neglected council estates might be provided with additional caretakers and maintenance workers. Tower blocks could be provided with reception staff, which would cut down on vandalism and humanize the environment. Extra workers could be employed to improve on cleaning and maintenance and thus reverse the sense of decline and squalor that increasingly pervades many estates. This programme would be complemented by support for local co-operatives and the continuation of the enterprise allowance scheme, both of which should be supervised by local authority economic development departments.

Provision for the long-term unemployed must also include a big expansion of training and educational provision. An allowance could be paid just as it will be for 16–18-year-olds, based perhaps on the levels of allowance currently available for TOPS schemes. We should aim to work as rapidly as possible towards the provision of a guarantee to the long-term unemployed of a job or an educational course or a training place on the lines of the YTS guarantee.

Clearly there is not space here to examine all the details of the suggested new approach. These are simply my first thoughts. Many questions remain to be settled. On national machinery I assume that we would retain the MSC which would continue to be funded through the DE as a counterweight to the Treasury. For 16–19-year-olds there should be a joint committee straddling the MSC and the DES to try to pull together the various education and training routes into a coherent scheme. All local supervision and monitoring would be controlled through local authorities which would complement the massive enlargement of their economic development responsibilities which will come with the implementation of the AES.

All of this would of course be only a part of the restructuring of the economy and training system. It will be assumed that provision for 16–19-year-olds and the long-term unemployed meshes into mainstream developments in economic and training policy. But without special provision for the unemployed they would be likely to remain at the back of too many employment and training queues. And some of the better lessons of special measures would be lost.

3. YTS: The Jewel in the MSC's Crown?

Dan Finn

Since its creation in 1973, the activities of the Manpower Services Commission (MSC) have affected literally millions of people and kept thousands out of dole queues – and unemployment statistics. Their schemes have also structured the experiences of an increasing number of school leavers as they have made the hazardous transition to work – or unemployment.

The programmes of the MSC represent the most active policies of the Conservative government for responding to the crisis of mass unemployment. As such, their interventions have become monetarism's panacea, obscuring the manifest economic failure of government policy and suggesting instead that the causes and cures for unemployment are to be found, not in the economic and social system, but in the capacities and skills of individual workers.

If we are to accept the ideology of contemporary Conservatism at face value, it would appear that we are in the middle of a dynamic, progressive and commonly agreed transition from recession to a utopian, new-technology economy where everyone will be fully trained and able to realize their hopes and aspirations.

The reality for the working class is nothing like this, and particularly for the young working class the outlook is increasingly bleak. Never having been able to rely on the education system for opportunities beyond 16, the majority at least could count on being able to gain independence and status through work. Now hundreds of thousands can only count on the offer of the Youth Training Scheme (YTS), an offer which does not deal with the situation, for the persistence of mass youth unemployment undermines YTS. Even a place for two years will inevitably end for many in unemployment. For already thousands of YTS graduates enter a depressed labour market where their job prospects are diminished by competition from experienced adults as well as a new batch, each year, of subsidized school leavers.

There is a yawning chasm between the stated objectives of the MSC's schemes and the practical everyday experience of trainees. It is in this context – where the oppressive realities of Thatcherite Britain were to be magically transformed and marketed as new freedoms and liberties – that the initials of the MSC have been given a new interpretation. In place of the technocratic and dynamic Manpower Services Commission, many see the emergence of an embryonic Ministry of Social Control.[1]

Since 1981 a bewildering array of training strategies and plans have emerged from various government departments. With little respect for conventional and constitutional niceties – like consultation with the schools and colleges who will be asked to undertake the work – radical proposals have been outlined to relate all public education and training provision to the new divisions being wrought in the economy by mass unemployment and the impact of new technologies. The work of further education colleges (FE), Skillcentres and Jobcentres, of voluntary organizations – and now of schools – is being transformed. In this process the individual needs of youth, both employed and unemployed, have been ruthlessly subordinated to commercialism based on a narrow and crude definition of employers' requirements.

Ostensibly, the MSC is now involved in a quantitative and qualitative expansion of its various programmes. The YTS, for example, is designed to accommodate over 250,000 school leavers each year. The TVEI – which strikes at the heart of comprehensive education – is now operating in most local authorities, and when fully operational, could be directly affecting up to 100,000 school pupils. The Adult Training Strategy (ATS) will cater for over 250,000 people. The MSC is starting to take control of a quarter of all non-advanced further education (NAFE) and has been given a direct role in the in-service training of teachers. The Community Programme (CP), which recycles the long-term unemployed at an average wage of less than £60 a week, is to be expanded to 230,000 places. The MSC will bypass ratecapped local authorities and be involved in what are described as 'inner city task groups' that will attempt to 'beautify' deprived urban areas. Most dramatically, the Youth Training Scheme is being expanded to two years on the grounds, that, to quote a Conservative Chancellor of the Exchequer, the YTS had proved 'a successful bridge between school and work'![2]

The long-term objective: a remade working class

The government has embarked on an extremely ambitious attempt to remake the British working class. It intends to resolve Britain's economic crisis by undermining the power of the organized working class to protect and advance itself, by creating a new generation of workers who will be pliant, adaptable, non-unionized, and grateful for any job whatever the conditions. Since there is resistance to this policy, monetarists are no longer relying on the free play of market forces. Through government control and intervention they are using education and training policy to create a new workforce – in the words of the Chancellor – 'with the right skills; one that is adaptable, reliable, motivated and is prepared to work at wages that employers can afford to pay'.[3]

The MSC worked hard to cultivate extensive support for each phase of its expansion. Despite acute reservations, particularly within the unions (see Chapters 1 and 10), a tripartite consensus between government, unions and employers has been carefully constructed around each new programme. Yet by examining YTS, the 'Jewel in the Crown' of this new generation of programmes, it will become clear that it offers little of real value to the young working class.

The government and the MSC have always dismissed their critics as misguided or malevolent, and from the start claimed a large measure of success for YTS. They pointed to the 450,000 training places created in the first year, the participation of many school leavers, most of whom, they claimed, had got jobs or a foundation training which would act as a permanent bridge to work.

It is as naive to accept these claims at face value as it is instructive to remember that even the present YTS is not what Conservatives wanted. When they first considered replacing the much-criticized and unpopular Youth Opportunities Programme (YOP), Mrs Thatcher's administration proposed the introduction of a one-year traineeship for all unemployed school leavers,[4] who would be paid only £15 a week and would lose their entitlement to supplementary benefit – then £14.30 a week.

This provoked considerable opposition. The Careers Service, voluntary organizations, FE lecturers and, significantly, some employers, were hostile to a programme that would virtually conscript the young unemployed into low-paid traineeships. The TUC stated unequivocally that they would not support the scheme unless there was a higher allowance and no compulsion. As a result, the MSC, which had initiated the debate, set up a tripartite working party – made up of employer, trade union and government representatives – to produce a more acceptable set of proposals.

The Youth Task Group duly came forward with their alternative.[5] They suggested a training scheme embracing employed and unemployed 16-year-olds and paying £25 a week. It was to be a 'quality' scheme wih voluntary participation. Their recommendations were grudgingly accepted by Norman Tebbit, then Employment Secretary, who later set to work with Cabinet colleagues to achieve Conservatives' objectives by other, more indirect, means.

Meanwhile, YTS claimed to guarantee a year's broad-based training, with 13 weeks off-the-job provision (including education) to all minimum-age school leavers at a national cost of about £1 billion. It was anticipated that 300,000 trainees would be placed on Mode A schemes – that is, schemes run by employers themselves. A further 160,000 were to be accommodated in a mixture of local authority, state and voluntary provision, to be known as Mode B schemes. Because Mode B often involved provision of new resources or programmes designed to meet the needs of specific groups, like young offenders or the handicapped, their places were more expensive than the places provided at employers' own workplaces in Mode A.

Individual proposals for schemes were to be approved and monitored by local Area Manpower Boards (AMBs), made up of individuals representing employers and trade unions, with minority representation appointed from other groups like the voluntary sector. It was anticipated – naively, it turns out – that YTS would not displace conventional jobs and that all schemes would have the approval of the relevant trade union.

This programme seemed at first to many who had been critical of the original white paper to offer a progressive way forward. For the trade union movement, in particular, it appeared to secure both the long-standing TUC policy of day-release education for all young workers and a new right of access to quality training for unemployed school leavers. More importantly, the YTS was able to attract broad public support in an election year because of extensive advertising (Saatchi and Saatchi handled its launch at a cost of well over £1 million). This portrayed YTS as a 'permanent bridge to work' and attempted to associate it with the new technologies intended to be at the forefront of employment creation.

In reality, developments in the first year of the scheme saw an abandonment of those election-year pretensions, as YTS was rapidly reduced to a mechanism for producing the kind of workforce that the Conservative government thought appropriate to the new realism of the late 1980s and beyond.

After the 1983 general election the YTS was increasingly characterized as an employer-led scheme. By contrast with the trainee-centred rhetoric and concessions embedded in the Youth Task Group Report, the government made it abundantly evident that so far as it was concerned, trainees should be exposed for as long as possible to the discipline of the workplace and individual employers. This renewed emphasis on employers' requirements reflected, among other things, the need to secure enough training places from employers at the start of the scheme.

It also signalled a series of important concessions. For example, employers retained complete control over hiring and firing trainees, and, where they use colleges, they have been granted special discounts on charges for educational provision. Employers were also exempted from the cost and responsibilities of several Acts which protect ordinary employees, so that YTS trainees were excluded from the Employment Protection and from parts of the Race and Sex Discrimination Acts. Lower standards of health and safety protection were another concession; as a result, trainees' health and safety protection was and is quite inadequate.[6]

Despite a recommendation from the Youth Task Group that the allowances should keep pace with inflation, it was only increased to £26.25 late in 1984, and has slipped back even further since. There has been some 'topping up' of the basic pay and some better conditions secured by trade-union organized workplaces, but over 80 per cent of trainees receive the pay minimum of YTS pay.

Nationally, the YTS actually worked out much cheaper for the government than originally anticipated. Rather than the much publicised, £1 billion, actual expenditure in the first year amounted to little more than £770 million, over £138 million of which in any case came from the European Social Fund of the EEC. Needless to say, this unspent surplus was clawed back by the Treasury for the government's own purposes instead of being used to improve the quality of the scheme or the amount of its allowances.

Failure of the Area Boards

The Area Manpower Boards, which were supposed to monitor and control the scheme, have been far less effective than was anticipated. A large proportion of schemes started without being approved by any trade union. These included schemes negotiated nationally by the Large Companies Unit of the MSC which account for a third of all YTS places offered by employers. Board members find these places are not subject to the approval of even the limited scrutiny of local AMBs. They also find that sponsors need only declare that there is no 'appropriate' or 'recognized' trade union for approval and schemes can proceed unhindered. Trade union officers have complained that MSC officials are working 'closely with employers in preparing proposals' so that it will be 'difficult to fault them' on paper.[7]

The work of Board members is heavily circumscribed. When visiting schemes, members have to be chaperoned and give a day's notice. They cannot insist on seeing the letters of trade union approval which each scheme not otherwise exempt is supposed to have (but many, it is suspected, do not). Lastly, AMBs have been overruled by the MSC when trying to protect local provision – for example, by preventing the participation of private training agencies or resisting cutbacks in provision, of, for instance, skill-centres or Mode B schemes (many of which were shut down within a few months of starting).

At best, the role of the AMB has become advisory, approving plans and programmes submitted by MSC officials; at worst, a rubber stamp.

A MSC survey of 464 Mode A managing agents found that 14 per cent aimed to make a profit out of YTS training. Despite MSC protestations to the contrary, private training agencies also became heavily involved in YTS. By 1985, of the 102,000 locally approved Mode A places covered by 20 AMBs, it was found that nearly 30 per cent were controlled by private agencies.[8]

Alongside these private agencies, a range of employer-dominated training organizations and local authority consortiums mushroomed into existence. There were 4,200 managing agents using in excess of 100,000 workplaces, which meant that many trainees were placed in small, non-unionized, low-paying workplaces.

Over half of the managing agents surveyed by the MSC provided their own work experience, but over a quarter subcontracted all of it to other employers. On average these schemes used 35 workplaces each and these were usually small establishments employing less than 25 workers.

In Birmingham, the National Association of Teachers in Further and Higher Education (NATFHE) investigated some of the private agencies involved in local YTS provision, and, in emphasizing how lax the MSC checks had been, established that many of these agencies had questionable business, let alone educational credentials.[9] Out of 30 agencies, for example, only ten were companies of any long financial standing. Seven had not filed up-to-date accounts at Companies House, as the law requires; two had had their accounts heavily qualified by auditors; three were not registered as companies at all; and seven had been formed only in the previous two years.

Apparently the MSC handed over millions of pounds of public money without even routine checks on YTS sponsors' financial standing. Some private sponsors – like the two large agencies, KBS and Computotech – collapsed spectacularly, leaving trainees adrift and the MSC (and ultimately the public) out of pocket.

Many of the Industrial Training Boards (ITBs) became YTS subcontractors and considerable inroads were made into the apprenticeship system, which had been steadily declining since the early 1970s. YTS accelerated the process in construction, road transport, hairdressing, catering, electricity supply, chemicals and agriculture because it became the new route into apprentice-level training. Other sectors are likely to follow, as government support for apprentice training is increasingly subsumed, as is intended, within YTS.

The MSC's survey of managing agents found that only 18 per cent of trainees in Mode A schemes were classified as apprentices or long-term trainees, and these typically enjoyed better wages (£41 per week in 1984) and far better quality training, spending on average 32 weeks in off-the-job provision.[10] In most of these cases the YTS year covered the first year of a three- or four-year programme, with most young people training for skilled occupations in construction or engineering. Many of these schemes had recognized trade union support in contrast to those run by small or non-unionised employers, where allowances, conditions and quality were far inferior.

What had emerged was a two-tier system within the single YTS scheme. The majority of trainees were being offered only a process of vocational preparation, which introduced them to the experiences and disciplines they would previously have received at work, while a minority were involved in the process of real vocational training on the lines of a first-year apprenticeship. For one university researcher, Malcolm Cross, the MSC's strategy was now evident: to use 'high-level training for a minority to assist economic restructuring . . . [but] to employ work experience, temporary work and work preparation [for the majority] as a substitute for employment'.[11]

Within an overall attempt to reduce the size of the public sector, the MSC has pioneered new and indirect means of achieving government programmes. Originally it operated its special measures through a large number of sponsors, but with YTS it introduced the concept of managing agents, organizations paid an operating fee who contract to provide the complete training programme for a specified number of trainees. Ideologically, this structure suits the Conservatives' free market strategy because it relieves the MSC of responsibility for monitoring what happens to trainees in individual workplaces, which is now the task of the managing agent, at the same time as enabling the Commission to keep much tighter financial and managerial control over a smaller number of managing agents.

But these factors mean it has negative consequences for the quality of MSC schemes. The increased bureaucratic control has had a particularly harsh impact on voluntary sector sponsors like the churches and certain charities. According to a report prepared by Church Action on Poverty, many sponsors who originally experienced 'a sense of partnership and flexibility', have since been 'reduced to the status of subcontractors delivering programmes to order', leaving 'very little room for manoeuvre if MSC policy changes'.[12] Indeed, because of a lack of recruitment of young people to YTS, and the government's insistence on an employer-led scheme, the MSC had to reduce the size of YTS by cutting the better-funded, trainee-centred Mode B provision by 20 per cent. The impact of these reductions fell on community-based agencies (like Dr Barnardo's Brent Warehouse Training Scheme, the Bradford Cathedral YTS Scheme, or Doncaster Metro Action Central which was closed with the loss of 255 places).

The first year of YTS was punctuated by public controversy, as established voluntary agencies were subjected to widespread disruption and cutbacks almost irrespective of the quality of their own training. (NACRO lost 428 of the 2,416 places, and the YMCA's 'Training for Life' programme lost 773 places and had seven projects closed down.) Yet only a few months earlier the MSC had been trying to persuade these very voluntary organizations to get involved in YTS.

The lesson was that when government priorities change, the sponsors – especially in the voluntary sector – have little chance of resisting the loss of their investment of time and effort, irrespective of the quality of their training or the need for their services by the groups for whom they were providing.

The use of managing agents also means that arrangements for monitoring individual employers are even less effective than they were under YOP; and there is virtually no MSC mechanism for ensuring that trainees do not displace employees. Drawing on the experience of 'agents, sponsors and trade union representatives', an independent survey from Income Data Services Ltd concluded that the 'MSC is in no real position to police the scheme thoroughly', and that its 'staff have neither the experience nor time to monitor schemes adequately'.[13] The monitoring that takes place concentrates on 'systems and supervising staffs, rather than [on] training and work placements'.[14]

Even on its own criteria something like a third of all schemes were not meeting MSC minimum standards during the first year; they had a 'poor definition of core and basic skills', 'inadequate assessment of trainees', and 'poor integration between on- and off-the-job training'.[15]

A key feature of the quality which was supposed to distinguish YTS from YOP was the requirement that there would be at least 13 weeks off-the-job training. However, because the financial support for each trainee was so inadequate, training was disproportionately concentrated in low-skill areas, and many managing agents experienced considerable financial pressure. This was particularly acute where they had problems recruiting or retaining trainees. Since the off-the-job component of YTS was the most expensive part of the scheme, it was 'in this area that cuts [were] made – with firms providing only the very minimum required'.[16]

Many LEAs and FE colleges had assumed that the bulk of the off-the-job training would be provided by the education sector.

This never occured – with consequent problems for the education service as its expected work failed to materialize. Colleges provided training for less than 50 per cent of schemes in the first year, and there were indications that this would contract further as more managing agencies provide their own off-the-job training.[17]

For Roy Boffey, an FE lecturer otherwise committed to the development of YTS, many of these agencies were 'functionally useless'. He pointed out that there were too many small, consortium-type agencies who were unable to provide quality training and were frequently 'unskilled, inexperienced intermediaries acting as blocks in the system rather than facilitators'.[18]

Low standards

An HMI survey of FE courses for YTS trainees found that 'attempts to provide a broadly based introduction to a family of jobs were not readily acceptable'.[19] The best results and most motivated students were found in the apprentice-type courses which provided narrower, more specific training, and led to nationally recognized certificates and diplomas.

Outside of these courses there was 'little evidence of integration or co-ordination of core skills, vocational studies and work experience', and 'no clear evidence of required standards of performance being understood or achieved'.[20] They also reported 'many instances of teaching and learning taking place in depressing conditions that failed to provide adequate practical working environments'.[21] It was stressed that the real learning difficulties encountered by many of the trainees were unlikely to be improved by the '40 to 50 teaching hours usually allocated to these subjects'.[22]

By far the most important element of the scheme, the on-the-job training, is not assessed in any conventional sense, and without adequate monitoring or skill testing, it is difficult to establish the quality of training offered. The MSC's survey of managing agents found that 40 per cent of trainees spent most of their time on their work experience assisting other workers to do their normal jobs, and 30 per cent doing work of their own that was similar to that done by ordinary employees. Only 30 per cent, including apprentices, were involved in systematic on-the-job training unrelated to production.

Many employers clearly preferred to train young people in skills which could be used immediately, and they also resisted the notion of broadly transferable skills. According to the Incomes Data Services survey, 'many schemes are not broad-based but specifically linked to the needs of the industry or company involved – in some cases to the complete exclusion of sections of the MSC's proposals'.[23]

The quality of public provision in FE has been, at best, variable, but few other sponsors have offered training leading to the attainment of recognized national standards. At the moment, all that most trainees obtain at the end of YTS is a descriptive certificate. Development work on the content of YTS training is overwhelmingly preoccupied with one aspect of assessment: establishing ways in which 'actual performance' can be recorded at work. This is likely to mean that trainee performance will be judged primarily by the subjective methods of YTS sponsors and managing agents. It is intended that the certificate will eventually consist of three parts: the first page, a summary statement of achievement, another few pages, a 'record of achievement', and the final page will describe the training plan followed.

It was argued by the MSC that this would amount to a 'recognized' certificate in its own right, but because of the uncertain response from employers and other examining bodies, and because it was decided to extend the YTS to a two-year scheme, the qualifications issue was postponed again by a working party set up in 1985 to review the structure of examination and certification systems for vocational education and training.[24]

It has been claimed that the YTS certificate will amount to a work-based alternative to conventional qualifications. David Young, when the chairperson of the MSC, asserted that the YTS certificate will 'be more important in employment prospects for young people than even O or A levels'.[25] These educational pretensions, never likely in any case, were shattered when the Department of Employment issued initial guidelines for the off-the-job provision. They specifically excluded YTS trainees from considering matters 'related to the organization and functioning of society in general'.[26] It appeared that these young people could learn how to complete application forms but they would not be allowed to discuss why they were unemployed! These guidelines were toned down after public criticism, but they signalled the government's intention of maintaining strict control over the content and methods of YTS in the interests of a restricted, employer-led definition of work socialization.

Between 1974 and 1984 the proportion of 16-year-olds who stayed on in full-time education increased by 10 per cent – to 45 per cent. Yet in 1984 only one in five 16-year-olds obtained a full-time job compared with more than three in five a decade earlier. By December 1983, although nearly half the 16-year-old school leavers had joined YTS, a further 38 per cent had obtained jobs outside YTS, half of which were in manufacturing and production, and 14 per cent were unemployed.[27]

Despite the collapse of the youth labour market, it appeared that some employers were less than convinced about introducing a training programme for their own young unskilled workers, and in some sectors there was considerable trade union opposition to YTS as well (see Chapter 10).

Originally the Youth Task Group envisaged that YTS would cover employed as well as unemployed school leavers. Some conventional employment was directly displaced by the YTS, but other segments of the juvenile labour market have been less susceptible to the blandishments of MSC publicity. The number of employed trainees anticipated on the scheme, therefore, had to be revised downwards from an original one-third of the total to a mere 5 per cent. Nevertheless, the MSC's survey of providers showed that 24 per cent of trainees were occupying jobs for young people which had been brought within YTS, and 7 per cent of trainees had been taken on in preference to older workers. Clearly, YTS was directly displacing employment.

At the same time YTS was also becoming a major channel of recruitment. Over half of managing agents and nearly three-quarters of work experience providers said they were using YTS to screen for permanent employment. At the time of the survey in 1984, managing agents anticipated taking on only about 15 per cent of trainees, work experience providers only a quarter of theirs. YTS may have been portrayed as a new deal for the young unemployed, but it appears instead to be providing employers with a pool of cheap trainees from which they can pick and choose for permanent work.

Although nearly half of the 16-year-olds who were apprentices, and other long-term trainees in England and Wales, were brought within the scope of YTS, this did nothing to reverse the cutback in long-term skill training. The number of apprentices recruited in

1979 had been 100,000; as early as 1983 this was down to 40,000.[28]

Paul Ryan showed that YTS offers little prospect of solving the chronic problem of training for key skills.[29] The subsidy available under YTS is broadly equivalent to that which existed previously, but placed alongside the real cost of apprenticeship training – in 1982 in construction and road transport about £5,000, in engineering about £12,000 – it hardly overcomes the disincentive to train.

Ryan emphasized that 'the number on YTS who continue on to complete a full apprenticeship is unlikely to exceed significantly the low levels of apprentice activity prevalent before YTS'.[30] The Engineering ITB pointed out that the 1984–5 recruitment of 3,000 first-year technician apprentices compares badly with the nearly 6,000 required merely to replace natural losses.[31] Technicians are a key group of workers vital to the diffusion and application of the new technologies, and government policy – despite the fanfare – has done little to remedy these skill shortages.

On the other hand, monetarists have had 'success' in reducing young people's relative earnings. First there was the Young Workers Scheme which subsidized employers who paid below trade union rates of pay. This has gone but in its place is a drive to exclude young workers from the coverage of Wages Councils and to alter the Employment Protection Act.

Young people's relative wages fell between 1979 and 1984, and in real terms workers under 18 were up to £2.50 a week worse off. Boys now earned barely a third of the wages of men over 21. Girls, who had been paid 56 per cent of an older woman's pay in 1979, were getting only 48 per cent by 1984.[32] Contrary to monetarist dogma that the young were 'pricing themselves out of work', these reductions in wage levels had little impact on young people's employment. Employers were still not willing to employ them.

The experience of trainees

At the end of the first year of YTS only 350,000 places had been taken up – less than three-quarters of the anticipated figure. In addition, one in five trainees dropped out of the scheme prematurely; and a third became unemployed. There is clear evidence that a substantial number of school leavers have been unwilling to become involved in YTS; and that substantial numbers leave before they complete it.

Many of these refusals took place in a context where the MSC's Jobcentres had to resort to sending threatening letters to unemployed school leavers. In the year preceding November 1984, as many as 10,701 young people had their supplementary benefit reduced because they left their YTS place prematurely 'without good cause'. A further 1,163 had their benefit reduced because they refused to take up a place.

YTS was originally described as a voluntary scheme of quality. Within a year of its start it looked more like a compulsory dose of work experience. By December 1984, in a 'Christmas gift' to future unemployed school leavers, Mrs Thatcher announced that her government would be taking steps to remove their right to supplementary benefit, declaring that 'young people ought not to be idle' and 'should not have the option of being unemployed'.[33] Not only had many of the young working class forfeited their right to work, but it now seemed they were to lose their right to supplementary benefit.

The lack of enthusiasm for YTS was not, however, the product of irresponsibility or feckless idleness. Despite the attractive image of MSC publicity, there were enormous variations within the scheme. Some employers offered good training, with the prospect of a job at the end, but other sponsors clearly offered what school leavers saw as an extension of YOP and experienced as a spell of cheap labour. Those who refused to join the scheme dismissed it as 'slave labour' doing menial work offering no real training.[34]

Irrespective of the presentation of YTS as 'quality' training, it was evident to HMIs inspecting the scheme that trainees saw it largely as an avenue into employment,[35] a view confirmed by many of the comments in the MSC's own surveys of ex-trainees. Many young people expressed positive responses to aspects of their experience on YTS but they hardly used demanding criteria. Almost universally, YTS trainees (as well as refusers) complained about the low level of allowance. This was experienced more acutely by those doing similar work alongside employees who were receiving normal rates of pay.

For trainees the vital element of the scheme was the work placement, which gave them a 'foot in the door' with employers. Where YTS was the agreed mechanism for recruitment into a skilled occupation – like agriculture or construction – trainees saw participation as an appropriate first step. But other trainees, according to the HMIs, saw YTS in a different light. Those with relatives or friends who were unemployed, or who themselves joined YTS after losing a job, often viewed the programme with some scepticism. In areas of high unemployment, it seemed that the training allowance – meagre though it is – was as much the incentive to joining as the prospect of getting work. Trainees regarded the YTS as a substitute for paid employment, and they 'rarely' stayed on it when jobs became available.[36]

Inequality reinforced

Detailed evidence, therefore, was revealing that the YTS, rather than transforming the labour market, was reproducing most of its essential characteristics. It was also reproducing the selective mechanism of education. Not surprisingly in an employer-led scheme, it seemed that many organizations used 'normal recruitment methods and selection procedures'.[37]

According to the MSC's surveys of managing agents, young people entering Mode A schemes did 'not face a rigorous selection process', yet at the same time it pointed out that a quarter of Mode A schemes did not accept either those with handicaps or disabilities, or ex-offenders – and a third did not accept young people with learning difficulties! Significantly, where YTS was the first year of an extended period of training, or was used to select people for permanent employment, entry standards were more stringent still. One in ten agents required prospective trainees to have at least three GCE O levels, and just over a quarter used tests of numeracy, literacy and manual dexterity when selecting trainees.

As a consequence, clear racial and sexual divisions emerged in YTS, especially between different modes and types of provision. Black youngsters were less likely to get on employer-based schemes[38] and the Commission for Racial Equality investigated 15 major Mode A employers to find that virtually no black youngsters had been recruited[39] (see Chapter 9 for a detailed discussion of ethnic minorities and the MSC programmes.)

Girls are also suffering discrimination in YTS, clearly being recruited to a far narrower range of occupations than boys, many limited to training for traditional 'female' work, and gaining only limited access to important MSC facilities like Information Technology Centres. (See Chapter 8 for a detailed discussion of girls and women in MSC programmes.) Instead of ameliorating inequalities, YTS is compounding them.

Economic and social divisions were also evident in the job prospects of trainees, which varied widely by region, occupational training area and previous level of qualification. Trainees with the best job prospects were located in administrative or clerical fields or in Large Company Unit Mode A schemes – like those with Debenhams, Marks & Spencer or British Rail – where more than 70 per cent of trainees got jobs.

Trainees with the worst prospects were found in, or sent to, Mode B schemes, and in areas of work with high unemployment. From the information contained in the MSC's regular monthly surveys of 15 per cent of YTS leavers' destinations, it seems that between June and October 1984 just over 56 per cent of leavers obtained jobs and over 31 per cent became unemployed. The remainder continued in education or training or left the labour market.[40]

Armed with YTS certificates, unemployed trainees were left to enter a depressed labour market where their job prospects were squeezed by competition from experienced adults and a new batch of subsidised school leavers. At the end of the first year, half of the country's under-18s, and one in four of the under-25s, were out of work. Half a million 25-year-olds had been unemployed more than six months, and 330,000 of them for more than a year. The situation did not improve in subsequent years.

It is these realities and the lack of quality in so many YTS schemes – not young people's alleged 'idleness' – which were and are having such serious implications for the public credibility of the MSC and the reactions of young people to it.

A two-year traineeship – any better?

The second year of operation of YTS had been described as one of consolidation, but when it became apparent that economic recovery was unlikely to reduce levels of unemployment, it seemed that additional measures would be needed to manage the continuing crisis of youth unemployment. On the one hand, this involved the creation of a two-year traineeship for 16-year-old school leavers. On the other hand, the Community Programme, which provides temporary part-time jobs for large numbers of unemployed 18– to

25-year-olds, was expanded to 230,000 places.

Thus in a keynote speech in 1984, Geoffrey Holland, Director of the MSC, called for a 'new deal' which would offer school leavers vocational education and training up to 18. The objective would be to increase the supply of 'qualified workers' by giving young people the chance to participate in work-based and work-related training and further education. The scheme was to be voluntary and would give school leavers a 'traineeship for today', involving the achievement of recognized competence in occupations or groups of occupations. It would offer young people a new recognized 'trainee status', which for the Director of MSC, was 'not taking young people out of the labour market. It is putting them in, but putting them in on terms which secure their entry'. The use of YTS simply to make young people more acceptable to employers had now been placed at the heart of the two-year scheme.

Most contributions to discussion about the two-year YTS repeat the arguments about quality training that were used earlier to promote the one-year YTS. As with YOP and YTS before it, another corporate consensus has been painstakingly constructed for a two-year scheme, and the TUC has pledged support. Not surprisingly, when the government's package emerged in the Budget Speech of 1985, it offered considerably less than the 'new deal' portrayed earlier by the MSC's Director.

The new scheme is simply offering a two-year training place to all unemployed 16-year-old school leavers, or a one-year place to 17-year-olds. Once again, it is employer-led. 135,000 more places will be provided, with additional resources of £125 million for the first year, and £300 million earmarked for 1987–88. It sounds generous, but in fact, most of this will come from the underspending on the one-year YTS and diversion of funding from the defunct Young Workers Scheme. The government says that it is 'expected' that employers will contribute more towards the costs of the scheme, but no mechanism or programme is provided for making that aspiration a reality. There is only a review and reorganization of vocational qualifications, so that young people enter the 'labour market with a qualification, either general or work-related, relevant to employment'.[41]

Making this policy a reality was left in the hands of the MSC, but for the government the expansion was intended to secure a key objective: 'it will constitute a major step towards our objective of ensuring that unemployment among young people under 18 becomes a thing of the past'.[42]

Opposition to YTS

From the start YTS has inspired cartoonists to set out the wide range of opposition YTS has encountered. In April 1985, in an unprecedented eruption of protest, up to 200,000 school students in over 60 towns and cities staged demonstrations and strikes against the YTS and the suggestion that training might be made compulsory.[43] This was the most spectacular public manifestation of the popular opposition that the MSC had been encountering for some time. Some trade unions, and many organized workplaces, have long made it clear that they will have nothing to do with YTS, and thousands of the young unemployed have refused places. This resistance, however, has been fragmented and localised. In part this has been the result of the TUC's unwillingness to debate its commitment to the MSC, but more realistically it has reflected the success of Conservative governments in exploiting the plight of the unemployed.

On a number of occasions the TUC, to its credit, has blocked proposals which were blatantly provocative – e.g. that adults should do 'voluntary' work for their unemployment benefit. But on each occasion, behind the closed doors of the MSC a compromise was established which gave immediate concessions to critics, but at the same time delivered programmes which offer little of real value to the unemployed. The MSC has kept its formal commitment to the trade union movement – e.g. on paying the rate for the job or no overt job substitution. Unfortunately, in reality these guarantees have been eroded, redefined and manipulated, so that in many respects the government and employers have been able to proceed as they see fit.

The response of trade unions has been polarized between those advocating a boycott of the MSC and its programmes and those who claim that existing guarantees are sufficient. Pragmatism has guided official TUC attitudes, but many trade unionists argue that TUC participation in the MSC has been largely ineffectual, and has merely given the TUC seal of approval to cheap labour schemes. It has also made it very difficult to create a strategy of opposition. (See Chapter 10 for a discussion of the MSC, the TUC and individual unions.)

The call for a boycott has created a gulf between those working within the MSC and those outside. The argument creates divisions because it avoids the reality that MSC programmes do respond, however inadequately, to some of the needs of the unemployed. In addition, a boycott could easily be portrayed as an attempt to defend the position of those at work or those who already have a monopoly of access to skill training. It would offer little to the workers and activists involved in MSC schemes, or to people who believe they have no other options but to enter MSC schemes.

TUC policy calls on trades unionists to report abuses of individual schemes to MSC Area Boards, to negotiate improvements, to recruit trainees to unions, and to monitor the impact of YTS. These are important activities which without more resources and a broader campaign are unlikely to be translated into reality, even in organized workplaces. Nevertheless, with the support of progressive local authorities, projects that monitor developments have been able to expose many of the inadequacies of YTS and other MSC programmes. In alliance with other groups – e.g. Women in Youth Training or Trade Union Resource Centres – such projects have begun to work at ways of challenging the effects of MSC policy. However, with the exception of the Youth Trade Union Rights Campaign's struggle against compulsion, little headway has been made nationally in creating an active relationship between young people and the trade union movement itself.

A progressive strategy

As the TUC is unlikely to withdraw from the MSC, it is vital that a progressive strategy is formulated which would transform the TUC's role from one of consensual partner to that of advocate of the interests of trainees. It should be required to use whatever power it has – and that is not inconsiderable – within the corporate structure of the MSC to block or delay policies which are against the collective interests of the young working class. Rather than await the arrival of some future Labour government, it should work now to establish the right of trainees to organize collectively and be represented at all levels within the MSC. In 1984, for example, out of 54 AMBs only two had representatives of young people sitting on them; and these were non-voting co-opted members. Most of all, the TUC should fight abuses and campaign systematically for real improvements in trainees' conditions.

There is beyond doubt a compelling economic case for more public investment in education and training if Britain is to exploit the new technologies and keep pace with our major international trading rivals. But the reliance on an employer-led strategy defies our historical experience, which has demonstrated consistently that employers in Britain take a short-sighted view of training. They are not prepared to devote the necessary resources to it.[44] The acute shortages in specific skills which are currently restricting the pace of technological change can be largely blamed on industry itself, which, during the recession, cut back on both capital investment and training. Even now, according to the Industrial Society, two-thirds of British employers spend less than 0.5 per cent of their annual turnover on staff training.[45]

The evidence is that employers, even when they can predict their needs with any coherence, will not train sufficient numbers in sufficient quality to meet either economic or technical requirements. To provide them with an enormous public subsidy, in the form of a two-year YTS, without any rigorous attempt to define and establish the needs of the labour market, or police standards in the scheme itself, is a recipe for a real 'great training robbery'. It will exaggerate all the trends and inequalities that have emerged in the one-year YTS.

For these reasons a statutory and public training system is essential. But, in contrast to the centralized corporatism of the MSC, a progressive strategy would aim to create a decentralized training system made up of democratic and accountable structures operating on a local, area or sectoral basis.

In addition to servicing the immediate skill requirements of the economy, such a training strategy could draw on the practical experience that now exists and establish a framework within which those groups who have been traditionally marginalised by the employment system would be given resources to explore, define and meet their own training needs. This would enable training needs to be identified, and planned for, according to a much broader definition than employers' immediate requirements, and it would give more control and influence over training resources to working people and to those groups now confined to the dis-advantaged 'secondary sector' of the labour market. At the very least, this would require a radical transformation of the MSC.

In the context of an expanding economy, such a training policy would be a powerful weapon for securing other elements of social advance. Through positive action programmes and as part of a concerted assault on racist and sexist structures in the labour market, a progressive training strategy could begin to release talents and energies of groups like married women returners, members of ethnic minorities, and older unemployed male workers – whom statisticians insultingly define still as 'unskilled'.

Training for social advance

In addition to providing foundation training for school leavers, a strategy of what has been called 'Training for Social Advance' would also provide for huge expansion in funding for adult training and retraining, with an adequate system of income support which would aim to equip people with the ability to criticize and shape technical change rather than simply respond to it.[46]

A progressive process of foundation training for school leavers would look very different from a two-year YTS. It would have structured into it the acquisition of real skills and qualifications, democratic participation, equal opportunities and properly nego-tiated rates of pay which reflect the value of the work performed by young people.

Such a foundation training would not just be concerned with the acquisition of technical skills, nor would it promote an employer-defined version of work socialisation. It would start from the reality that even those going into unskilled jobs requiring little training do continue their education, as do those now consigned to unemployment.

In the process of growing up working class most of the lessons are harsh, negative and alienating. It is about time that the entry into work of the vast majority of young people was consciously designed so that the experiences encountered and the skills developed could be integrated and extended as part of their general education.

The conditions and prospects of young people placed with employers must remain within the scope of collective bargaining. As in France and West Germany, young people should be employees on a wage, with legal rights to further education and

The Youth Training Scheme 73

training. On this basis, it might be possible to talk about a 'new deal' for the young working class and discuss how that process would be integrated with other forms of continuing education and training.

As it is in Conservative Britain, many young people are simply being consigned to the margins of the economy to alternate between badly paid jobs and long spells of unemployment. Instead of creating an integrated and comprehensive structure of education and training which could begin to provide equal opportunities for 16-year-olds, the Conservatives have created a scheme which reintroduces a three-tier structure of opportunities (both outside and within educational institutions). At the same time, it creates a pool of cheap labour for employers from which they can recruit as and when they see fit. In this crude experiment in social engineering, the needs and aspirations of young people are being manipulated and their expectations systematically reduced.

In this situation, and confronted by such powerful forces, the task of educators and trainers is immense. Somehow we must resist the imposition of priorities which reflect a narrow and vulgar commercialism, which are attempting, as R. H. Tawney once put it, to provide 'cannon fodder' for industry. Simultaneously, we must attempt to exploit and develop those educational spaces that are opened by courses and schemes, which, however inadequately, start from the real destinies and interests of the young working class: the 'world of work'.

1. F Coffield, 'Is There Work After the MSC?' *New Society*, 26 January 1984.
2. Nigel Lawson, Budget speech, March 1985.
3. *Ibid.*
4. White paper, 1981.
5. MSC, The Youth Task Group Report, April 1982.
6. Youthaid, 'Health and Safety; the New Evidence about YTS', *Youthaid Bulletin*, No. 18, October 1984.
7. NUPE, 'Notes of the Meeting of Divisional Officers and NUPE Officers who were AMB Members on Tuesday 20th September 1983, at the Great Northern Hotel, London', National Union of Public Employees, 1983.

8. Hansard, Answers to Parliamentary Questions, 6 February and 16 May 1985.

9. NATFHE, *The Great Training Robbery: An Interim Report on the Role of Private Training Agencies within the YTS in the Birmingham and Solihull Area*, Birmingham Liaison Committee, Trade Union Resource Centre, Birmingham, 1984.

10. MSC, YTS Providers' Survey (YTB/85/14), presented to the Youth Training Board at its 25th meeting on 14 March 1985.

11. M. Cross, *Equality of Opportunity and Inequality of Outcome: The MSC, Ethnic Minorities and Training Policy*, Centre for Research in Ethnic Relations, Warwick University, 1985.

12. T. Addy, 'MSC and the Management of Unemployment', *Christian Social Concern: Two Contemporary Issues*, The William Temple Foundation, Occasional Paper No. 12, Manchester Business School, 1984, p. 6.

13. Incomes Data Services Ltd, *YTS: A Review*, Study 311, April 1984, p. 1.

14. *Ibid.*, p. 9.

15. MSC, Monitoring (YTB/84/13), presented to the Youth Training Board at its 17th meeting on 17 April 1985.

16. Industrial Relations Services, *IRS Guide to the Youth Training Scheme, Industrial Relations Review and Report*, 1983, p. 38.

17. Incomes Data Services Ltd, *op. cit.*, p. 19.

18. R. Boffey, 'Some Thoughts on Year One', *NATFHE JOURNAL*, October 1984, p. 24.

19. Department of Education and Science, *The Youth Training Scheme in Further Education 1983–4: An HMI Survey*, report by HM Inspectors, 1984, p. 6.

20. *Ibid.*, p. 25.

21. *Ibid.*, p. 21.

22. *Ibid.*, p. 9.

23. Incomes Data Services Ltd, *Youth Training Scheme*, Study 293, July 1983, p. 2.

24. *Education and Training for Young People*, HMSO, Cmnd 9482, April 1985, p. 9.

25. HMSO, Fourth Report from the Committee of Public Accounts, Department of Employment, MSC, Special Employment Measures, Session 1983/4, 1983, p. 41.

26. Draft Memorandum on the Political Content of YTS courses, quoted in 'Youth Scheme Rejects Political Memo', Melanie Phillips, *Guardian*, 12 October 1983.

27. Department of Employment, 'First Employment of Young People', *DE Gazette*, October 1984.

28. G. Holland, 'The Challenge of Long-Term Unemployment', address

to the Stock Exchange, 18 June 1984, para. 23.

29. P. Ryan, 'The New Training Initiative after Two Years', *Lloyds Bank Review*, April 1984.

30. *Ibid.*, p. 40.

31. Engineering Industry Training Board, *Economic and Industry Monitor*, March 1985.

32. Paul Lewis, 'The Price of a Job', *Youthaid Bulletin*, No. 19, December 1984.

33. Prime Minister, BBC, 17 December 1984, quoted in 'Thatcher Backs Out of School Leavers' Benefits', by Colin Brown, *Guardian*, 18 December 1984.

34. The Fawcett Society and the National Joint Committee of Working Women's Organizations, *The Class of 84: A Study of Girls in the First Year of the Youth Training Scheme*, London, 1985, pp. 32–3.

35. HMI, *The Youth Training Scheme in Further Education 1983–84: An HMI Survey*, DES, 1984.

36. *Ibid.*, p. 5.

37. Incomes Data Services Ltd, *YTS: A Review*, Study 293, July 1983, p. 1.

38. S. Fenton, J. Davies, R. Means and P. Burton, *Ethnic Minorities and the Youth Training Scheme*, MSC Research and Development, No. 20, MSC, 1984.

39. Commission for Racial Equality, *Racial Equality and the Youth Training Scheme*, 1984.

40. Information from Progress Reports submitted to the Youth Training Board between May and July 1985, MSC, 1985.

41. HMSO, *Education and Training for Young People*, Cmnd 9482, April 1985, p. 6.

42. *Ibid.*, p. 7.

43. *Times Educational Supplement*, 3 May 1985.

44. Morris Kaufman, 'Is there a Future for Training?', *NATFHE Journal*, May 1981.

45. Industrial Society, *A Survey of Training Costs*, London, 1985.

46. Greater London Council, *Training in Crisis: The New Training Initiative 1981–1984 Policy Review*, Greater London Training Board, 1984.

4. TVEI: The MSC's Trojan Horse

Clyde Chitty

TVEI – The Technical and Vocational Education Initiative – was introduced into some of our schools by the Manpower Services Commission (MSC) in 1983 with indecent haste and the promise of manna from heaven. Although it claimed to be a scheme to provide 'technical' and 'vocational' education for the 14-18 age group, it had involved no consultation with local authorities, teachers or parents, or the schools or colleges traditionally responsible for running and providing education. In this it represented an ominous break with the past.

Yet for many local authorities and schools, starved of resources after years of cuts and the prospect of ratecapping, the large amount of MSC funding that went with the offer made TVEI an irresistible gift. In the first year £46 million was promised to the 14 authorities initially deemed worthy of launching the programme on a pilot-scheme basis. There was money for new equipment, new staff, new curriculum development, new in-service training and new building to house TVEI units in schools. But it was to cover only five years and involve only 13,830 students and 144 schools and colleges – on average, about half a dozen in each authority and only from authorities whose proposals passed the government's selective criteria. Authorities soon fell into line. A further 48 schemes got off the ground in 1984, including five in Scotland.

Today the ground rules are known and TVEI money is available to any authority which wants to participate on the terms offered. The white paper of 1985, *Education and Training for Young People*, anticipated that TVEI would one day sweep into every authority. Yet a sizeable minority still refuses to accept the gift. Many teachers, too, remain unconvinced. In 1985 the main Scottish teachers' organization, the Educational Institute of Scotland (EIS), boycotted TVEI's introduction in at least one area – as part of its industrial action but also because teachers were suspicious of it.[1] In England and Wales, a teacher writing in a National Union of Teachers' publication a year earlier had already notified the education world that just because teachers bid for TVEI money 'in no way means they support the MSC's intervention in the school curriculum'.[2]

Although in 1985 the pilot version of TVEI had only about 3 per cent of all 14-year-old pupils spread over only 8 per cent of secondary schools, from the start there were misgivings. First, because TVEI plans had the potential to distort the curriculum for all schools eventually, but also because only certain pupils and schools were to receive the manna. Selection between schools – some receiving extra resources for basic educational development while others are not – is quite contrary to the comprehensive principle and increases disparity between schools in all authorities with TVEI. In the same way, within TVEI schools, disparities between departments which get TVEI money and those which do not (or students who get to use the equipment and those who do not) presents further difficulties to those attempting to implement the equality principle in an education system already coping with a significant level of curricular and exmination inequality between 14 and 16 – to say nothing of the struggle against structural inequalities based on sex, class and race. That TVEI has involved more boys than girls from the start (see Chapter 8) is alone cause for alarm.

For these reasons a few schools which accepted TVEI money have tried to make TVEI resources available in some form to all pupils in their schools. Very quickly, however, the MSC has reminded them that TVEI is a selective scheme for TVEI pupils only. Similarly, local authorities – like Clwyd, which proposed spreading TVEI money between all their schools, rather than spending it all on half a dozen 'designated' schools – have run into the same prohibition. The MSC has made it clear that during this pilot phase 'technical' and 'vocational' money is not to be spread fairly between all schools – or within a school, between all pupils. Even when 'replicated' at the end of the pilot period, it isn't designed to give 'technical' or 'vocational' education to all pupils, only to a minority.

Incipient attempts to make TVEI compatible with comprehensive principles have thus been thwarted. The reason the MSC can enforce compliance is because it has the power to stop the money if schools do not carry out its policy the way it wants. In addition to entrenching inequality, TVEI had therefore brought significant moves towards direct manipulation and centralized government control of the school curriculum, another even more ominous break with the past.

Background of TVEI

Although it was hatched in furtive collaboration with Conservative education and employment ministers, TVEI was very much the brainchild of David Young, Chairperson of the MSC from 1982 to 1984. TVEI's original inspiration lies in the private trade schools run by employers on the continent. France has several, started by the Organization for Rehabilitation and Training (ORT), the Jewish philanthropic organization which started life in Czarist Russia and whose British director used to be David Young. ORT operates in 32 different countries; its attitude is wholly utilitarian.

In France vocational schools make themselves available for those pupils not considered 'suited' to academic education, and thus draw pupils out of mainstream secondary schooling. However, from the evidence collected by the BBC, it seems that the French government – like many other advanced industrial governments – would now like to see vocational education postponed, possibly until the age of 18.[3] Their concern is that vocational education started too early leads to an undesirable concentration of institutions – private or state – catering for the same clientele: working-class and immigrant children from large families and poor areas. Some of the young people interviewed by the BBC were glad to be free of scholastic schooling; but others made it clear that they realized only too well that because they had given up their places in mainstream education they now had very diminished life chances.

Vocational education in this narrow sense does not open doors for youngsters – it closes them. Yet the pressures of rising unemployment will always make vocationalism for the 'less able' pupils seem beguilingly attractive at first, particularly in a system still dividing pupils by prejudged 'ability'. The same BBC TV programme saw David Young being taken round Coventry's three training workshops where secondary pupils are introduced to the 'world of work', to find trainees saying obediently for the cameras that 'it is much better than school'. Some of them then turned back to the mindless tasks which modern capitalism has in store for them for the rest of their working lives – that is, if they are lucky enough to have 'working lives'.

In the event, segregated trade schools for Britain were only a scare – a tactic the MSC has often used to coerce public opinion to accept what it is planning anyway, as the lesser of two evils. Nevertheless, in launching TVEI, David Young used the scare to the full by making it clear 'that the MSC has the power and the authority to open its own establishments, so let me say at the outset that we have no intention of doing that as I believe and hope we can work as partners with the local education authorities. If that did not prove possible, then we might have to think again.'[4] Not much scope in that threat for dissent or negotiation.

Elected authorities – as well as teachers – were deeply suspicious of the MSC's motives and of the intentions behind David Young's statement that TVEI was to be a 'short, sharp shock' to the education system. These fears were well, and prophetically, expressed in a cartoon in the *Times Educational Supplement* at the end of 1982 showing Young as a masked burglar making off with our children's precious education.[5]

A few months later there was criticism from the 1983 conference of the Council of Local Education Authorities which Young made use of to announce yet more money found for a 'second round' of TVEI pilot schemes. A number of delegates were understandably critical of the ease with which the MSC was able to find money for such projects at a time when local authorities were being forced to cut spending on education, and so many schools and educational programmes were starved of funds. The Deputy Leader of the ILEA, which had refused to bid for TVEI money, said to Young: 'You are in fact belying us if you are suggesting that we can work in partnership, because what we have seen in TVEI is a real erosion of our powers and responsibilites'.[6] The conference passed a resolution which called upon the government to deny unequivocally any intention of centralizing the education service through the MSC. But by then the Trojan Horse was already being wheeled through the gates.

Ever since the Great Debate in 1976, when curriculum questions were diverted from the issue of how best to develop a curriculum suited to comprehensive education, and became instead a matter of how schools can best serve industry, the potential for government takeover of education has been there. But it was only under Young and the Conservatives that the MSC was given the power to pursue this process to the full.

The MSC's ostensible excuse was that vocational education would lead to a better-trained workforce and thereby help Britain to move out of her recession. Young even blamed comprehensive schools for helping keep us in recession by failing to 'vocationalize the curriculum' and suggested simplistically that much of the problem would be solved if schools simply trained youngsters to fill suitable jobs.[7] Ignoring the fact that whether youngsters were trained or not, the jobs were simply disappearing, and once again conjuring up the old 11-plus theory about certain pupils not needing education, along with fears of rioting youth, Young claimed that 'a lot of young people are not naturally academic, so they major in truancy. They leave school unprepared for the world outside.'[7] Yet recent American studies show that training programmes in schools or colleges do nothing to create new jobs (nor has YTS created any in Britain). Instead, such vocational education creates a caste system by imposing on students an assumption of personal failure.[8]

It seems clear that the sudden arrival of TVEI raises a number of fundamental questions about the nature and objectives of secondary education. Most important of all: should education be about the development of attainment and the initiation of youngsters into key aspects of our culture; or should it be directed towards practical skills for particular ends? Should the 'able' be selected for the academic work; the practical work reserved for the 'less able' and the working class? Or might we begin to think in terms of a new synthesis which combines education for work by hand and brain for everyone alike, since the life development of individuals – whether at work or not – requires the combined education of both?

Since the Great Debate, a lot of partial and contradictory pronouncements have been made on the matter. James Callaghan, who initiated it, had no hesitation in opting for a utilitarian approach in his famous Ruskin College speech of October 1976: education should 'equip children . . . for a lively, constructive place in society and . . . fit them for a job of work'.[9] But since much hostility to TVEI centres on just this narrow view, others since – like TVEI Project Director, Christopher Lea – have said that

What we are striving to develop within TVEI is . . . a moderation of the harsh distinction between education and training and an approach to the presentation of the curriculum that more readily generates the motivation and builds the confidence of many young people from the age of 14 to 18.[10]

David Young takes yet another view: 'Training should not be confused with education. Training is about work-related skills and is intimately connected with employment'.[11]

David Young's view is apt to carry the most weight still and to reflect accurately MSC thinking. We can assume that in future the vast majority of 16–18-year-olds, and perhaps up to a third of 14-year-olds will be 'trained', while the top 20 per cent will continue to be 'educated' via GCE grades in the new GCSE, A level, higher education and the professions. Those in between will get a variety of pre-vocational 'options' in schools, followed by the 'option' of a variety of narrow vocational courses after 16.

No-one debating the matter at national level has as yet considered the comprehensive development of education and training for all alike. The most the MSC does – to placate widespread fears from teachers and parents that TVEI will recreate the narrow technical stream, or be a dumping ground for the pupils that schools want to get rid of – is to insist that TVEI is open to children of all abilities. But being 'open to children of all abilities' is not the same as having pupils of all attainments represented. The secondary modern school, for example, was always open to all abilities. YTS is a good example of another MSC scheme which the MSC constantly reminds us is designed for all abilities, but which everyone knows gets 90 per cent of its intake from pupils who are not in GCE streams in schools.

Not only do the MSC's assurances on this fail to allay fears, they also cause concern about the MSC's attempt to redefine the comprehensive principle itself. As one teacher wrote in the NUT's annual careers guide,

despite all disclaimers, a careful study of the scheme in operation displays in many cases an unacceptable level of selection . . . despite insistence from the TUC that the criteria should include maintenance of the comprehensive principle, there is still selection. The [MSC's] Steering Group seems to have adopted 'available across the ability range' as their definition of a comprehensive, whereas I would argue that the true definition is 'available to all'.[12]

Many of us would go further and say it means 'experienced by all'. TVEI is certainly not experienced by all, nor is it meant to be available to all in future. These are fatal flaws for a programme attempting to succeed in a school system still ostensibly purporting to be about the continued development of comprehensive education.

Breaking up comprehensive education

Thus, despite the MSC's ambiguous assurances, it is widely believed TVEI can, and is possibly intended to, break up the developing comprehensive system and reestablish the differentiation at all levels that the white paper, *Better Schools*, shows to be at the heart of all Conservative policy.[13] In primary, secondary and tertiary education, development in future is to be through separate classrooms, separate teachers, separate streams, separate curricula, separate exams, separate papers and separate courses according to prejudgements about which kind of 'ability' different groups of pupils possess. The thinking is pure '11-plus' once more – except that it is extended to every age.

Although TVEI is supposed to be a separate and complete course (rather than a new arrangement of existing subjects) through from 14 to 18, the reinsertion of 11-plus thinking is implicit rather than explicit so far. To a certain extent there is also a vagueness about the schemes' 'target group',[14] as well as some evidence that early TVEI schemes showed wide variations between and within different schemes.[15] But evidence since gives more credibility to the idea that by its implicit operation TVEI will result in the reemergence of the old hard-line tripartite system inside schools as well as between schools and further education colleges, where the 'tertiary modern sector' after 16 is being concentrated (see Chapter 5). A review in The *Times Educational Supplement* of three local authority schemes confirmed that most programmes were for pupils not on O-level courses, and that even where 'flyers' were added, they were there in small numbers as token additions, and their work was not integrated.[16] Wigans's TVEI co-ordinator admitted that the inability of teachers to explain exactly where two years of technical and vocational education might lead in terms of qualifications, largely explained the schools' inability to persuade many potential O-level candidates to take part.[17]

What we see emerging, therefore, after 14 is a divided system where 'able' pupils take an unchanged grammar-school-type course – leading to separate, high-level academic examinations and higher and professional education, augmented by the new A/S levels devised just for them; a middle band reincarnating the old technical streams and schools of the past, heading for a variety of qualifications – some old, some new; and below that a new and separate prevocational education for the 'practical', augmented by new and separate programmes for the 'slow' or the 'remedial' along the lines of the government's Low Achievers' Programme, already running in pilot form in several areas.[13] Later there will be vocational courses combining social and life 'skills' and 'work experience' on YTS, and the new and narrow Certificate of Prevocational Education (CPVE) will provide a further extension of vocationalism in the tertiary modern curriculum, particularly for those staying on for one extra year (see Chapter 5).

The question put to the Conservative Education Secretary, Keith Joseph, some years ago – which he deflected – now seems quite shrewdly asked: did he intend to 'hive off the non-academic pupils in our schools to an organization more concerned with training them for work than preparing them for life?'[18] Just as it is now clear that the MSC's youth employment schemes are specifically intended to provide employers with cheap labour and to undercut wage levels won by trade union pressure over the years (see Chapters 3 and 10), so TVEI beginning at the age of 14 is designed to undermine the whole concept of an invigorating, rigorous, broad, balanced and non-segregated curriculum experienced by all alike from 14 to 16; and equal and open choice of education and training after 16, regardless of any individual's sex, race, social background, level of attainment or capacity to support herself or himself during the period of education and training.

The government finds it difficult to argue openly against so popular a concept as a comprehensive curriculum, a local comprehensive school, or genuine choice in education. In addition, its attempts to bring back grammar schools to the state system have failed. Thus its only option is to prevent comprehensive development inside schools and colleges themselves by even deeper differentiation and segregation. Its supporters in education go even further and articulate theories discredited for years – like Beverly Shaw from Durham University who now maintains that there 'must be a return to the former selective system by the front door', not even the back.[19]

Most Conservatives have always agreed and even at this late hour they are hoping to extend the already massive public subsidies to the private sector by reintroducing more fee-paying, publicly funded grammar schools[20] as well as to extend the Assisted Places scheme. Few of these schools are likely to be involved in TVEI. In a TV discussion on TVEI in 1985, the headteacher of one said his school did not do TVEI because his was a school for 'academic' boys hoping to go to university.[21] That really gave the TVEI game away.

Evidence from the state system about how far this divisive thinking has now gone comes from Devonshire, an area with TVEI in operation which held a conference on 'The Management of Change in the 14–19 Sector' in 1984. Joslyn Owen, the county's Chief Education Officer, stated firmly that: 'we must decide to vocationalize the education of those who will not pass examinations and tackle the main problem which has arisen, namely that we have to identify two halves of a school population which are now educated together.'[22] He went even further to say that having taken note of what had happened – or not happened – to the disadvantaged half of the school population considered decades ago in the Newsom Report,[23] Devon must consider 'putting vocational education and examination-aimed education into separate categories of education from the age of 14'.[22] What more could the MSC and the Conservative government want in the way of compliance?

Opposition from teachers

Not surprisingly, there has been opposition to TVEI in addition to the fundamental disagreement expressed by comprehensive school teachers already mentioned. Some relates to TVEI specifically, some to the sinister reputation the MSC has earned in its dealings with the education service at a more general level.

At 1985's conference of the National Association of Teachers in Further and Higher Education (NATFHE) a resolution was passed opposing YTS and resolving to work for changes. Earlier in 1983 a resolution was passed relating to fears that TVEI posed a 'fundamental threat to comprehensive education', risked further privatization of education, and could well lead to 'vocationally specific' education before the age of 16. Nothing that has happened since has lessened fears, and much has increased them, particularly the MSC's directive to those in charge of its schemes to prohibit young people discussing matters 'related to the organization and functioning of society in general'. Young people can learn how to fill in application forms but not, it seems, engage in dicussion as to why they are unemployed. There was a good deal of adverse reaction, and A.G. Watts, writing in *Liberal Education*, called this directive 'a shameful statement for an education minister . . . in a society that aspires to be a democracy'.[24] Although ministers later toned it down, attempts to proscribe free discussion of social and political issues on YTS courses are widely reported, a fact which the *Guardian*'s education correspondent once pointed out does not enhance the MSC's 'reputation for impartiality towards the content of the curriculum.'[25] No more does a government minister's statement in the House of Commons about the educational objectives of YTS,

> The Scheme is not a social service. Its purpose is to teach youngsters what the real world of work is all about. That means arriving on time, giving of their best during the working day and perhaps staying on a little longer to complete an unfinished task.'[26]

This makes it clear that training youngsters to fit certain jobs is only part of MSC strategy; just as important is the inculcation of the 'right' attitudes, beliefs and behaviour patterns. With the introduction of TVEI the 'benefits' of what can be described as a new model of capitalist training are now to be pushed back into the period of compulsory schooling. Youngsters must be 'taught' loyalty to the firm and to the principles of monetarist economics, or as Keith Joseph put it, 'Schools should preach the moral virtue of free enterprise and the pursuit of profit',[27] political indoctrination apparently being quite permissible if it comes from the Right of the political spectrum.

Objections to TVEI do not only come from radical sources or from teachers. Members of the *Black Paper* group have also expressed misgivings about government dictation leading to a distorted curriculum, including the swing away from traditional classical education that commerce-tied programmes involve.[28] And in September 1983 Sheila Browne, the then retiring Senior Chief Inspector of Schools, expressed her concern about the possible effects of TVEI on vulnerable areas of the curriculum. Her fear was that TVEI would push up unit costs and force some LEAs to cut traditional subjects, particularly at sixth-form level.[29] The MSC's deputy director of TVEI did not deny that some subjects – like History or Geography – might 'atrophy'.[30]

This, of course, is very much tied up with the question of the deployment of teachers once TVEI spreads through the system. Now that over half the local education authorities are involved, have we enough qualified teachers for the expansion of computing and technology courses? One of *Education*'s staff writers summarized it as a fear 'that there will not be enough technical teachers to go around – particularly in non-TVEI schools, since teachers will be lured away by the challenges and in some cases the promotions associated with TVEI'.[31]

As things stand at present, LEAs are expected to take over the funding of TVEI when the MSC's five-year pump-priming money runs out. The theory is that MSC funding will have enabled LEAs to develop cost-effective schemes which they can then 'replicate' throughout the authority. But many believe that government determination to limit local authority spending may make this very difficult, particularly where purchasing hardware is concerned. There is also the question of what happens when MSC money is withdrawn and new teachers, often with scale posts, recruited under the scheme, have to be reabsorbed into the system. Or when teachers suddenly discover that in the new 'high-tech' age their subjects are no longer fashionable or 'relevant'?

Compatible with comprehensive education?

Schools operating TVEI and wishing to continue developing comprehensive education at the same time do their best to integrate TVEI work within the existing fourth-and fifth-year curriculum, even, perhaps, to the extent of spreading the financial benefits across an entire year group rather than restricting them to a named group of students. Where teachers understand what is going on, they will be vigilant to ensure that the experience of comprehensive education is not fatally compromised. Yet it is not easy to outmaneouvre the MSC. The criteria for accepting programmes within its Technical Education Initiative are not negotiable and include 'clear and specific objectives . . . with a technical/vocational element throughout . . . broadly related to potential employment opportunities with arrangements for regular assessment.'[32]

This makes comprehensive compatibility hard to achieve inside any school, as was made clear at a conference organized by The Right to a Comprehensive Education (RICE), where the Vice-Principal and the TVEI Co-ordinator from Countesthorpe College in Leicestershire described their school's attempt to devise a scheme that was compatible with their (well-known) comprehensive practice in the rest of this school catering for the 14–18 age range.[33] Their starting point was that there should be open access to the new provision, and therefore that it would not be feasible to establish separate TVEI groups in the fourth year. Thus they do not have students who regard themselves as 'TVEI students', as in other schools, but let students, irrespective of subject choice, negotiate with tutors to spend time in areas with TVEI support.

The aim is to distribute TVEI resources through open access but not to spread them so thinly that there will be no measurable impact. Thus all students who choose to work in the 'enhanced areas' funded by TVEI money will benefit from the additional resources. Those who choose to work only in such areas benefit the most. There were 50 at the time, but one factor that stood out clearly was how greatly boys predominated over girls in both groups 'choosing' to work in TVEI areas (see also Chapter 8).

What sounds simple and straightforward is not, and other schools trying to make TVEI compatible with the principles of equality inherent in comprehensive education have found this out as well. Clwyd is an authority which has won commendation from MSC chiefs and many others for its wholehearted and imaginative TVEI operations (which enabled the school to introduce a modular system of short courses upon which it had long been working). Until recently it was expected that Clwyd would be able both to spread its MSC money to all pupils inside its five 'TVEI schools' as well as to the rest of its 16 secondary schools. But the MSC stepped in to say MSC money can be spent only on the 250 designated pupils in the five designated schools and on no others, and MSC inspectors are being sent to see that this is obeyed. Clywd's TVEI co-ordinator called the MSC's action puzzling in view of the MSC's declared intention to get TVEI into all schools eventually.[34] In fact, it is not puzzling, since TVEI has been intended from the start to be selective.

Those who campaigned so vigorously for comprehensive education in the 1960s and 1970s could not perhaps have envisaged that it would be quite so easy to undermine the reform. The movement, which gathered momentum after the promulgation of Circular 10/65, based on the pioneering work of certain progressive local authorities in the previous decade and supported by a modest crop of pressure groups, attracted converts with a wide variety of aims and aspirations. This was always a source of strength and weakness: ensuring strong local support for a vast number of first-class genuine comprehensive schools, but, at the same time, preventing the comprehensive movement as a whole from establishing its own clearly defined criteria for success.

It is certainly clear, as Brian Simon has argued,[35] that the transition to comprehensive education was seen to be 'necessary', in some senses at least, 'for the maintenance and smooth functioning of the existing social order.' It was widely believed, particularly among reformist sections of the Labour Party, that the new system would both reduce the wastage of the human abilities so urgently required as a result of technological change and economic advance as well as ensure an amelioration of social-class differences through the pupils' experience of 'social mixing' in a common environment. Yet there were many, including of course Professor Simon himself, who demanded the transition for a quite different and more positive reason: namely a belief in the educability of *all* children and in the futility of forcing them into outworn and prejudged categories. It is this more fundamental comprehensive principle which is under threat with the talk of 'separate categories of education from the age of 14' and even the possibility of lowering the school leaving age to 14 so that the 'academically minded' elite will not be held back by 'unruly' and 'disruptive' elements who are judged more 'suited' to work experience programmes or vocational courses.

Benefits of TVEI

Despite TVEI's implicitly negative implications for long-term comprehensive development, it would be churlish to deny that, as could also be expected, in the shorter term some of the latent talent and enterprise locked up in rate-starved local education authorities would be able to surface. Money from TVEI has enabled teaching in some of the new courses to break new ground, and there are imaginative new forms of organization of the school day. As with Newsom, innovations and education during the years after the school leaving age was raised, much of the pioneering work being undertaken is both exciting and challenging. The 'modules' in the newly reorganized curriculum at Ysgol Emrys ap Iwan, Abergele, for example, were developed as a result of the TVEI initiative and the personal expertise of individual teachers who worked on short courses in computing, electronics, electronic music and television production. They are available to those who do not choose traditional examination courses, as well as to those who do.[36]

There is a real place in the 14–16 curriculum for techno-aesthetic experience. Neglect of this area and of expressive areas of education in general is one of the major shortcomings of the grammar school model. The point is, however, as Maurice Holt has argued, that if it is to be integrated into the rest of a comprehensive curriculum for all young people, 'it should stem from an educational appraisal of key forms of doing and making, *not* from vocational pressures and employment-led skills.'[37]

Uppermost in the thinking of the MSC and the Conservatives is the need to prepare youngsters for society and the world of work as they now exist: education for jobs in a divided society rather than useful work and personal development in a society where jobs are planned to meet social needs.

Yet if vocational education is to exist, there is no reason for it – even now – to involve the separate preparation of one set of pupils for university entrance and the professions, while another set is being trained for the butcher's shop or the building site. Vocational education in comprehensive schooling must be about the world of work as a whole, and all the jobs people do. It must be education about work, not socialization of specific groups into specific lower levels of work. It must be about the wide variety of workplaces – and why they differ and how conditions have changed (or not) over the years. It must be about the growth of trade unions and workers' rights as well as the way employers and governments spend and distribute the wealth all have created. It must be about the need for full and active and wholly equal participation in local, national and international life. No education system can by itself produce a democratic society, but it can be personally and collectively egalitarian and liberating only when it seeks to help youngsters understand from the start that the existing social and economic arrangements were not ordained by God and can therefore be changed by human activity and struggle.

In any case, it is unlikely that the vocational education now being developed by the MSC and DES is in any sense 'necessary' for the majority of the school population. Dan Finn's research into the experiences and aspirations of fifth-year students in schools in the Midlands challenges the myth that today's youngsters are ignorant of work routines and disciplines, as so many claim.[38] Three-quarters of the teenagers interviewed had had some involvement in the juvenile labour market already and knew all about work – as well as exploitation – from the inside.

In seeking to alert people to the dangers inherent in the new vocationalism, we need to go on arguing for a broad and balanced and non-segregated curriculum which avoids the perils of premature specialization, and where the common elements account for a significantly large proportion of the pupils' working week. Designing such a curriculum is concerned with establishing those kinds of knowledge and areas of experience to which it could be argued all youngsters should be introduced by 16 – a cultural analysis model which owes much to the ideas put forward by Raymond Williams, for example, in *Culture and Society* in 1958 and *The Long Revolution* in 1961.[39]

That is why developments in the 1970s, when it seemed that both HMI and the Schools Council were moving in this direction, were so encouraging, and why it is such a tragedy that the political impetus has been lost. The HMI's *Curriculum* 11–16, often called the 'Red Book', dates from 1977, and much of it is based on the principles of cultural analysis – with inspectors highly critical of what Denis Lawton has called the 'cafeteria' curriculum where everyone picks and chooses in a lopsided way.[40] HMIs define a common curriculum as a:

body of skills, concepts, attitudes and knowledge, to be pursued, to a depth appropriate to their ability, by all pupils in the compulsory years of secondary education for a substantial part of their time, perhaps as much as two-thirds or three-quarters of the total time available.[41]

The 'Red Book' argues for a curriculum conceived in terms of 'areas of experience' rather than subjects. Although the checklist below can be translated into subjects, subjects are simply the means by which learning is to be organized. A common curriculum should not be 'trapped in discussions about the relative importance of this subject or that'; it should be about what HMIs maintain all pupils should have and without which no pupil's curriculum can be considered valid: adequate coverage of these eight areas – aesthetic, creative and practical; ethical; linguistic; mathematical; physical; scientific; social and political; and spiritual.

In urging us to plan education 'by looking through the subject or discipline to areas of experience and knowledge to which each may provide access, and to the skills and attitudes which it may assist to develop', HMIs take a courageous path, far more radical than the DES secretariat's more limited approach which views the curriculum in terms of an irreducible 'core' of specified and limited subjects.

Common curriculum not enough

There is clearly much to be said, therefore, in favour of a 'liberal-humanist' model for the curriculum whereby all young people without exception have experience of all the main areas of culture available in society through the medium of the common curriculum. But a radical perspective on education needs to go further than this. A cultural analysis approach should also aim to promote the ability of all students to function effectively within society and to use their talents to change that society in the light of future and developing aspirations. This is a far cry from the utilitarian viewpoint which looks to schools to provide the systematic preparation of youngsters for their future occupational roles.

At first sight it is not easy to unite the left on this particular platform. Contributors to *Schooling for the Dole?*, for example, argue rightly that the current controversy centres on whether schools should produce ideal workers to help solve the economic crisis or critical and independent people who can develop their own capacities to the full.[42] Yet they reject both models in favour of a radical approach which is rooted in working-class life and experiences. John Clarke and Paul Willis outline the book's general thesis with the following argument:

> most working-class children have never been concerned with what the ideal models are supposed to be. Their concern is not the ideal future worker to solve the problems of capitalism, nor is it with the ideal citizen to solve the problems of democracy, nor is it with the self-developed individual to solve the problems of civilization. Their problems concern survival in scarcity and the need to make material adjustments and plans to cope with their real – and future – situations. Gaining a wage to survive; hoping to enjoy power as a buyer and consumer through the wage; going through the adolescent sexual dance and setting up the working-class home in straitened circumstances; adapting to the strengths and enablements as well as the oppressions of quite strictly policed gender identitities – these are the real themes of working-class apprenticeships to adulthood in our society. In relationship to this apprenticeship there is often a general and uneasy sense of the irrelevance of the school. School is often rejected, rebelled against or treated as a comic interlude before 'real life' begins.

Despite the attempt at an honest appraisal of working-class attitudes, all this comes across as being somewhat patronizing and condescending, as well as betraying a very limited view of the role of education in society. Inadvertently, it lends itself to David Young's analysis of school's irrelevance and to Conservative arguments that 'real education' is appreciated only by the elite few.

Admittedly, schools should take into account the material culturalism of growing up in the working class, and many teachers are quite ignorant here. But why does this have to rule out the discussion and treatment of wider political and social issues? It would seem to be peculiarly defeatist and counterproductive to view working-class aspirations as being rooted for all time in the stark reality of everyday life – today's life at that. If working-class adolescents are not to be concerned with the problems of equality, monopoly capitalism, democractic change, and the distribution of the world's resources, they leave a vacuum which will be filled only too readily by those with a vested interest in exploitation and control.

Our opposition to TVEI's new vocationalism and to the narrow educational developments associated with YTS, must be based on a confident and optimistic assumption that everyone is capable of benefitting from education and that teachers and learners can bring about human development through the educative process. We must seek to demonstrate that it is part of reactionary monetarist philosophy to view youngsters not as whole human beings and potentially active citizens but simply as fodder for industry and employers.

Without this perspective we will not be aware of the implications of the MSC's initiatives for education. As we have seen, TVEI represents at the very least a distortion of the secondary school curriculum for some; at the worst, a return, in a disguised or overt fashion, to a deeply divided system of secondary schooling. This may well mark the end of any attempt to move towards a common curriculum, a movement essential to the advance of education and of the working-class majority. In 1983 Alan McMurray, Principal of Hind Leys College in Leicestershire, called TVEI the enemy's Trojan Horse:

> it is a beautiful and attractive gift, which has already seduced and bemused many; but when we are least expecting it, the supporters of grammar schools, selective education, privilege and elitism will come pouring from its belly, and the citadel of comprehensive education will be lost.[43]

Drift towards state control

TVEI is clearly far more than a short-term curriculum innovation. It is part of the drift towards vocationalism at all levels of education, as well as part of the Conservatives' determination to tighten the government's grip on the nation's schools. At first sight it may seem to bemused onlookers that the introduction of the new TVEI and other vocational and training programmes are the outcome of some sort of bitter power struggle between the DES and the MSC, but this would be to misread the present situation. There is no conflict between the two, and a more accurate interpretation might be that the DES is quite happy for the MSC to take over those pupils and students not 'suited' to academic education and to take charge of all vocational education.

This leaves the DES free to set about exercising control over other key areas of the curriculum in schools. Having failed in their attempts to determine what goes on in schools through documents like *A Framework for the School Curriculum*[44] and *The School Curriculum*,[45] they can now succeed by another route, namely their control over the national criteria for the new examination syllabuses at 16 plus. These will accompany the GCSE, the examination ostensibly developed to unify the assessment system and end the invidious divide between GCE O level and CSE, but in fact retaining the invidious divide and adding a third divide in the form of a new 'merit' level.

Between them, the DES and the MSC are now in a strong position to exercise formidable influence over the education and training of all the youngsters in this country. Far from senior officials at the DES being ready to defend the old liberal consensus, there is evidence they are quite prepared to concede that social control is a key objective of the government's overall strategy. In a recent study of the relationship between economic recession and government education policy, with particular reference to the new vocational examination at 17 plus, Stewart Ranson argues that 'the state has sought to control and restructure education in order to facilitate and regulate a period of rapid socioeconomic change.'[46] In the words of one chief education officer quoted in the study: curriculum changes are designed by the state to 'facilitate social control as much as encourage manpower planning.'

Clearly there is concern at senior levels in both the DES and the MSC about the social consequences of an oversupply of highly educated young people in a period of contracting job opportunities, and what effect higher levels of education might have. One DES official articulates government fears:

> We are in a period of considerable social change. There may be social unrest, but we can cope with the Toxteths. But if we have a highly educated and idle population, we may possible anticipate more serious social conflict. People must be educated once more to know their place.[47]

A coherent alternative

TVEI must not be viewed as an isolated initiative but as one of a series of government measures designed to establish effective control of the secondary school curriculum in order to exert effective social control more generally. Other measures include: the instigation of examination changes through the new hierarchical GCSE, the Certificate of Prevocational Education for 'vocational' students and the Advanced Supplementary levels for 'academic' ones; the control of teacher education through the introduction of the Council for the Accreditation of Teacher Education; and the proposal, outlined in *Better Schools*, for central control of in-service training for teachers by means of specific grant. TVEI is only one part of the wider attempt to vocationalize and stratify the curriculum for the majority in the perceived interests of the state and of employers.

Elaborate schemes of vocational preparation have as their chief rationale the necessity of fitting young people into established social relations of production. Workers in the new capitalist Britain will be at all times 'schooled' to be industrious, flexible, obedient, and above all, unquestioning in their loyalty to management, the state, the nation, and the social status quo. Deregulation, including the abolition of Wages Councils and employment protection for young people, is the new watchword of that efficiency which will help to patrol the aspirations and ambitions of the majority. Meanwhile, the advantaged continue as before, monopolizing the positions of influence and power, and increasing their already commanding occupancy of places in the elite schools, the major professions and the universities.

To assist this outcome, the secondary school curriculum is to be so structured as to provide sharply differentiated experiences beyond the age of 14 – the same differentiation provided in the old days by separate schools. In the new order, education is seen as a mere servicing process for capitalism, a provider of specifically trained youngsters matched in terms of number and education levels to the particular and immediate needs of the economy. Forty years after the passing of the 1944 Education Act which inaugurated, even if it did not specify, a divided system of secondary schooling, the wheel has come full circle with strategies that are, if anything, more ruthless and interventionist than in the days of explicit selection.

But comprehensive education and the democratic tradition have a good grounding. Moreover, they have much popular support. The Conservative state is right to fear the enhanced knowledge and understanding of the majority. It is the responsibility of the radical Left to ensure that Conservatives do not succeed in undermining the advances that the majority have made in the past 20 years.

1. *Times Educational Supplement*, Scotland, 3 May, 1985.

2. Harry Dowson, 'My Fears for TVEI', *NUT Guide to Careers Work*, 1985.

3. Information given during the screening of *Panorama*, 'Good Enough for Your Child?', 28 February 1983, which was devoted entirely to TVEI.

4. David Young, quoted in *Times Educational Supplement*, 26 November 1982.

5. *Times Educational Supplement*, 3 December 1982.

6. Ruth Gee, Report in *Times Higher Educational Supplement*, 22 July 1983.

7. Speech delivered in Sevenoaks, Kent, reported in *Sevenoaks Chronicle*, 14 December 1984, and also in *Times Educational Supplement*, 4 January 1985.

8. W. Norton Grubb and Marvin Lazerson, 'Vocational Solutions to Youth Problems: the Persistent Frustrations of the American Experience', *Educational Analysis*, Vol. 3, No. 2, Summer 1981, pp. 91–103.

9. Speech printed in 'Towards a National Debate', *Education*, 22 October 1976, pp. 332–3.

10. Christopher Lea, Project Director, TVEI, Education and Industry Centre at the City of Birmingham's Education Department, writing in *Forum*, Vol. 26, No. 2, Spring 1984, pp. 47–8.

11. Speech to the Institute of Directors, *The Director*, 1983.

12. Harry Dowson, 'My Fears for TVEI', *NUT Guide to Careers Work*, 1985.

13. *Better Schools*, Cmnd number 9469, March 1985.

14. See Caroline Benn, 'NTVEI: Time to Speak Up', *The Careers and Guidance Teacher*, Spring 1984, pp. 16–20.

15. Maureen O'Connor, survey for the *Guardian*, October 1983.

16. *Times Educational Supplement*, 14 October 1983.

17. Interview in the *Guardian*, 4 October 1983.

18. Keith Joseph, *Listener*, 3 March 1983.

19. Beverley Shaw, *Comprehensive Schooling, The Impossible Dream*, Basil Blackwell, Oxford, 1983.

20. Announcement that the government intended to propose returning the direct grant to private schools, *Times Educational Suppplement*, 19 July 1985.

21. Martin Rogers, Chief Master, King Edward's School, Birmingham, speaking on *Open Space*, 'Class Encounters of the Secondary Kind', BBC 2, 6 February 1985.

22. Speaking at a conference, 24–27 September 1984, reported in Devon County Council/Institute of Local Government Studies, *Report of a Conference on the Management of Change in the 14–19 Sector*, September 1984.

23. HMSO, *Half Our Future*, (The Newsom Report), 1963.

24. A. G. Watts, *Liberal Education*, Autumn 1984.

25. Maureen O'Connor, *Guardian*, 4 October 1983.

26. Peter Morrison, House of Commons, July 1983.

27. Keith Joseph, *Times Educational Supplement*, 26 March 1982.

28. Enoch Powell and Brian Cox, quoted in Adrian Harvey, 'MSC (Social Engineers) Ltd', *NATFHE Journal*, April 1985.

29. Sheila Brown, *Times Educational Supplement*, 23 September 1983.

30. Quoted in Caroline Benn, 'TVEI: Time to Speak Up', in *Careers and Guidance Teachers*, Spring 1984, p. 16.

31. Diane Hofkins, 'A Pattern for the Future?', *Education*, 31 August 1984, p. 173.

32. Quoted in *Times Educational Supplement*, 4 February 1983.

33. Report of proceedings and contributions to conference on 'Is TVEI Compatible with Comprehensive Education?' held at the University of London Institute of Education, 1983; printed in Issue 48 of *Comprehensive Education*, 1984.

34. Adrian Farlam, quoted in *Times Educational Supplement*, 15 February 1985.

35. Brian Simon, 'Problems in Contemporary Educational Theory, a Marxist Approach', *Journal of Philosophy of Education*, Vol. 12, 1978, pp. 29–39.

36. John Williams, 'Abergele – Trailblazers in TVEI', *The Careers and Guidance Teachers*, Spring 1984, pp. 20–25.

37. Maurice Holt, 'Vocationalism: the New Threat to Universal Education', *Forum*, Vol. 25, No. 3, Summer 1983, pp. 84–5.

38. Dan Finn, 'Leaving School and Growing Up: Work Experience in the Juvenile Labour Market', in Inge Bake (ed.), *Schooling for the Dole? The New Vocationalism*, Macmillan, London, 1984, pp. 17–64.

39. Raymond Williams, *Culture and Society*, Penguin Books, Harmondsworth, 1958; and *The Long Revolution*, Penguin Books,

Harmondsworth, 1961.

40. Denis Lawton, 'The Curriculum and Curriculum Change', in Brian Simon and William Taylor (eds.), *Education in the Eighties: The Central Issues*, Batsford Academic, London, 1981, pp. 111–123.

41. HMI, *Curriculum 11–16*, DES, 1977.

42. John Clarke and Paul Willis, Introduction, in Inge Bake, (ed.), *Schooling for the Dole, The New Vocationalism*, Macmillan, London, 1984, pp. 1–16.

43. Alan McMurray, 'Comprehensive Schools: Threatened or Challenged?', *Forum*, Vol. 26, No. 1, Autumn 1983, pp. 15–16.

44. DES, *A Framework for the School Curriculum*, HMSO, 1980.

45. DES, *The School Curriculum*, HMSO, 1981.

46. Stewart Ransom, 'Towards a Tertiary Tripartism: New Codes of Social Control and the 17 Plus', in Patricia Broadfoot (ed.), *Selection, Certification and Control: Social Issues in Educational Assessment*, Falmer Press, Lewes, 1984, pp. 221–44.

47. *Ibid.*

5. The MSC and the Three-Tier Structure of Further Education

Andy Green

The history of further education over the past decade has been one of continual change. Developments in educational provision for 16–19-year-olds have brought both an unprecedented expansion of new courses, as well as changes in the quality and nature of post-compulsory education and training. Most significantly, there has been widespread organizational and structural change brought about by the institutionalization of a new philosophy of 'training' for working-class youth. The major outcome has been the emergence of a new 'tripartite' structure in further education, which prefigures similar changes in other education sectors.

The immediate origins of these new divisions lie in the intervention of the Manpower Services Commission in youth training from the mid-1970s onwards, and the attempts of various governments to resolve new social and economic problems concerning youth, through the agency of this powerful quango.

Prior to 1976, further education was primarily concerned with the education and training of employed youth. The traditional student was the craft apprentice, typically white and male, whose attendance in FE was, since the 1964 Training Act, a part of the apprenticeship agreement. In addition there were a growing number of students on business and technical courses, both full- and part-time, and a new clientele of school leavers choosing college rather than school for traditional sixth-form work. This last group is increasing with the growth of tertiary colleges – over 50 now – which concentrate post-16 education in various forms. In most cases these colleges represent the rationalization of resources for this age group, but in some they arise out of the wish to promote a more comprehensive organization of the system.

The potent traditional image of the technical college was as a provider of 'second-chance education' or as an alternative route to social mobility for working-class youth. While the reality of the alternative route may have been gradually eroding,[1] the solid link between college education and job opportunities was such that the mythology of social mobility partially masked the existence of the hierarchy of opportunities within FE. There was a small top tier of students headed for university or professional training, but the majority were in a second tier, where at least they were destined for skilled and technician level work; with both, day-release attendance or night school classes were clearly instrumental in this. Any three-tier structure in FE was only latent, defined by the absence of its lowest tier. This is because those likely to enter unskilled work, and many others besides, simply did not come to FE colleges. Prior to the Youth Opportunities Programme (YOP), which began in 1978, 60 per cent of school leavers had no further education after leaving school.[2]

The situation since 1983 has been very different. The vast majority of 16-year-olds now receive some form of education or training. By 1983 30 per cent stayed on at school, 13 per cent went into full-time FE, 22 per cent went on to a Youth Training Scheme (YTS), and a further 7 per cent were employed and attended part-time at FE colleges.[3] Of the remaining 28 per cent, half of whom were unemployed, many registered on part-time FE courses and claimed supplementary benefit. Some of these, however, were forced to limit their study time by the notorious rule which stopped their benefit if study exceeded 21 hours in any one week.

This rapid incorporation of all sections of youth into post-compulsory education and training can be dated quite precisely from the immediate post-1976 period. The major mechanism by which this has been achieved is the youth training programme of the MSC. In order to understand this extension of access to FE, and why it has taken on a three-tier form, one must look at the social and economic factors which underlay the particular 'educational solution' offered by the MSC.

Unemployment and social control

The primary reason for the development of youth training was, without doubt, the precipitous growth in youth unemployment between 1976 and 1978. Although the Crowther Report had predicted as far back as 1959 that further education would be the next battleground of English education,[4] there had been precious little impetus for change from within the educational system. It was only the fear of social problems arising out of high youth unemployment, particularly severe amongst blacks and girls (see Chapters 8 and 9, and inner-city youth, which promoted action from governments. It is also this awareness of social and economic problems which provides the key motif in the seminal Holland Report of 1977 on employment for young people.[5]

Another critical issue for governments after the mid-1970s was the collapse of the youth labour market. The latter involved the disappearance of young people's jobs through recession and new technology as well as the breakdown in the institutional mechanisms whereby youth labour was reproduced. Put simply, whereas in the past young people were socialized into work through their first jobs, now they were unable to get this experience until lengthy periods of unemployment had already undermined their motivation for work. Governments saw the answer to be the development of a mass youth training programme which first appeared in the form of the MSC's Youth Opportunities Programme in 1978.

There was a timely concurrence of these social developments with certain new educational forces. These latter had been crystallized from the Great Debate of 1976 onwards in the form of demands for a more industrial and vocational bias in secondary education. But the primary impetus for change clearly came from the perception of the economic and social problem with the state. The MSC was certainly not an organic offshoot of the education system.[6]

The drive to concentrate these new developments within further education is easily explained. Firstly, FE has always had a strategic location between school and work, which makes it a 'natural' site for a system designed to smooth this increasingly bumpy passage for young people. Secondly, its typically 'entrepreneurial' character[7] has made it fertile soil for implanting ideas in education that are based on a market philosophy. These two characteristics have been fully exploited by the Conservative government.

Training and market economics

Two factors emerge very clearly from recent developments. One is that recruits to the third tier – sometimes called the tertiary modern sector – have been thrown up by rising unemployment and not by demand for an extended or comprehensive post-compulsory education provision. The other is that the character of training offered to this third-tier group has been determined largely by a particular political solution, designed to counter economic and social problems. That is to say, it has been more a question of 'keeping them off the streets' than a matter of extending rights to comprehensive education and training.

The development of a new training philosophy for unemployed school leavers has clearly followed these economic and social imperatives, and it is important to define the nature of this philosophy and its roots in market economics. The dominant educational or training paradigm in this new tertiary modern sector of FE is that derived from policies which have been formulated in connection with the MSC's youth training schemes, and its clearest expression can be found in the New Training Initiative[8] and the white paper, *Training for Jobs*.[9]

The philosophy has been described both as 'the new vocationalism' and 'narrow vocationalism',[10] but neither term is fully adequate since it is neither vocationalist nor narrow in a traditional training sense. Vocational education has normally meant preparation for a particular job and its connotations of 'calling' are clearly tied up with a protestant work ethic and the middle-class preoccupation with choosing a career. Youth training schemes, however, are explicitly concerned with training for work in general and not preparation for a particular job, and there is precious little real choice for most young people involved. Furthermore, one of the defining characteristics of youth training is that it does involve broad-based skills training and specifically eschews skill specialization. Although it may be narrow in other, and especially, educational senses, the use of the term would be confusing in the training context. Perhaps the best designation is simply 'the new training philosophy'.

The 'new training philosophy': deskilling the majority

The main objective of 'the new training' is, in the words of the MSC Task Group Report, to 'develop and maintain a more versatile, readily adaptable, highly motivated and productive workforce'.[11] On the face of it there is nothing new in this. Education and training have always involved an explicit relation to work and the preparation of the future workforce, and arguably this was the dominant paradigm even within the old social democratic tradition where the Fabian stress on national efficiency always jostled for supremacy with the Tawneyite goals of equality of opportunity and developing the individual.[12] What is new here, however, is the exclusive emphasis on economic goals and the way the relationship between youth training and economic need is presented as a direct correspondence. This is evident not only in the almost total absence of traditional educational objectives in MSC training proposals, but also in the extreme restrictiveness and instrumentalism embodied in the notion of its basic skills training.

Underpinning 'the new training philosophy' is a clear perception of present and future economic need, as defined by monetarism. Shorn of their technocratic rhetoric and playing on the need for new technological skills, all MSC programmes display four central assumptions about the labour market:

1. that most manual work is becoming deskilled;
2. that new skills needs are largely at scientific and higher technician levels;
3. that the majority of young working-class youth will be employed in unskilled manual jobs or junior white-collar jobs in the service and manufacturing sectors;
4. that for most people, working life will consist of frequent job changes and intermittent periods of extended unemployment.

Training for working-class youth is based on the premise that what is valuable is exclusively that which contributes towards their socialization and 'skilling' for this kind of working life. This can be seen at a general level in the insistence that training be geared towards locally available work rather than for work meeting wider or national needs. *Training for Jobs* constantly reiterates that training should be 'to agreed standards of skill appropriate to the jobs available' and the 'supply of skills training for unemployed people should relate more closely to identified local employment needs'. The conclusion we draw is that 'training for stock' or training beyond immediate necessary skills levels, is unnecessary.

The application of this restrictive and short-sighted policy is evident in the MSC's decisions to cut back adult industrial training courses (TOPS) in areas where skilled manual work is declining as well as in proposals to reduce the length of traditional apprentice-ships. The deskilling of manual work has its corollary in the deskilling of youth training. The only area of training where genuine 'UP-skilling' is envisaged is in 'high tech' – hence, while *Training for Jobs* talks of revitalizing training in colleges as a whole, the only area which actually warrants a specific mention is robotics. Further evidence of this narrow equation between training and work can be found in the specified contents of youth training schemes. Each one-year course of the YTS, for example, should contain work experience, a minimum of three months off-the-job training in 'core skills', and social and life skills training (SLS).

The dominance of the work experience and the relative brevity of off-the-job training in most schemes ensures a minimum of surplus skills training, and wider, general education. In addition, the essence of both the practical skills training and the SLS training is not the mastery of technical skills but the inculcation of appropriate work attitudes and social and 'communications' skills – all of which rank high in MSC priorities for unskilled work. As the Industrial Research Unit reported, 'Job skills hardly merit consideration in young people's jobs'.[13] What counts now in youth training is the cultivation of adaptablility and the willingness to accept the fact that many working lives are likely to consist of a succession of unskilled jobs.

What is new and distinctive about the MSC's training philosophy is not that it relates to future work but how it does so and for whom. Whereas vocational training for the middle class has always been only loosely tied to economic need, training for working-class youth is now to be bound fast. Training for the professions – e.g. for doctors or lawyers through higher education – has always exceeded both in numbers and content actual economic need. Moreover, few would claim that three years' university education involved only essential skill acquisition for those going on to practice professional occupations. Nor would many suggest that places and grants for higher education and professional training be restricted to economic or local job need alone. In the past craft training has not been based purely on these criteria either. The new training philosophy can be defined as one which embodies a purely and narrowly instrumental relation between training and economic need. Applied in today's context of deskilling and job loss, it also produces a paradoxical result: much of the MSC's youth training is actually 'skills training for deskilling' and 'job preparation for unemployment'.

The evolution of a tripartite system in further education arises, then, out of the incorporation of a previously excluded segment of working-class youth into further education, and their subjection to a new training philosophy not applied to other social groups. While this process may bring 'access' to tertiary education to new groups, e.g. black youth, it also beings increasing segregation and segmentation of the student body in a way that starkly exposes the limitations of a politics of education based solely on the calculus of access. The most pertinent questions to ask of further education now are not about who goes, but what they do when they are there.

The three tiers inside the colleges

In many ways the enormous diversity and constantly changing nature of FE courses defies easy categorization, but, broadly speaking, we can identify three tiers, differentiated by their educational practices and related to the assumed future positions of their students in the occupational structure.

Tier One comprises students on full-time higher, technical and business courses (B/TEC) and those doing GGE O and A levels. Potential occupational destinations include professional, managerial and higher-grade technician and technologist jobs.[14]

Tier Two includes craft courses and junior clerical courses (with qualifications from the RSA and the City and Guilds) and implies access to craft-level technical jobs and junior office jobs.

Tier Three includes a disparate array of courses, including those for MSC trainees – from part-time general education to full-time vocational preparation. The Certificate of Prevocational Education (CPVE) will be the main form of certificate on many of these courses in future.

It will be immediately apparent that these three tiers include potential overlaps. For instance, a high percentage of those doing O levels will fail and will have to accept occupational destinies similar to those doing prevocational courses. Under the new MSC training many craft apprentices from the second tier are now absorbed within YTS (see Chapter 3) and therefore work alongside Tier Three students. In the present situation, Tier Two is inherently unstable due to the decline of skilled work, which presages an imminent polarization in the structure that corresponds with an increasing division in society between intellectual and manual labour.

The existence of a tripartite structure does not, of course, depend on mutual exclusivity and the impossiblity of movement between levels, or an absolute correspondence with different occupational outcomes. The tripartite system created by the 1944 Education Act did not imply any of these things. The existence of an emergent tripartite structure can be deduced from the existence of different educational practices prevalent in each tier, which in turn assume different occupational outcomes.

Differentiation can be found in the following four areas: objectives (including the curriculum); methods (the pedagogy); organization; and teacher role.

The contention here is that at each level there is a dominant 'mode' in operation, which, while not necessarily determining the practices of every course at that level, defines the terms and sets the agendas of change.

Tier One – curriculum and teaching methods
The dominant mode of courses at Tier One level is still traditional. The curriculum is largely determined by the requirements of externally set and marked examinations like GCE (with their future link to higher education), or, in the case of B/TEC courses, certification through examination and continual assessment.

Assessment for Tier One work is designed to test the acquisition of certain forms of knowledge and linguistic and other skills, where a high premium is attached to conceptual understanding and the manipulation of language symbols in written form. Although, as Geraldine Lander has pointed out, business and technical courses have incorporated some of the oral and social skills involved in YTS,[15] the primary skills remain traditional. Although B/TEC courses are narrow and vocationally related, knowledge and linguistic ability at this level is not determined by the requirements of a specific future job — any more then they are with GCE courses.

Education at this level has never been instrumental in a narrow sense. The most appropriate model to characterize them is Bourdieu's notion of 'cultural capital', whereby 'academic education' is seen to provide a knowledge, ideology and style (i.e. culture) which has 'arbitrary'; but real, symbolic power.[16] That is to say, a certain 'culture' is acquired which, although not strictly functional to particular social roles, gives easier access to them.

Teaching methods at this level tend to be based on traditional models of instruction or 'transmission'. A certain body of knowledge is transferred from the expert (lecturer) to the student. Student progress is carefully monitored against 'objective' criteria, i.e. the ability to 'pass' a particular form of assessment. While there may be some 'democratization' of classroom practice, minimal use is made of counselling, group interactive work and experiential learning through outside visits.

Tier Two

At this level courses are largely traditional and much of the above description would apply here also. Some of these courses – like City and Guilds Craft courses – are currently under review.

Tier Three

Tier Three methods and objectives are harder to specify since there exist a variety of courses and competing pedagogies. Nevertheless, it is possible to identify the dominant paradigm as 'the new training philosophy' of the MSC; and to posit a gradual diffusion of objectives originating from here to other courses not funded by the MSC. The fundamental objectives, as we have already seen, concern primarily the inculcation of social skills and attitudes. However, this can sometimes translate into educational practice unexpectedly, as, for instance, in language borrowed from child-centred progressivism. Such borrowing was necessary for the MSC in order to reach educators, for the MSC has few educational credentials itself and speaks in an industrial, not educational language. It has had to rely to a certain extent on a set of interlocutors. Most notable here are the Further Education Unit (FEU) which grew out of the Department of Education and Science. The FEU has produced a prolific quantity of educational 'theory' in the field of prevocational education.

The objectives of the MSC and the FEU, however, are far from identical, and so in practice what has happened is that MSC objectives have been translated into FE practice through the mediation of the FEU. The result is a practice that owes something to each: the raw objectives of the MSC garnished and modified by the FEU, the sophisticated pedagogy of the FEU tramelled and constrained by the structural limitations of YTS courses.[17] The resultant amalgam has certain distinctive features which must be summarized briefly.

Most notable of these is the distinctive shift away from 'knowledge and understanding' – as in traditional education – to 'competence' and 'effectiveness'. This is paralleled by a preference for 'doing' and for 'execution' over conception and analysis. This can be seen in several ways. Firstly, 'general (or liberal) education' has been largely replaced by 'basic skills' and 'personal effectiveness' or social and life skills (SLS). Such categories are, of course, notoriously slippery but if one takes a concrete example the meaning is more apparent. A particularly crude but clear one comes from the checklist of items for the much-used prevocational course, City and Guilds 365. Out of 14 entries in its Vocational Preparation Profile, there are five which refer explicitly to attitudes: 'working with those in authority', 'working with colleagues', 'self-awareness' and 'coping with problems', while only one deals with 'reading and writing', only one with technical skills ('using equipment') and none with 'general knowledge'. Similar criticisms have also been made of the Certificate of Prevocational Education, the new prevocation course being designed for school leavers, although it is more sophisticated than previous projects and appears to give more weight to the formative values through analysis and critical judgement.[18]

While the 365 checklist – or CPVE's suggested 'topics' – do not represent a syllabus in a traditional sense, both are clearly intended to include what the syllabus for vocational education imparts, i.e which skills; and while the study of general topics may be used as a vehicle for the organization of these skills, the range and depth of study will be much curtailed, if not altogether dropped, by the need to emphasize skill acquisition.

In addition, the structural parameters of YTS will largely determine how much can be learned. In practice, a three-month equivalent of college education, which is all that is allowed for, can allow little room for literacy and numeracy work, let alone the study of 'general topics'. Therefore, while the FEU, in their influential document, *A Basis for Choice*,[19] may advocate an 'appreciation of the physical and technical environments' and 'sufficient political and economic literacy to understand the social environment and participate in it' (note: participate only, not transform), the in-built constraints will militate against the attainment of any such objectives in practice.

Another illustration of the shift from knowledge to competence and from concept to practice, is in social and life skills (SLS) itself. The main objective of SLS is to promote social and communicative skills for 'coping' in the worlds of work and unemployment. Even where the emphasis is on 'personal effectiveness', implying assertiveness rather than passivity, the primary objective is to adapt to given situations, not to analyse or change them. Preferred, or dominant, methods of teaching in these vocational areas reflect these objectives and their distance from traditional education. Where the latter stresses 'transmission' and 'instruction', SLS emphasizes participation and 'self-discovery'. Where traditional education is seen to be knowledge- and paper-based, SLS attempts to be experience-based and skills-based, thus stressing the 'active' as against the 'reflexive' aspects of learning.

Furthermore, the centrality of social skills acquisition in this paradigm requires the development of a variety of new pedagogic techniques, not least the use of intergroup dynamics drawing on an eclectic array of counselling and therapy techniques. The extensive use of visual materials – like videos – and of visits, residentials and other learning 'experiences' is also characteristic of this Third Tier mode, and much less prevalent in others.

Organizational or structural divisions buttress and make concrete the hierarchical distinctions in teaching modes and course content. This can be seen in terms both of the internal organization of FE and in its external relations with its funding bodies.

Internally, there are now clear institutional divisions between the three tiers in many colleges starting with a typical physical separation of Third Tier work from other areas of college activity. YTS courses and other so-called non-examination (or 'Appendix Two') courses have often been located in annexes and buildings away from main college sites, which has led inevitably to the feeling that young unemployed students are being 'ghettoized'. Furthermore, where this has involved a high concentration of black students in particular buildings, it has often led to stereotyping of student behaviour and the mobilization of racist responses both amongst individuals and in the institution as a whole (see also Chapter 9).

Concurrently, there are the growing organizational divisions in FE work. One result of the growth of prevocational work in General Education Departments has been that they have often swollen beyond 'manageable' proportions, which has often led to their being split in two along 'academic' and 'non-academic' lines. This institutional division has exacerbated the isolation of the young unemployed student. Not only is he or she separated physically from other mainstream areas of college life, but the likelihood of through or upward 'routes' from one course to another, when they cross departments, is effectively impeded.

This lack of effective through-routes is reinforced by the singular status of the young unemployed student or trainee, constructed, as it is, primarily out of negatives. He or she is defined in educational and training terms as 'non-academic' and in work terms as 'unemployed'; neither student, apprentice, nor employee, the young trainee is in limbo, and he or she is in a period of transition from school to work.

This transitional status is reinforced by financial dependence on the family, which can only be escaped through entry into work, which however has been indefinitely delayed. Despite the elevation of youth training to YTS from an unemployment scheme like YOP, and its extension from six months to one year – and now to two – the trainee is still encouraged to enter work as soon as possible, and consequently to see his or her period of training and education as short and transitory. With such an identity, the young trainee is unlikely to think in terms of an extended period of vocational training or academic study, such as would be required to gain higher qualifications. Under such social determinations it is not surprising that the student often 'chooses' not to go on the other courses, thus making the three-tier system appear to be an institutional reponse to the market where individual choice rather than a social construction into which these young people are fitted.

Such divisions in the internal structures of FE have been institutionalized further by new arrangements governing external control and finance. Already the MSC finances, and therefore part controls, 10 per cent of non-advanced further education (NAFE).[14] This is planned to rise to 25 per cent, which will mean an increasing separation of 'vocational' from 'academic' education. The latter will remain solely financed by the LEAs, but a considerable part of work-related education will be controlled by a non-elected and unaccountable central government agency.

It is important to mention, finally, how the role of the teacher has been affected by 'the new training philosophy'. This cannot be dealt with at length.[20] Most notable amongst the changes has been the enormous extension of administrative, planning and pastoral work connected with new courses, and the growth of curriculum development and in-service training. Where this work has been delegated to Lecturer I level (basic grade), it represents generally a heavier workload and therefore an erosion of conditions of service, since no additional pay is received. Another change is when the subject specialist has been replaced by a generalist, the basic skills teacher.

Taken all together, these changes mean the teacher's role is less concerned with subject expertise and becomes increasingly managerial and technical in the sense of utilizing new educational technology and managing and organizing increasingly diverse and numerous courses. Lecturers on prevocational courses can now spend almost as much time on non-teaching duties – like counselling, liaising with outside agencies, careers advice and supervising work experience – as in actually preparing and conducting lessons. The work also includes management of students, which in the context of demoralized unemployed youth, can seem to some increasingly like 'soft policing'.

In an important article on education in America, Michael Apple[21] comments on the prevalence of 'teacher-proof' and prepackaged learning materials and the increasingly technical nature of work, where teachers 'process' students through learning units designed and produced by commercial firms. He goes on to remark that while the deskilling involves the loss of craft and the on-going atrophy of education skills, the reskilling involves the substitution of the skills and ideological vision of management. The growth of behaviour modification techniques and classroom management studies strategies, and their incorporation within both curricular material and teacher's repertoires, signifies these kinds of alternatives.

While the use of commercially produced, prepackaged teaching units is not yet extensive in this country, Apple's analysis provides a suggestive commentary on the changes in the role of the college lecturer outlined above.

The tertiary modern sector

The primary objection to tiered systems in education is that they reproduce social divisions. Students are inserted into different tiers whose curriculum and pedagogic styles are determined by what is considered appropriate for particular social groups. At this stage in life it is usually on the basis of prior assumptions about future work roles. This may be legitimated by reference to ideological constructs which posit different natural abilities for different groups – as in the 'age, ability and aptitude' clause of the 1944 Education Act which was used to justify the divisions in the 11-plus system – or simply by an 'innocent' invocation of principles of 'relevance', as in recent writing on vocational education.

The invariable result is that most of those students placed on particular tracks will follow them through to their predestined outcomes, with the groups corresponding largely to existing class, race and gender divisions in society. The outcome is the same whether we want to argue that selection for different tiers is caused by social bias in the system or results from student self-selection – as in Boudon's model of 'positional theory' whereby students make educational choices for social mobility on the basis of the relative chances and costs involved, these varying for different social classes.[22] Where an educational system is differentiated it will necessarily reproduce differential outcomes, since forms of certification available – and teacher expectations — will substantially determine student performance at each level.

With the creation of a tertiary modern sector in post-compulsory education we can see this social reproduction in its crudest and most instrumental form. A large portion of working-class youth, disproportionately large in the case of blacks, is being trained almost exclusively for a combination of unemployment and semi- and unskilled work, often in the poorly paying 'secondary' labour market. Furthermore, within the training sector there is a hierarchy whereby racial and gender divisions are superimposed on class divisions (see Chapters 8 and 9). Whatever the reality of 'alternative routes' in traditional FE, it is clear that with the 'new training philosophy' a 'second chance' means no more than being required to requalify for unemployed and semi- or unskilled work. As David Raffe has concluded, 'Far from advancing the supply of technically necessary skills, or generating alternative routes or chances for working-class youth, these divisions have tended to lock students into pre-existing class and gender divisions'.[23]

More than anything else, the development of the 'new training philosophy' of the MSC has served to institutionalize the generation of low aspirations for many working-class young people, and to legitimate in their own eyes their educational failure and poor employment prospects.

The limits of progressivism

It may seem strange that such a manifestly illiberal educational philosophy has implanted itself so quickly in further education and received support from many teachers who would claim to be progressive in their educational beliefs. The answer to this does not lie solely in trade union pragmatism at a time of retrenchment, nor can it be explained purely by the absence of educational alternatives for unemployed youth, although both these factors are important. A critical factor has also been the way in which the training paradigm has evolved precisely by drawing on key progressive themes and elaborating them in new ways.

Central amongst these have been the concepts of curriculum 'relevance' and experiential or active learning. The 'new training philosophy' shares with progressive educationalism an antipathy towards 'over academic' or 'bookish' learning and the traditional 'transmission' model of teaching, whose meaning is best conveyed in the idea of 'instruction', with all its authoritarian and undemocratic connotations of experts and passive receivers. Social and life skills and work experience are therefore justified in terms of their supposed relevance to the concerns of working-class youth, while the experience-based model of learning gains credence through its apparent appropriateness to those who have demonstrated their aversion to academic teaching in schools.

At one level one can say that what is occurring in prevocational training is simply a question of good ideas being used for bad ends. No one could object to the idea that learning should be relevant to the needs and culture of the learner, nor to the proposition that learning occurs best where the learner internalizes what is learnt, through an active process. Similarly, other typical practices in prevocational work – like counselling, learning in workshops using individually negotiated learning programmes, and the use of positive, criterion-referenced assessment in student profiles – are surely positive contributions to the development of more appropriate teaching strategies. What has gone wrong in MSC courses is that these progressive techniques have been pressed into the service of reactionary ends. Thus relevance is unduly restricted to 'work-oriented' learning, experiences are carefully selected so that they involve mainly experience of work, and counselling and group dynamics are used for social control, and so on. The use that is made of the idea of experiential learning clearly falls into this category of distortion. Whereas J.S. Bruner, the doyen of 1960s and 1970s progressive teaching, advocated a form of discovery learning to develop conceptual understanding, the MSC advocate the same to develop 'competences'. The 'experience' is characteristically different and so, also, is the objective. While the experience for Bruner involved exploration of the physical and social world through symbolic representations (books, maps, charts, photographs, etc.) and concrete experiences, the emphasis in SLS is biased towards the concrete, where the concrete is usually something to do with work, either real or simulated. So too the objectives. For Bruner the aim was to take children through the 'spiral' of conceptual learning, from simple to higher levels of generalization, arising from different concrete instances, so that, as he optimistically claimed, you could teach any child anything at any age – by which he meant concepts. SLS, however, is notable precisely for its studied avoidance of concepts in learning.[24]

There is no doubt that some of the criticisms that are made of SLS can be put down to bad practice and that some of the fault lies not in the teaching strategies but in the framework in which they are deployed. This account is seductive, not least because it leaves many of the cherished ideas of progressivism unscathed - they are simply being revised. But this analysis, however comfortable it may be to hard-pressed practitioners, is, in my view, mistaken. It is partly this failure to reexamine the ideas of progressivism amongst socialist teachers and educational theorists, with a few notable exceptions,[25] that has allowed the present lurch into educational reaction. There are two dimensions to this. First, it is clear that when the *Black Paper*-ites first threw down the gauntlet on standards, discipline and parental choice, progressive education failed to stand and fight, leaving the Right ample opportunity to mobilize popular opinion around a set of hopelessly contradictory and anachronistic slogans which nevertheless had popular reverberations. Second, in some important respects it is the very same progressive ideas, which many thought constituted the strength of progressivist theory, which have been taken up and used by the educational Right.

The crucial issue here is the question of what is a 'relevant' curriculum for working-class students. Progressive education has offered various answers to this question, but common to all has been a critical evaluation of the hierarchy of knowledge and a positive assessment of working-class, and latterly, minority cultures. Clearly, in general terms, these are necessary and correct starting points. Uncritical acceptance of what has passed for legitimate knowledge in school clearly leads to elitism and a failure to understand those cultures brought to school by students not only demonstrates prejudice – class and racial – but would and does lead to unsuccessful education.

The problem for progressivism is that this necessary critical stance has often led to an epistemological relativism which is at best confused and at worst anti-intellectual and ultimately patronizing towards working-class youth. What has been called the 'new sociology of education' begins by 'rejecting the assumption of any superiority of educational or 'academic' knowledge over everyday common sense available to people as being in the world.'[26] Unfortunately, the critics of knowledge hierarchies never specify the terms in which teachers, or for that matter, sociologists, should evaluate what is legitimate knowledge, or what should form the basis of the curriculum. Leaving it to students, in a situation where choices are constructed and constrained by the institution, was never an entirely viable alternative. The dangers here are two fold. First, whereas it is certainly true that 'school knowledge' is ideology constructed through class, race and gender discourses, and should be approached critically, it is also true that the acquisition of this 'academic' culture gives access to power, and that the oppression of those denied it will work through lack of it. Second, the uncritical celebration of working-class cultures is often problematic, as we surely should have learnt from analysis of racism and sexism.

The points are so obvious that they really should not need restating, and yet the history of the misapplication of progressive ideas is such that they certainly do. The instances where progressive ideas have been used to justify utterly reactionary positions are legion. The MSC's invocation of 'relevance' to justify 'work experience' and SLS, the demotion of literacy and numeracy as priority goals, and the replacement of education with a diluted form of social therapy, are merely the latest instances. But they are made possible by crucial simplifications and ambiguities that were lodged in progressive ideology from the start. Most dangerous was the naive assumption that you could bypass the problem of class ideology and class power by simply turning away from the 'academic curriculum' and developing a school curriculum out of the culture that children brought to school. What has followed from this stance – it cannot be called a theory – is the failure to develop a potent rationale for a schooling which would involve high levels of general education for all, and hence the withering away of the whole basis of the comprehensive idea.

The stance has, as Stuart Hall points out, involved a considerable degree of 'bad faith' on the part of teachers:

> The bad faith, to put it brutally and polemically, consisted of teachers, who had themselves learned to manipulate, symbolically at least, two worlds, in effect patronizing kids with their view that all they needed to know was what they had already absorbed through their pores from the 'great university of life', when they themselves wouldn't be caught dead subscribing (nor would they consign their children) to the textbook of the street alone. The error of thinking which underpinned this was that 'experience itself' is alone the great teacher. Relevance in this sense is all.[27]

The danger of 'instant relevance' is that in its earnest desire to 'meet kids where they're at', it ends up leaving them exactly there – in the case of working-class kids, in working-class jobs, excluded from the culture of power. The danger of confining working-class children to this non-education is greater today than ever before, since increasingly class power is organized around a sharpened polarity of intellectual and manual labour, where access to positions of power requires daily greater facility in conceptual and symbolic thought. In a world where computers now manipulate information one may adapt the old proverb and say that today, in a limited sense, 'conceptualization is power'. Education without concepts and analytical tools, is education for subordination.

Any socialist theory of education must concern itself with the ways in which working-class children, including black children and girls, can gain greater power through education. It was Antonio Gramsci, perhaps more than any other social theorist, who understood the centrality of education in the politics of socialism. Himself a tireless educator, both through journalism and at first hand in the factory councils, Gramsci understood the fundamental importance for the working class both of generating working-class intellectuals (organic intellectuals) and of developing a counter-hegemonic culture within the working class; that is, a culture sufficiently rich and 'expert' to meet the technical and intellectual demands of challenging, and assuming, power. This involved both the appropriation of all that was powerful in traditional – bourgeois – culture and the transformation of popular common sense. Gramsci's approach to popular culture – or common sense – which he decribed as 'thinking without having critical awareness, in a disjointed and episodic way', was to extract and transform the good sense, i.e. 'that healthy nucleus which exists in 'common sense' and which deserved to be made more unitary and coherent'.[28] Education had to be an uncompromising 'struggle against folklore' but starting from the grounds of common sense. Education was, in this sense, a

> criticism of 'common sense', basing itself initially, however, on common sense in order to demonstrate that 'everyone' is a philosopher and that it is not just a question of introducing from scratch a scientific form of thought into everyone's individual life, but of renovating and making critical an already existing activity.[29]

Well aware of the cultural gap between teachers and pupils, Gramsci was at pains to point out that the teacher must know and understand 'folklore' in order to transform it. No one has put it better.

It is also of interest to note that Gramsci opposed vocational education in schools, instead calling for a full 'humanistic' education for the people, which aimed amongst other things at a full command of the standard form of the national language. What is equally important, perhaps surprising to some, is that Gramsci also viewed this education as a hard struggle, involving 'pain and tears', and one that inevitably required considerable discipline and rigour.

Conclusion

In analysing some of the changes in further education as a result of the Manpower Services Commission and the influence of the new training philosophy, and being largely critical of the outcomes, does not mean we should argue for a return to the previous status quo. Prior to the MSC's intervention, colleges not only failed to provide for the majority of school leavers, but what they did provide – City and Guilds of London Institute and GCE – was wholly inadequate. At that time education authorities, and indeed educationalists and academics, had given little thought to the design of a post-compulsory education system adequate to the needs of an age of mass unemployment. At the least, the MSC can be thanked for raising the issues and highlighting the problems for tertiary education.

The tragedy is that now, when the opportunity to rethink post-compulsory education has been forced upon us by the decline of work, the solutions offered should be so pitifully inadequate. The objectives of YTS and the new training philosophy are both narrow and short-sighted. To derive the objectives for post-school education and training from the immediate requirement of existing jobs, when these are becoming by and large less skilled and less numerous, is by definition short-sighted, and surely unwise by any reckoning. What YTS offers is not in fact, as its apologists claim, a watershed in post-16 education, nor a new deal for school leavers. In important respects it is more of the same; a continuation of the historic inadequacies in the British education system. The elitist division between liberal and practical education, the under development and institutional marginalization of technical education, and the failure of the British state to create institutions that offer a popular mass general education to high levels, are all historical problems traceable, at least, to mid-Victorian Britain. Far from being a corrective to this, YTS is essentially in the same mould. Its primary objective is social training for working-class youth and its mission, as Victorian educationalists would have said, is to teach the people to know their 'station' in life. If it differs, it is only in its more utilitarian idioms, 'gentling the masses' through the teaching of good telephone manners.

Viewed in a comparative light, British post-compulsory education is distinctively underdeveloped. Britain offers fewer opportunities for extended post-compulsory education than almost any other major industrialized country. Taking available comparative statistics, in Japan in 1982, 94 per cent of those reaching school leaving age continued in upper secondary education, and 36 per cent of those who finished lower secondary education three years earlier were in higher education. In the USA in the same year, 19 per cent of the civilian labour force had had four years of higher education, and 78 per cent had obtained a high school diploma at the age of 17 or 18. In Sweden, 94 per cent of the 16–18 age group stayed in upper secondary education in the comprehensive *gymnasieskula* – for which all receive a grant – whereas in Britain a mere 9.3 per cent of boys and 6.7 per cent of girls went on to do degree courses, and only 16.7 per cent stayed on at school after the compulsory leaving age.[30] By 1984 – even with the MSC's new programmes – it was still only 30 per cent staying on in school and 13 per cent in full-time further education.[31]

The promise of a two-year YTS with several months off-the-job training for any who need it, looks, by comparison, a poor deal, and barely touches the problem. Even in Germany, which has like Britain a traditional preference for vocational and work-based training for school leavers, the concept of training extends far beyond the needs of existing jobs. Although many Germans are now rethinking their own 'dual system' of education vs. training, there is still a clear recognition that training for stock is economically and socially worthwhile. It means that 80 per cent of those who leave school do three-year apprenticeships – with day release – up to craft level. As the National Economic Development Council put it in a recent survey of international training systems prepared for the MSC, 'It is believed that it is better to be unemployed and skilled, than unemployed and unskilled.'[32] When will the MSC listen?

The argument is not, however, that the German model is enviable or that training beyond immediate need is a sufficient criterion. A better starting point would be the recognition that in the future the majority of the 16–19 age group and large sectors of the adult population will be unemployed and that while we must campaign for more jobs and a more equal sharing of work, we must also see to it that for the unemployed there is adequate material assistance and opportunities to develop their talents through extensive periods of continuing education and training. What is required is both a new structure of opportunities and a new structure of expectations. In search of the latter, we could do worse than contemplate, in the old utopian fashion, the meaning of the 'education of desire'. Especially so since, whereas on the ground the return of so many unemployed and unwaged adults of all ages into further education demonstrates an urgent and keen instance of the meaning and potential of 'permanent education', our policy makers have, for the most part, barely assimilated the words into their lexicon, and certainly, as to their true meaning, it is barely dreamt of in their philosophies.

The development of expectations is important because, clearly, education is about more than simply 'putting on courses', especially where we are considering, as we must, the development of something radically new. However, we are not without guidelines. If we are to do more than sanction an education system that merely reproduces in the old way workers 'by hand' and 'workers by brain', we must generate a system of post-school educational opportunities whose aim is to encourage higher levels of general and technical education for all, and whose structure is such that the words 'universal' and 'comprehensive' achieve renewed potency and meaning.

1. D. Raffe, 'The End of the "Alternative Route"'? The Changing Relation of Part-time Education to Work-life Mobility Among Young Male Workers', *Youth Training and the Search for Work*, ed. D. Gleeson, Routledge & Kegan Paul, London, 1983.

2. G. Holland, *Young People and Work*, MSC, 1977.

3. HMI, *Report on the Youth Training Scheme in Further Education 1983–84*, DES, 1984.

4. Central Advisory Council for Education, chaired by Geoffrey Crowther, *15 to 18*, HMSO, 1959.

5. G. Holland, *op. cit.*

6. For arguments about parallel changes in the DES see S. Ransom, 'Towards a Tertiary Tripartitism: New Codes of Social Control and the 17-plus', in *Selection, Certification and Control, Issues in Educational Assessment*, ed. P. Broadfoot, 1984.

7. D. Gleeson, 'Further Education, Tripartitism and the Labour Market', in *Youth Training and the Search for Work*, ed. D. Gleeson, Routledge & Kegan Paul, London, 1983.

8. *A New Training Initiative, A Consultative Document*, MSC, 1981.

9. HMSO, *Training for Jobs*, White Paper, cmnd no. 9135, 1984.

10. See P. Cohen, 'Against the New Vocationalism', *Schooling for the*

Dole? ed. Inge Bake et al., MacMillan, London, 1984.

11. MSC, *Youth Task Group Report*, 1982, 4.3c.

12. See *Unpopular Education*, Centre for Contemporary Cultural Studies, Hutchinson, London, 1981.

13. Industrial Training Research Unit, *A–Z Study*, 1981.

14. This tier would include students in so-called 'advanced further education' (AFE) and some of those in 'non-advanced further education' (NAFE). The latter is defined as 'provision offered by local authorities through colleges of further education at qualifications much below degree, high diploma, higher certificate and professional courses of equivalent level'. See *Training for Jobs*, White Paper, 1984.

15. G. Lander, 'Further Education and Corporatism: The Signficance of the Business Education Council', in *Youth Training and the Search for Work*, ed. D. Gleeson, Routledge & Kegan Paul, London, 1983.

16. P. Bourdieu, 'The School as a Conservative Force: Scholastic and Cultural Inequalities', in *Schooling and Capitalism*, ed. R. Dale et al, Open University, Milton Keynes, 1976.

17. See C. Searle, 'FEU and MSC: Two Curricular Philosophies and their Implications for the Youth Training Scheme', *The Vocational Aspect of Education*, May 1984.

18. See C. Benn, 'CPVE — Learning your Place', *Teaching London Kids*, Issue 22, 1985.

19. FEU, *A Basis for Choice*, DES, 1979.

20. See M. Moos, 'The Training Myth, A Critique of the Government's Response to Youth Unemployment and Its Impact on Further Education', in *Youth Training and the Search for Work*, ed. D. Gleeson, Routledge & Kegan Paul, London, 1983.

21. M. Apple, ed., *cultural and Economic Reproduction in Education*, Routledge & Kegan Paul, London, 1982.

22. R. Boudon, *Education, Opportunity and Social Inequality*, John Wiley, 1974.

23. D. Raffe, *op. cit.*

24. J. Bruner, *Towards a Theory of Instruction*, USA, 1966.

25. K. Jones, *Beyond Progressive Education*, Macmillan, London, 1983.

26. M.F.D. Young, 'Taking Sides Against the Probable', *Education Review*, Vol. 25, No. 3, 1973.

27. S. Hall, 'Education in Crisis', in *Is There Anyone Here from Education*?, ed. J. Donald and A.M. Wolpe, Pluto Press, London, 1983.

28. A. Gramsci, *Selections from Prison Notebooks*, ed. Q. Hoare and G.N. Smith, Lawrence & Wishart, London, 1971.

29. A. Gramsci, quoted in *Antonio Gramsci*, Conservative Schooling for Radical Politics, ed. H. Entwistle, Routledge & Kegan Paul, London, 1979.

30. National Economic Development Council, *Competence and*

Competition, MSC, 1984. British figures are for 1981.

31. HMI, *Report on the Youth Training Scheme in Further Education*, 1984.

32. National Economic Development Council, *op. cit.*

6. The MSC and Adult Education

Eric Robinson

Edward Heath's Conservative government had few notable successes. One of them was its conception of the Manpower Services Commission which was then fostered by the next Labour government. When Margaret Thatcher took office she announced her intention to reduce the number of 'quangos'. But the greatest quango of all was to continue to grow and to extend its power. The MSC grew during her government into a most dangerous monster. Its dismemberment or abolition in its present form must be one of the highest priorities for the next Labour government if it is to begin to reconstruct a democratic system of education and training.

To say this is not to disparage indiscriminately all that the Manpower Services Commission has done, nor even to deny that it has done some valuable things. But much of the MSC's work has been based on false or even iniquitous assumptions. It has sponsored much mistreatment of people and has done little to enhance human dignity. Its structure, procedures and the directions of many of its policies constitute a massive threat to vital democratic principles on which the British education system has been progressively developed since the great Education Act of 1870.

The basic appeal of the assault of the MSC on the education system has been that democracy is inefficient, and that non-accountable central control by officials is efficient. It has been sustained by a massive and expensive public relations campaign of defamation of the education system and highly selective reporting of the works of the Commission. The Labour movement is inhibited in recognizing all this by two things: the fact that the last Labour government first introduced the MSC into the education service and the fact of continuing, albeit ineffective, participation of the Trades Union Congress in the Commission.

Undermining adult education

It is perhaps difficult but it is necessary for socialists and radicals to acknowledge that we have in Britain an inheritance of democracy and liberalism that is valuable and worth defending. The contempt of Margaret Thatcher and her associates for these British achievements and traditions is manifest. Class hatred, materialism, avarice and selfishness are the values that they are perversely attempting to elevate to the status of virtues, but they were not the only Victorian values. There was also a Victorian tradition of compassion, and liberalism which liberated British children from servility to Mammon in the fields, factories and mines of this country. One of its great achievements was the Education Act of 1870 in which were laid down the democratic principles on which our education system has been based ever since. This system has been the envy of many countries, the model used by many. The great threat of the Manpower Services Commission is the destruction of the system for undermining its foundation.

The most important principle of British education is that the prime beneficiary of education should be the pupil or the student: that education is for the child, the individual.

When he introduced to the House of Commons the Education Bill of 1870 Mr W.E. Forster described 'the principle on which our Bill is based . . . the ultimate force which lies behind every clause' as 'the education of the people's children by the people's officers, chosen in their local assemblies, controlled by the people's representatives in Parliament.' Section 76 of the 1944 Education Act reads,

> In the exercise and performance of all powers and duties conferred and imposed upon them by this Act the Minister and local education authorities shall have regard to the general principle that, so far as is compatible with the provision of efficient instruction and training and the avoidance of unreasonable public expenditure, pupils are to the educated in accordance with the wishes of their parents.

These are the principles on which the public democratic system of education in Britain has been based.

In contrast, the MSC is not locally controlled, it is not responsible to parliament and it is developing an education system in which pupils and students are educated in accordance with the wishes of the employers and the state, as represented by an unaccountable bureaucracy.

The enemies of democracy subordinate the individual to the state or to the corporation. To them the individual is merely the instrument of the corporate body. For them the education of the student is for the benefit of the state or the employer or the employer who might eventually appear. This is explicit in the statements of the leader of totalitarian states. It has become explicit in this country only recently in the statements of Margaret Thatcher, Keith Joseph and the leaders of the Manpower Services Commission. The failure of the education system for which they have such contempt is that it has not been hesitant in abandoning its sacred duty of primary concern for the individual.

The Manpower Services Commission did not *create* the chaos in the provision of education and training opportunities for adult people: it has merely compounded that chaos. Whereas in the field of 16–19 education the MSC has pursued a fairly straight course of malevolent corruption, its activities in post-18 education and training have been of a much more random and naive character. The theme of the succession of youth schemes is the conviction amongst the MSC bureaucracy that it is more efficient than democracy in determining and directing the 'training' of the young people from poor homes for whom the aspirations generated by 'education' are not to be encouraged or even tolerated. It is a totalitarian approach to the 'education' of youth in the service of the state in which neither the youth nor his/her parents has any legitimate rights.

In the adult sphere the MSC has hitherto operated on rather different lines. Here it has insisted that the voluntary principle is paramount, that training is the responsibility of employers and that the MSC should generally intervene by pressure, bribery, preaching or any other means available to encourage employers to undertake training and even to contemplate their future labour requirements.

The British tradition of vocational training of workers by their employers is almost nonexistent. British industrial and commercial management have generally been supremely indifferent to training, to say nothing of retraining, and have stubbornly resisted any change in this even under the pressure of the technological advances of recent years. This is recognized in the comparative study of vocational training in Japan, West Germany, USA and UK recently published by the MSC and the National Economic Development Office (*Competence and Competition*, 1984).' The outstanding facts emerging from this study are that those in power and those with influence in the most highly industrialized capitalist countries believe that high expenditure on education and training is vital both to national economic prosperity and to the success of individuals and corporations. In the UK they do not. In the other countries the private money and effort that goes into vocational education and training is vastly greater than in this country, both in respect of investment of companies in their employees and expenditure by individuals on themselves and their families. The Thatcher government, while ostensibly encouraging adult training of the 'right' kind, has in fact grossly neglected it. It has dismantled much substantial work in educational establishments. It has reduced capital investment in education and training to a trickle, grossly inadequate even to check depreciation. It has introduced through the MSC, financed largely by the EEC, a sequence of insubstantial gimmicky schemes. The main contribution of the MSC to adult training has been a large volume of documentation in its own distinctive jargon urging both employers and the unemployed to snap into action to make good the shortcomings of a government with no policy for reducing unemployment or creating a workforce to meet the future needs of industry or society.

Undermining democratic tradition

One of the trademarks of the Manpower Services Commission has been its total and overt contempt for the education system, the educational institutions, the educationists and the educational processes. It has sought popular support and political support by exploiting every possible element of resentment, prejudice and antagonism against academics and teachers. In this it has not distinguished between the academic tradition and the vocational tradition which are quite distinct in British education. The MSC has found it useful to pretend that the technical college tradition is not significantly different from the grammar school tradition. The whole of education has been defined as hostile or indifferent to industry and employment. Indeed, both the government and the MSC have been unashamed to imply that the education service is responsible for the sickness of the economy. Part of the MSC anti-academic ethos is that it has no need of the concept of truth. It has therefore found it unnecessary to acknowledge a strong, distinctive, British tradition of vocational education and training that exists, namely the 'night school' tradition, the mechanics institute tradition inherited by the further education colleges. Most of the Whitehall civil servants, the MSC officials and the Tory politicians know little of this, but the people of Britain know it. The British tradition is that if you want to improve yourself you go to classes at 'night school' or 'the tech', and you help yourself with the assistance of the local council. You don't expect anything from your employer. The Tory government and the MSC have rubbished all this, but they have put nothing in its place apart from a few half-baked, very expensive 'initiatives' such as TOPS, Skillcentres and the Open Tech, and a large volume of propaganda about adult training. While one gimmick after another has tumbled out of brainstorming sessions behind locked doors at MSC headquarters, often supported by large sums of money it has found difficulty in spending, the system of adult and further education in evening institutes, colleges, polytechnics and universities has been starved and squeezed mercilessly without any serious attempt to assess its value.

The rise of the MSC coincided with the attack on the educational budget. The savaging of university budgets and the steady deterioration in the value of students grants have been well publicized: in general the university cuts hit the more prosperous sections of the community. Much less publicized but more savage were the cuts in the provision of further and adult education for the less prosperous in the colleges of further education and the evening institutes. In contrast with the predominantly middle-class university students, the students in the less prestigious institutions often pay fees, they get small grants or no grants at all and they are even ineligible for social security. Evening institute and college budgets were cut and cut again. Teachers were made redundant, equipment became obsolete and libraries deteriorated. Fees were increased, public transport became more expensive or disappeared. For the individual, motivated student things became steadily more difficult. Many abandoned their studies to go on the dole so that they could eat.

While this was happening the Manpower Services Commission

financed new training schemes — the Training Opportunities Programmes mainly in the colleges and training courses in Skillcentres. Often the content of these courses was hardly distinguishable from courses that were being closed in the colleges. In some cases Skillcentres were established with newly established workshops duplicating those that were under-used in the colleges. Untrained and inexperienced instructors were engaged by the centres as experienced trained teachers were discharged by the colleges. There were differences – most importantly that the 'trainees' had no rights as 'students'; their courses were short and intensive; they obtained no recognized qualification; they were encouraged to learn nothing that was not strictly practical towards doing a job that existed, even though the necessary skills were to be obsolete fairly soon. Now many of the Skillcentres are to close unless they can be 'self-financing'. It is not expected that a full financial report of the ultimate cost of these centres will be published. The MSC is not accountable through any democratic process. It can afford to bury its mistakes.

Overriding it all has been the basic assumption on which the MSC has never wavered – that the people themselves cannot be trusted to judge what they need. Big daddy knows best and he reserves the right to change his mind overnight, so that in some cases big expensive schemes disappear almost as quickly as they were invented. There must be few adult training or education establishments in the country that have not had experience of establishing schemes with MSC support and enthusiasm to find them abandoned a year or two later, sometimes with little or no explanation: simply that they no longer conform to the fashion of the moment. Skillcentres have been opened with ballyhoo and closed with a whimper. TOPS schemes have flowered, and faded. Community Programme subsidies have been withdrawn. Who does not have friends who are employed by the MSC who have no confidence that their employment will last beyond the end of the year or the end of the month, apparently at the whim of some faceless official of the Manpower Services Commission?

In the field of adult training the MSC has been anxious to respond to the immediate vagaries of the labour market. Training for jobs that really exist has been the objective, but how many have completed a MSC training scheme only to find that the jobs were no longer there? The demands of employers are notoriously transient and conservative. It is difficult for an employer under severe financial pressure to think of the long-term future.

Many MSC schemes have reinforced work patterns that were already doomed. The labour market segregates men from women, blacks from whites, and the MSC has loyally responded. When the TOPS scheme was at its height the MSC boasted that nearly half of its trainees were women – but nearly all of them were training for jobs that were defined as women's jobs, notably in typing and secretarial work which was in rapid decline in response to computerization. Then around the corner appears a MSC white horse promoting equality for men and women and boasting to the world of its tokenism: that it is training a few women engineers. Let them eat cake. The most recent emphasis is an insistence that the training system must be employer led, with sublime indifference to the fact that the employers generally will lead by giving priority to white men.

Undermining freedom of thought

If there is a justification for such a body as the Manpower Services Commission, it is that it should undertake the preparation of some long-term national planning. But this it has notably failed to do. It is understandable that when its creation was quickly overtaken by the onset of large-scale unemployment the Commission should have been asked to give a priority to short-term measures to alleviate unemployment. When, however, it became clear that unemployment was a long-term problem, the Commission should have been required to concentrate on long-term issues rather than encouraged to rampage across wide areas in which it had no legitimate role.

What is the likely pattern of labour in this country 20 or 30 years hence? What industries will there be and what types of jobs? What patterns of education and training are now in need of development to anticipate these labour market needs? In place of credible answers to such questions as a basis for policy, the Commission has mere guesswork and prejudice imposed by the wishful thinking of politicians. Science and technology are in. Almost everything else is out. Education is bad and training is good (except of course for the sons and daughters of statesmen). Creators of wealth, by which we mean those employed in the private sector, are good. Those working in the public services are parasites so that a hustler or an advertising model or a stock exchange gambler is a creature producer, whereas a nurse or a sewage worker or a teacher or a road mender is not a producer but a parasite. These are the lunatic values to which the Manpower Services Commission has to respond.

There is considerable evidence that the economic future of Britain cannot lie mainly in manufacturing and that the provision of services is a much more likely national preoccupation. Although it is certain that familiarity with science and technology will be of great importance in the future, it is by no means certain that we will need more scientists and technologists. It could well be that in the twenty-first century our most important natural resource will be our language and our most valuable skill the ability to communicate in it. Even some of our traditional educational concerns, for which this government and the MSC have such contempt and of which they are so destructive, could be of the greatest economic importance, to say nothing of their social, cultural and spiritual value.

Perhaps the most important economic and social need is the improvement of skills not in technology but in human relationships. If there is a characteristically British industrial weakness, it is not in scientific and technological invention and skill but in the human and social constraints upon their effective use. The cultivation of social skills is obviously vital to the many social and personal services. It is also vital to every aspect of business and industry. We have a Secretary of State for Education and Science who has decided to abolish social science. We have a Manpower Services Commission which values amongst the social skills only those of obedience and conformity.

In so far as the long-term objectives of the MSC are ostensibly defined, they are, to say the least, unconvincing. But in one thing the MSC and the Thatcher government are right, by their own standards. Education and training must not encourage independent thought, imagination and nonconformity.

A plausible workforce planning body, having identified the objectives of education and training, would carefully appraise the existing arrangements for education and training and then consider ways to adapt them for future needs. The Manpower Services Commission presumes to design a national training strategy without making any substantial appraisal of the existing arrangements. How much and what kind of adult training is carried out in industry, business and the public service; in the colleges, polytechnics and universities; in the evening institutes; in private training institutions? We have only the vaguest of information about much of this. For example, each year several million people attend 'night school' classes in further education colleges and evening institutes. How many of them attend classes designed to be of vocational value? How many attend for vocational reasons? How well are they satisfied? How much demand for such opportunities is not being met? Nobody knows because nobody has attempted to collect this information. For years the DES has simply defined as 'vocational' those courses leading to an examination and those as 'non-vocational' those which do not! Thus a navigation course for gentlemen yachtsmen is 'vocational' and a reading course for illiterates is 'non-vocational'. It is on the basis of data collected with this type of superficiality and naivety that we are confidently assured that the education system has failed to respond to the needs of demands of industry or has failed to prepare people for the labour market. Anyone who has worked in the field of further education knows that many if not most colleges have for many years been submissive to a fault to the 'needs of industry' as defined by all and sundry; that they have struggled against massive apathy to obtain the interest or participation of employers in their work; and that they have been encouraged particularly by Whitehall to neglect the evening students in favour of day students, preferably full-time day students. They also know that the lot of the part-time student has grown steadily more difficult, even heartbreaking, with contraction of the service, increasing fees, more expensive books and materials, rising transport costs, decay of public transport and almost total lack of support from grants or scholarships. Over past years the personal investment of so many of these students in their educational improvement has been massive – private expenditure on education and training that the government and the MSC claim so earnestly to encourage. Yet this is the very effort which they have done so much to disparage and dismantle. The main reason for this? Perhaps it is because people who spend their own money decide for themselves what they will do. In this field our masters seem strangely mistrustful of private enterprise and judgement.

A new education act

What then should and could be done? Government must have
confidence in the intelligence of people, collectively and individually,
and plan to help them to cultivate that intelligence and the
confidence to use it. Most people want jobs, even careers, they want
to do them well and they want to be successful. The essence of a
democratic system is simply to help them to get the education and
training they want! In this field, above all, a Labour government
must avoid policies of central control and direction. A Manpower
Services Commission that is undemocratic and tries to prescribe
from London or Sheffield a national formula for the education and
training for the whole nation is an utter nonsense. Anyone who has
experience of forcing piano lessons on an unwilling child knows a
fundamental truth about teaching: it works effectively only if the
pupil wants it. The role of government and institutions in education
can only be to provide facilities and teachers to help people to learn
what they choose to learn. A policy of providing educational
assistance to meet the demands of the people yields a large bonus in
the form of the time, effort and resources that the people themselves
will contribute. This will far outweigh the losses imagined in effort
wasted on useless education.

The Manpower Services Commission has had success in exploiting the failures of the education system to respond to popular
demand and in this it has done a useful service. It has given priority,
particularly in its youth schemes, to many who have been neglected
by the education system. It has been an effective iconoclast in
challenging traditional educational hierarchies, prejudices and
rituals. It has blown a refreshing breeze of amateurism into some
cosy professional corners. It has demystified, but it has developed
its own mystique.

The forecasting of future labour market demands, the provision
of specialist skill training, the creation of jobs, the sponsoring of
community programmes are all of importance and should be the
tasks of special agencies of local and national government. These
tasks should not be confused with the provision of a service of
education and basic training for all. In particular, spurious labour
planning should not be used to restrict educational opportunity.
Specialist skill training must not be mistaken for education.
Creation of jobs and of work experience must not masquerade as a

substitute for education, and trainees must not be exploited as cheap labour. Most important of all is that the control of education must not pass into the hands of employers and the labour movement must not be seduced into believing that this is acceptable provided it is moderated by the participation of trade union representatives.

Continuing education for all who want it is an objective that is now within reach of the industrialized countries. This does not mean that we can all go to Oxford for three years whenever we feel like it. Indeed, it may mean that fewer of us will have such an opportunity even once in a lifetime; but it is reasonable that we should all expect to get something.

The Labour Party National Executive Committee is right in calling for colleges, polytechnics and universities to open their doors more widely to give access to many more people. It should be more courageous in acknowledging that difficult decisions of priority and power structure have to be taken. The education and training effort of the MSC should be firmly relocated, with its substantial funding, within the democratic control of local and national government. In the short term the assurance of a system of national provision of education and training beyond school should be obtained by using the 1944 Act in a way that it has not been used – by requiring every local education authority to submit for approval a plan for further education provision. The efforts of a strong national team in a new major adult branch of a Department of Education could then go into the oversight and co-ordination of local initiatives.

In the longer term, but certainly during the next parliament, the way should be paved for further progress along these lines by major legislation — the next great Education Act is long overdue. Its principles and content are clear. It should reinforce the principles of mass education established in 1870 and extended in the principles of comprehensive education as developed by Labour governments since 1944. And it should extend these principles to education beyond school. This means establishing new rights to educational opportunities for adults and new duties for authorities to provide educational assistance and facilities for them.

A people's democracy has no need for a commission to provide a service of manpower. It needs instead, and it will have, a commitment to provide a service to enable people to exercise power.

7. The MSC and a New National Training System

Morris Kaufman

'Nelly' might be regarded as the patron saint of British industry, for 'sitting by Nelly' to learn how to do the job has traditionally been the favoured national training system. For more than a century the failure of this cheap-jack way of nurturing and developing the required skills progressively became more evident until in 1964 a Tory administration recognized that voluntary training without statutory pressures was synonymous with inadequate training. It introduced a Training Act.

Conscious of the extent of employer resistance to 'government interference', the government did not through the Act insist on training. It created a system of about 25 Industrial Training Boards (ITBs), each with the task of raising the qualitative and quantitative level of training within given industries or groups of industries. Each ITB had the power to levy companies within its industry a sum of money, generally of the order of 1 per cent of its payroll, which might be returned to the company if it could persuade the board that it was training 'reasonably'.

The ITBs were set up over a number of years amid much complaining and threatening, particularly on the part of smaller companies, which had so far done little or no training themselves, but who were quite content to continue to poach the few people trained by others. 'The Great Training Robbery' was a rallying cry in the political campaign of the day to destroy the effort to establish a more effective training system for British industry. By 1971 the anti-ITB pressure was strong enough to force the government to publish a green paper called 'Training for the Future', which conceded most of the case of the protestors and was clearly meant to pave the way for the quiet demise of the statutory system. However, wiser heads prevailed and the ensuing Training and Employment Act 1973 in effect strengthened the system with the introduction of the Manpower Services Commission (MSC). This was to be the central national body which was to give coherence and direction to what had so far been 20-odd disparate ITBs.

But that 1973 Act turned out to be but a temporary reprieve. The protagonists of 'sitting by Nelly' regrouped and persuaded the more sympathetic Thatcher administration to destroy the training system by its Act of 1982. By that Act it abolished 16 ITBs leaving a rump of six or seven degutted and demoralized Boards together with an array of a hundred or so futile voluntary so-called 'non-statutory training organizations' to provide a fig leaf to cover the government's shame and complete lack of interest in training for industry.

Nobody familiar with the statutory training system between 1963 and 1982 could possibly claim that it did not suffer from some fundamental inadequacies. But it did provide a base upon which the nation and industry could build. It did by its very existence proclaim the central importance of more and better trained personnel and the fact that a national training system is vital for the future of the country.

It would appear that the present government and the interests it represents have lost faith in the future of Great Britain. They make this evident in many ways, not least by their indifference to the demolition of the national industrial base. In such circumstances the absence of an effective training system is not likely to be considered of any great moment.

However, those who are concerned with the re-establishment of a strong, viable and competitive industry must get to grips with the design and construction of a mechanism that will stimulate and facilitate the training of the personnel required to run it. The absence of a system now gives us the space on which to build a better structure, one which incorporates the lessons learned from experience. But the problem is urgent. We shall need all the time between now and the end of this government to get the answers right.

What, then must a national training system be able to deliver? Its major objectives must surely include:

1. That it will as far as possible ensure that adequately trained people are available at all levels to meet the changing needs of industry and commerce;

2. That it will make it possible for people to train and retrain

throughout their adult lives;

3. That it will facilitate a smooth and fruitful transition to the world of work and to adulthood for all school leavers;

4. That it will seek to maintain high-quality training throughout the system;

5. That training will be available to all sectors of the work force without restrictions imposed by traditional concepts and stereotypes relating to sex, race or other preconceptions.

Realizing the above list, or any other list of possible objectives, immediately brings into focus the relationship between, if not indeed the identity, of training and education, and the need to consider how a national system can best reflect this reality. This is not the occasion to discuss and theorize about the relationship. But there will be little disagreement, at any rate among people in industry, that while specific skills are obviously necessary, fast-changing technology makes these skills obsolete within the lifetime of a worker. This puts a premium on his or her education and versatility which allows them to master problems at work and adapt to new situations.

Thus provision for education and training can be considered only as a unity and the problems that have been encountered between the MSC and the world of education are a clear warning of the inevitable troubles that arise when this truth is ignored. The logic of this argument leads directly to the creation of a Department of Education and Training at the highest government level, instead of the present DES and MSC under the Department of Employment arrangement. The operation of such a government organization would have much to commend it but one must concede that other considerations impinge on such a decision. The politics of government as well as less arcane politics make a decision on the precise form of organization at this level difficult. Be that as it may, it is vital that administrative and political considerations do not vitiate the unity of education and training. That said, industry and commerce have specific objectives by way of education and training, such as have already been indicated and these will have to be catered for within the total national need.

It is in this connection that we have to consider the nature and function of the MSC and examine how much it could contribute in its present form and how useful it might be, if at all, in a modified form. The role of the MSC has changed considerably from its founding conception in 1973. Then it was conceived as a tripartite body, composed of representatives of the employers, trade unions and education (including local government), responsible to the Secretary of State for Employment but with a large degree of independence. Now, whatever the formal situation, it operates still on a tripartite basis, but more or less as an arm of central government. The question therefore arises, should we continue with a tripartite system and if so how can we safeguard its integrity?

In our society wherein industry and commerce are still largely based on private and nationalized enterprises as well as much local government activity, it seems desirable to operate a system in which all the interested parties are involved in policy formulation and decision. The question for discussion is how far is this compatible with strong central government direction as operated under the present government? How far indeed, is it desirable or acceptable from a trade union point of view to be bound by decisions of the MSC, particularly when its policies owe so much to strong government pressures? A related question is how can the MSC be structured so that it becomes responsive to the experiences and pressures generated regionally and locally?

The MSC has moved from its original conception in other ways. In the scheme of things it was the apex of a system created to stimulate more and better training. It was to co-ordinate efforts across industry and commerce to develop and operate an appropriate national manpower policy. But the destruction of the ITB system has deprived the MSC of its links with industry and at the same time the government's unemployment policies have required the MSC to become its instrument for handling the growing unemployment. In particular, a great part of MSC preoccupation and resources have been concerned with the consequences of unemployment among the young.

The paucity of MSC thinking and its lack of concern with training for industry was well illustrated by the 1984 white paper of the Secretary of State for Employment called 'Training for Jobs'. It dismisses adult training in six short paragraphs. Some of these deal with the unemployed, others with a futile campaign 'to raise awareness of the need for adult training'. All of them are quite minor when compared with the functions of the MSC as originally conceived. It adds nothing of significance to the solution of the urgent problems of the supply of trained people.

But it would be wrong to imagine that the MSC, even in its halcyon days, was able to contribute effectively to the development of national training policy. It provided even less in its implementation. There were various reasons for this and the following were among the significant deficiencies:

1. The system provided the MSC with no effective means of getting its policies adopted in practice. Its only instrument was the prospect of money as an incentive and this proved to be inadequate.

2. It has no real means of developing local, regional or Welsh or Scottish policies. There was no means of generating the necessary feed of local information and policies nor was there a mechanism for translating policy decisions, if any such were taken, into local action.

3. MSC staff were, on the whole civil service bureaucrats with little or no expertise or even interest in training. There were a few people who could discuss training and training problems intelligently, but so few that they were completely swamped. As a result, as I know from personal experience, contact between the MSC and the ITBs was restricted to exchanges about finance. Only on very rare occasions were matters of training the subject of discussion. Nor have matters changed more recently. With a total staff now of more than 20.000 the MSC can muster less than 100 trainers.

The national training system as a whole, as it evolved through the operation of the 1964 and 1973 Acts, had its strengths as well as its weaknesses. In addition to the points already made specifically in relation to the MSC, experience of the system overall suggests that it produced the following positive results:

1. The placing of training on the agenda of industry. There is no doubt that, particularly through the regular visits of ITB Training Advisers to companies and their friendly relationships with company management and staff, the contribution of training to company performance was the subject of conscious consideration.

2. The development of a pool of professional expertise on training which was very familiar with the reality and problems of industry and was available to it. In particular the body of ITB Training Advisers made it possible to convert what might have been a bureaucratic exercise into a fruitful exchange between

companies and ITBs. Of course the quality of that exchange was not uniform. It varied between and within ITBs, but it was a feature of the British training system that was unique internationally. The government has largely dissipated that pool of expertise. Most of the Training Advisers are now doing other things and many would not willingly expose themselves again to the uncertainties and problems of a training system which was under attack for most of their lives as Training Advisers. Nevertheless, our experience of their operation and contribution is a strong recommendation for re-establishing a widely based core of professional, peripatetic advisers.

3. Training Boards based on industries often built on the reality of an industry identity which facilitated the development of forms of training and training organization which corresponded closely to the needs of the particular industry. While this was not always a simple relationship, the existence of trade associations, research associations and so on attest to the fact of industry identity and in the best cases the ITB became an integral part of the structure of its industry. Such a relationship should be nurtured and where possible built into the continuing industry organization.

The weaknesses of the system emerged in a number of ways:

1. ITBs were conceived as instruments to deal with training needs, industry by industry. Within limits, they did this reasonably well. What they could not do, was to consider the changing labour needs of a locality or region. But this is a vital requirement. The changing industrial scene is expressed as the opening up or closing down of establishments in different parts of the country, as well as the changing profile of a given industry. The introduction of a large new enterprise, for example, into a town or region may have its repercussions on companies in a wide variety of industries in the vicinity or further afield. The opening up of the new Ford plant at Bridgend in Wales sucked in engineers from such industries as plastics processing and chemicals, as well as printing and ceramics. Industrial Training Boards were not able to deal with such problems, particularly since the MSC without an effective regional training structure could give no strong lead.

Another aspect of the weakness of a system based solely on given industries became manifest in dealing with types of workers who are found in a range of industries, for example, managers, office workers, engineering craftsmen, etc. In spite of attempts to deal with such training problems together, ITBs never satisfactorily solved the problem.

2. The system was incomplete. It covered about 15 million of a working force of about 25 million. Part of the difference was well catered for in British Rail, the armed forces, the electrical industry and others, but a considerable swathe was not covered at all. This was because of a failure of nerve of the government which set up ITBs over a period of several years and opposition to training measures deflected it from its original intentions.

3. The existence of more than 20 ITBs each reflecting the nature of its industry, some big, some small, each with its distinct type of leadership and staff, inevitably gave rise to a fissiparous response to common problems. It placed a premium on strong central leadership. The MSC had generated neither the authority nor capacity to provide it.

4. The system was tripartite, i.e. it comprised the employers, trade unions and educationists. In practice, the union contribution was weak. Not uniformly so. There were issues and moments when the TU contributions were decisive, but on the whole the TU presence both at MSC level and on the boards reflected the relatively low priority which unions accord to training. There were few occasions when they presented and fought for a training initiative. They often defended classical trade union positions in defence of wages and conditions for workers, but they did not often put forward training propositions. The same might of course be said of negotiations on the shop floor.

5. A major fundamental problem arose from the contradiction between the essential unity, or identity, of education and training on the one hand, and the quite separate organizations of the MSC and DES to administer what they choose to define as education and training. Administrative convenience and politics have often clashed with the needs of the clients and with the necessity to develop sensible and effective methods to meet those needs. Nor were these problems confined to the topmost levels of administration. The division between the education and training systems at all levels has been obstructive, frustrating and harmful and most obviously in the education and training of young people.

These comments on the strengths and weaknesses of the system are, of course, by no means exhaustive but they do perhaps indicate issues which ought to be considered in any new national training structure.

Finance

Perhaps the single most important problem in the design and operation of the national training system has been posed by what system of financing training should be used. The issue might be expressed in another way: how far should the system aim to cover the cost of training by statutory means? The question is quite crucial because the cost of training is the major determinant in shaping the attitude of companies towards it.

Experience in the UK over a very long period has demonstrated quite conclusively that any system relying on the voluntary decision of most companies to train is doomed to failure. That historical experience has been confirmed in the few years since the government destroyed 16 ITBs because, it said, it was convinced that voluntary bodies from those industries would stimulate the necessary training without the expense and bureaucracy of statutory organizations and controls. Doubtless the government was just as aware as everybody else of the lessons of history, but the last two or three years demonstrate that British employers are unwilling to allocate the resources necessary for training. As a result we live in a situation in which the diminishing number of employers who do pay for training are very likely to lose their investment to competitors who do not. The former are therefore discouraged and the total volume of training, never adequate, is now declining catastrophically.

The 1964 and 1973 Acts were designed to extract part of the total cost of training from industry as a whole and to redistribute most of the proceeds among companies that train. It did so by levy/grant/exemption system operated by the ITBs. However attractive the scheme looked on paper, it failed in its purpose. The system was complex and cumbersome in action and proved to be a continuing irritant to most companies. Although the iniquity of the levy was the slogan under which some companies went into the battle against training, the size of the levy, which represented only a small part of training costs, was never enough to make its loss an effective inducement to carry it out. Thus the levy/grant system, while an irritant, was an ineffective instrument.

The situation in this respect in the surviving rump of ITBs is interesting. The level of the levy is fixed by purely 'political' considerations. The employers on the ITBs apply pressure progressively to diminish it, the trade unions and ITB staffs try to maintain the level, while the government fixes the rules and circumstances to ensure a steady fall. This has the effect of curtailing the activities of the ITBs so that they become simply irrelevant without the government having to incur the odium and bother of wielding the axe again.

The levy/grant system has failed on a number of counts. Most important, it has not increased the quantity of training nationally. It has not spread its cost between companies benefiting from it, nor has it persuaded companies of its equity.

With hindsight we can see the reasons for its failure. One reason seems to have been a confusion of objectives of the financing system. This is well illustrated by a comparison of the wording of the 1964 Act and of an official Ministry of Labour *General Guide to the Industrial Training Act*. Section 4(1) of the Act laid it down that, 'For the purposes of raising money towards meeting its expenses an ITB shall from time to time impose a levy on employers in the industry'. In other words, the levy was to pay the cost of running the boards. On the other hand, the Ministry of Labour Guide explained that one of the three main objectives of the Act was 'to share the cost of training more evenly between firms'. It continued in paragraphs 9 and 10 to answer the question, 'How will the board ensure that enough people are being trained?' in this way: 'its main weapon will be its obligation to impose a periodic levy on employers and its power to make grants to those whose training courses are approved by the Board'. Further,

An employer who provides no training will have to pay a levy but will get no grant; one who does approved training will pay the levy but may receive grants towards the cost of training. In this way an employer will have a greater incentive than before to see that his employees receive training. . .

Even if we accept the intention as explained in the Guide, then experience has clearly demonstrated the flaws in that thinking. The levy/grant system has never provided a decisive incentive to employers. The grants paid out have in the main depended on the kitty provided by the levy and the levy has with one exception been low in relation to the cost of training. That exception was the initial demand of the Engineering Industrial Training Board (EITB) which was for $2\frac{1}{2}$ per cent of the payroll. It was calculated on the cost of engineering industry-wide training. But the EITB levy came down quickly. Other Boards fixed their levels at 1 per cent or fractions thereof and so tacitly accepted that the incentives offered to companies would fall far short of the actual cost of training.

The ITB levy/grant system was thereby reduced to a marginal financial issue which was quite readily ignored by many companies. In effect, ITBs said to companies within the ITB scope, 'We will statutorily extract a sum of money from you. If you train satisfactorily you will get that money back; if not you will lose it, or part of it. In any event you will have to pay the cost of training.' To companies not convinced of the need for training, especially when they could get other companies to pay for it, this was not a very compelling argument. To many it was merely an irritant. It did little to spread the cost of training.

The intention to divide the burden received a further blow when it was decided to exclude 'small' companies from the obligation to pay the levy. Boards defined 'small' at different levels but it was no doubt true that in many cases the cost of collecting the levy was bigger than the levy itself. Thus, while the exclusion of small companies from the levy/grant could often be justified administratively, it vitiated the basic aim of the system, particularly as small companies are as a group not known for their training activities.

A possible alternative national training system

The finance of training must be the central issue in the design of any new national training system. The design must take into account the general lack of training tradition in Britain and the unwillingness of most companies to spend money on it of their own accord. They must all contribute to the creation of a national pool of trained personnel into which they can all dip, if the manpower needs of industry are to be met.

The architects of the 1964 Act in the event explored a cul-de-sac. The only reasonable alternative for providing the wherewithal to ensure an adequate flow of trained personnel to staff an ever-changing industry would appear to be a training tax which all enterprises employing labour would be obliged to pay. It would be based on the number of people employed. The money raised would not find its way into the general coffers of the Treasury, but rather would form a 'training resources pool' from which companies would be reimbursed according to the amount and type of training which they carried out. Such training would, in the normal way, be in response to the needs of the company, but it might go beyond that to satisfy specific industry or national needs.

In this way the cost of training would not be borne by individual establishments. Instead the cost would be spread over all those who would benefit from the availability of trained personnel. Companies would not lose their investment if people they had trained decided to move off to pastures new.

The training tax would be much simpler and cheaper to administer than a more complex levy/grant, or series of levy/grant systems as devised by the individual ITBs. It would also remove the complaints of companies making adverse comparisons between the different levy/grant systems operating in different industries. Of course, payments for training would have to reflect in some degree the inevitable complexities of industry and naturally there would be political opposition to the introduction of such a tax. However, no serious attempt to ensure adequate and continuing training in industry can evade such opposition. The issue will have to be confronted.

The administration of education and training

The previous discussion has emphasized the dilemmas posed by the division between the administration of education and training. The division has its origins in history, administrative convenience and a class-divided system of education. It in no way corresponds to the aims of a system which sets out to provide for the efficient and effective education and training of the citizens of this country.

A Department with a Secretary of State encompassing all important aspects of education/training would seem to be a strategic requirement of any attempt to avoid this division. Such a department would aim from the outset to have this fusion mirrored at all levels of the process. Achieving a real unity of approach would no doubt present difficulties to the department dealing, as it would have to, with both the educational establishment and with industry (i.e. manufacturing and service industries, be they public or private). However, a structure capable of dealing with both, but dedicated to the single task of education/training of the population, can surely be envisaged.

The MSC, or its analogue, should find a place beneath its umbrella and just as at present it should be autonomous while answering to the Secretary of State. It would be primarily responsible for the education/training of those who had left full-time education. This autonomy would not be an altogether new concept in the operation of a department. Although quite different in form, the system under which the LEAs operate independently while under the general aegis of the DES shows that this is quite feasible, as does an earlier period in the workings of the MSC.

The MSC should retain its tripartite form to reflect the interests of those primarily involved. Some members of trade unions might argue that when the MSC becomes an arm of government, as it presently is, they would be giving a hostage to fortune by continuing as part of the MSC. Our current experience demonstrates that when the MSC becomes an arm of government the unions are caught up in the prosecution of policies which may not be their choice. That seems indisputable. But it seems equally obvious that the representatives of workers should be vigorously involved in the formulation of training policies which have such an important bearing on their lives at work and outside.

While the composition of the MSC should remain tripartite, its functions must change considerably. It should no longer be the principal administrator of the government's unemployment policies and schemes, but should be the central body to plan and co-ordinate the manpower strategy of the nation in close conformity with industrial, economic and educational policies.

To do this the MSC would have to develop close working links with the regions and with the world of education, both centrally and in the regions. Hopefully the relationship with the latter would benefit from the fact that they would be parts of a single government department and we should be spared the takeover type of behaviour which has characterized the MSC in this context.

At the moment, the MSC is a fairly isolated body, in spite of the fact that it has a large number of employees distributed around the country. As a result its real influence is limited. Because it is non-democratic in the way in which it reaches its decisions, it cannot draw on the vast fund of knowledge and activity that is available in the regions and localities. The formulation of local policies and activities which translate otherwise futile national decisions into living events depends on the involvement of people down the line and this is only possible when they believe that they have a say on policy and when they control resources.

To date no such organizations exist. It might be said that the Area Manpower Boards (AMBs) created to administer the Youth Training Scheme (YTS) can be regarded as prototypes for the job. In principle they seem to offer interesting possibilities. They are at the 'coalface' and they are composed of local people. In their present manifestations, however, they suffer from some crucial shortcomings. They are 'toothless tigers' in that they cannot, or at any rate do not, make the significant decisions and they are not informed enough to make those decisions even if they were allowed to. It is not possible here to discuss the 'why' or 'how' of this situation but it is incontestable, for example, that the members of AMBs play little real part in the approval or otherwise of specific YTS schemes, despite it being their formal duty to make these important decisions. They are made by the local MSC officials working to guidelines laid down by the national headquarters.

If local or regional organizations are to form a vital part of the national training system, and they must, then they will have to be different from AMBs in significant respects. In other words, we are speaking of real devolution of powers from the centre to truly representative local bodies. They and not senior MSC civil servants working in the field must make the decisions.

The representative local bodies would be wider than present AMBs in their composition. In addition to the presence of commercial and industrial interests, including the local chamber of commerce, major individual companies, the Trades Council and appropriate trade unions, there should be local authorities, LEA and other educational agencies, such as the Youth Service and local FE college. Organizations representing local community interests would also seem to be appropriate together with local representatives of the MSC and relevant ITBs.

This sort of representation would make the body well able to act as the agent required to synthesize the various aspects of an education/training strategy into an integrated and coherent plan of local action. It would translate national policy and guidelines into local terms. It would bring together the occupational and regional aspects of industrial manpower requirements and it would mobilize the local resources of 'education' and industry to satisfy the developing needs of a changing local economy. These representative local bodies would be truly nodal points of the national training system and should command resources commensurate with their responsibilities.

Reference has just been made to the presence of ITBs in the local bodies. Earlier discussion commented on their positive contribution while it also suggested that a system based solely on a number of such discrete organizations representing individual industries did not, and could not, provide an integrated response to national and local needs. The scheme outlined so far therefore throws much greater weight on the contributions of the functions of the central MSC and the regional bodies. But that would not obviate the need for industry-based training organizations. ITB-like bodies would still have a role to play. Based on the identity of their industry, they would develop training schemes and programmes for their specific needs. They would each also organize and maintain a network of training advisers to visit companies in their industry and to represent it on local and other bodies.

There would thus be three dimensions to the training system: central, regional and industrial with the ITBs very well integrated into the other two.

Young people

The role of the MSC as the government administrator of unemployment schemes has turned its attention away from a real concern with training. The major Youth Training Scheme occupies MSC staff on bureaucratic and financial details. But even when the MSC seriously addresses its national manpower responsibilities, the training and education of young people will inevitably occupy a great deal of its concern. YTS, or a more worthy successor, is likely to become a permanent feature of the education/training scene.

In putting forward the following proposals, I think it may be useful to preface them with the fundamental beliefs on which they are based.

A major proportion of young people will continue to opt to leave full-time education at 16. Most will be right to do so, and it would therefore be a disservice to them individually or en masse to persuade them to remain in full-time education. But their choice should not condemn them to follow the 'tramp's road' through life thereafter, while others opting for higher education are thereby routed onto the 'royal road'. Those who leave school at 16, even if they become unemployed have every right to follow the career of their choice thereafter without incurring the penalty of a lower status and of being denied the support of further education and training, both on and off the job. This support should help them achieve their goals not only in a narrow vocational sense but also in their transition to adulthood and into the world of work.

A number of important implications follow from this approach and even from the professed objectives of YTS. Perhaps the most important is the assumption that learning at work is a crucial element of the development of young people. This is not posed as an alternative to learning off the job, still less is it conceived in conflict with learning at college. On the contrary, it is seen as the complement of such learning and to be integrated with it.

But all this casts industry (or the world of work in the wide sense) as an essential component of the educational system. While most employers recognize that young people's learning is implicit in their employment (if they are employed), most of them deny that it is their function to provide time and resources for the learning process. The purpose is to provide a product or service and, in many cases, to generate profit. They are therefore not prepared to assume the role in which they have been cast, and so ready support from industry for serious and costly education/training of their young employees or trainees cannot in most cases be assumed. This reluctance is in fact a major reason for the poor quality of YTS and its predecessor YOP.

The question of how the true cost of a high-quality YTS is to be met cannot be permanently left under the carpet. The fiction that the managing agents' fee for taking on a trainee covers the cost of training rather than exploiting the youngster can be perpetuated only at the expense of the scheme itself. The number of cynics about YTS in the ranks of the trainees, trade unions and employers can only grow. It would seem that the costs of a genuine YTS will have to be a factor in fixing the rate of the proposed training tax.

But finance is not the only important factor. Given the will, industry does not at present have the trained people necessary to run the scheme. With between 300 and 500 thousand young trainees to be provided for, the number of supervisors to be trained will constitute a very serious problem. So far the MSC has genuflected to this need by setting up its so-called Accredited Centres, but the way in which they were established and their financial basis suggests that they may well be done to death on the same dusty road as the Skillcentres.

Maintaining a reasonable minimum quality of training in the myriad of companies and colleges involved would be a massively difficult task in the best of circumstances. But with no serious commitment of the MSC to standards in YTS one can only commiserate just now with the small section which formally has the task of establishing quality controls in the scheme. When that task is taken more seriously the local representative organization will doubtless be heavily involved in the monitoring of standards.

Training quality depends also to a large extent on the integration of the various elements of the programme and as these take place both over and off the job, one can readily understand how things can go awry when good liaison is not built into the scheme and then maintained. But that is easier said than done, as our general failure to achieve the desired objective of industry-education collaboration, despite our oft-repeated commitment to it, makes clear. Nor is it difficult to appreciate the obstacles which stop it happening. The objects of industry and education are so different. So is their ethos and their mode of working.

The administration of education/training centrally, and even more locally, has a crucial responsibility for seeing to it that the practical conditions for real integration exist. But this goes beyond the setting up of appropriate mechanisms. It reaches to the heart of the question of curriculum and the purpose of the whole exercise. It is bound up with the reality of the bridges said to be available to all for progressing up the education/training ladder, those bridges which have so far played such a relatively small role in the lives of our people. A local education/training board as described earlier should be well placed to discharge the responsibility.

Liaison cannot be limited just to industry and education beyond the age of 16. School must be involved because the transition of young people, with which we are concerned, is a single, gradual and continuous process beginning well before 16. This is not the occasion for a discussion of the school curriculum, but if it is to meet the needs of most of its clients and not predominantly those who are moving on to higher education, then the school curriculum for all will have to respond to the implications of the post-16 changes.

The more we consider the different elements of the total education/training requirements, the more they turn out to be inextricably interwoven. That is just as true in the field of higher education which we have not had a chance to discuss here. How necessary then that they be dealt with by a unified and integrated Department of Education and Training.

Summary of proposals for a national industrial education training system

1. There should be a single integrated government Department of Education and Training.
2. A tripartite MSC type of organization forming one element of the Department of Education and Training should plan and co-ordinate a national manpower strategy.
3. A powerful network of regional or local education and training boards should be established to ensure the satisfaction of regional/local industrial manpower needs. These boards would be powerful by virtue of their representative nature and by the powers and resources delegated to them. They would be responsible for the application of national policies locally.
4. Industrial Training Boards based, as now, on individual or groups of industries would supplement the local dimension with an industrial element and would be responsible for teams of professional training advisers maintaining a continuing advisory service to enterprises. The ITBs would with their professional training capacity be responsible for the initiation and maintenance of training standards. They would form an important element of the local boards.
5. The cost of industrial training and education would be generally shared through the operation of a National Training Fund financed by a training tax.
6. The local education and training boards would take over the work of the Area Manpower Boards which are now nominally responsible for the YTS operation. The new-style boards would

be particularly concerned to ensure the monitoring of the quality of YTS and to facilitate the integration of industry, FE and schools in the schemes.

8. Women and the MSC

Sheila Marsh

In its National Training Survey which identified 396 jobs,[1] the MSC found that over half of all women in paid employment were located in only four types of work: clerks, typist/secretaries, cleaners and shop assistants. Clearly the MSC was not responsible for this stark and wasteful limitation of women's employment opportunities, but this statistic reflects the nature of the MSC's operating arena, and the need for change.

Training is a tool for changing knowledge, skill and attitudes, and in the process changing who determines and owns them . The MSC, which is taking the role of 'national training authority',[2] has a policy which acknowledges the inequality women face in the labour market. But although it proclaims equal opportunity, it limits this to 'equal treatment' of women and men, an approach that makes equality a constant rather than a goal that has yet to be reached. It also mistakenly assumes that equality can exist regardless of discrimination continuing from the past. It even forgets that the Sex Discrimination Act (SDA), inadequate as it is, recognizes that a so-called 'equal treatment' policy is frequently a cause of indirect discrimination itself, since it results in situations which affect women disproportionately – e.g. some age restrictions can effectively exclude women with young families.

MSC policy also fails to acknowledge the deep and difficult nature of striving for equality for women in our current social and economic context, where the division of labour between women and men has two separate dimensions, related in origin and effect. Firstly, the division of domestic labour is one which is scarcely a division since women bear the overwhelming burden. This leads to the so-called 'double shift' of paid and unpaid work, whereby women return from low-paid, menial employment during the day to equally undervalued but unpaid domestic labour in the evenings and at weekends (and indeed during lunch breaks).

Secondly, the division of paid employment between men's and women's work shows the latter to comprise the least valued and worst-paid occupations with the least prospects – such as cleaning, clerical work, catering, and looking after the sick, the old and children. These jobs are seen as extensions of women's domestic role, therefore not skilled and not of particular value. Historically, it has been the role of training to reinforce these divisions. How the MSC has responded to this is therefore crucial to any goal of equality it espouses.

The MSC's unequal training inheritance

Before examining the work of the MSC in detail, it is important to consider the training issues it inherited.

To most working people – and parents and teachers – training has meant apprenticeships. They set the pace and provided standards of excellence, transmitting and matching cultural values and aspirations. With the exception of trades dominated by women – like clothing, hairdressing and catering – which account for only about 15 per cent of apprentice training in any case, apprentice training has been in male-dominated industries such as engineering, construction and printing. Trade unions used training to regulate entry and standards for the benefit of their members, and apprentices were practically never women. Women were to be found in the 'secondary' labour market, often relegated permanently to temporary work considered of little or, at best, transitory value, or in the less well paid and unskilled occupations vulnerable to employers' changing demands for labour, where they acted as buffers to skilled men's jobs. Apprenticeships meant power in the labour market and recognition of skill ownership. This strength has been systematically denied women.

Despite developments over the last decades and new approaches to standards and institutions adding other elements of industrial training and education, women are still excluded from apprentice-ship-type training. Research sponsored by the Equal Opportunities Commission (EOC) and the Social Science Research Council (SSRC) showed that training for skilled manual work formed 45 per cent of all training activity, and that only 2 per cent of participants in this were women.[3] Similar forces operate in other forms of industrial training – e.g. women account for only 10 per cent of general managers in industry, and, significantly, had a mere 3 per cent share in management training. Since such training is often provided by firms at some expense and makes up about 28 per cent of all training, denying women access to it obviously affects their advancement. It points to an almost total lack of investment in women by employers; and helps account for the fact that women often overoccupy the lower ranks of many hierarchies in industry and the professions. In education, for example, women are 62 per cent of Scale 1 teachers in secondary schools but only 16 per cent of headteachers.

The arrival of Industrial Training Boards (ITBs) after 1964 had little impact on women's training opportunities, even in industries where women were numerous, like clothing and distribution. The Boards themselves were dominated by men, representing employers, trade unions and education, who tended to concentrate on higher-level skills training, from which women were excluded. By the late 1970s, in response to pressure, most Boards had at least one person working on women's training, but this work was limited in its value for the majority of women because it concentrated on management and promotion training, often at senior levels.

The role of education

The pervasive assumptions in society about women's role are reflected at home and at school as well as at work. These are the socializing influences which channel and lower women's and girls' expectations and aspirations. From nursery education onwards, both in hidden assumptions about sex-appropriate activity and in 'choice' of subjects studied at school, there are explicit and covert assumptions about girls' interests and aptitudes that are narrowing and discriminatory.[4] A recent study of young women on Youth Training Schemes (YTS) found that most had also experienced appallingly limited careers advice at school; while experience of the Careers Service later indicated that many girls felt deprived of advice and, in pointed contrast to the experience of young men, said their desires to depart from traditional options were not encouraged.[5] In adulthood, Jobcentres act as effective gatekeepers, excluding women from applying even for entrance tests to MSC TOPS courses in non-traditional areas, as evidence from women now on non-MSC funded courses testifies.[6]

The latest statistics show little change in the damaging occupational 'clustering' experienced by young women in the past. Indeed, as academic specialization increases, so occupational choice narrows. More young women may enter further education than young men, but the majority study stereotypical subjects like secretarial skills[7] and are not expected to work for long. By contrast, the expected duration and implicit importance of boys' education and training is reflected in the fact that 36 per cent in employment were getting day release training compared to only 15 per cent of girls.[8] In higher education, 'clustering' continues: 93 per cent of entrants to university courses in engineering and technology were male (94 per cent in polytechnics), while 65 per cent of entrants to language and literature courses were female (73 per cent in polytechnics).[8]

The situation also reflects the fact that parents too are often prepared to put more effort, encouragement and money into their sons' rather than their daughters' education and training. In 1984, when the GLC advertised apprenticeships in women's magazines, a stream of mothers applied for their sons. Social conditioning makes parents think of high-skill training only in relation to young men.

If opportunities are unequal for women in general, they are even worse for black women. Racism adds an enormous dimension to the sexual division of education and labour (see Chapter 9). It is estimated that in London, for example, one-third of black women have no formal qualifications at all. Many endure extreme marginalization in the labour market, where work is limited to the least-skilled, worst-paid manual jobs in industries like transport or the health service. This makes black women invisible and saps their self-esteem alongside black men in the hardest, least-valued work.

Discrimination produces pressure for change but the impetus for change comes from several sources, each with its own strengths. In the 1970s the Sex Discrimination Act (SDA), along with the Equal Pay Act, resulted from pressure for a legislative framework to reflect women's increasing demands for equality. The SDA provides minimum standards for day-to-day practice and the Equal Opportunities Commission works to indicate best practice and promote change.

Continuing pressure has also come from UK membership of the EEC, both to fall into line on legislation concerning 'equal pay for work of equal value' and through the working of the European Social Fund (ESF). The ESF provides significant resources to the EEC countries for employment and training work, and its criteria specify 'operations designed specially for women who are unemployed, threatened with unemployment, underemployed or wishing to return to work, to promote a more even mix of the sexes in jobs in which they are underrepresented.'[9]

The political climate in Britain was set both by the influence of the Women's Movement and by MPs like Jo Richardson – as well as by women trade unionists, MSC employees, and Industrial Training Boards, even some employers. From the late 1970s this pressure focused on training and the preconditions required for women to get access to training. Despite limited resources, most trade unions now have a national women's officer and put emphasis on negotiating equal opportunity agreements which affect recruitment, selection and promotion. Some employers, notably local authorities and large companies like Thames Television, have pursued active policies, exploiting the SDA provision for positive discrimination in training their existing employees for jobs where women are underrepresented.

Experiments in women-only training and in initiatives to attract women to 'male' options have also come from ITBs – for example, the Engineering ITB's Insight scheme to give young women a taste of degree course work, and the Inter-Board Liaison Group on Training Opportunities for Women. Importantly, individual feminist groups worked to provide alternative training resources – in Leeds, Bristol and the Lambeth area of London – and campaigned for mainstream provision to cater for women through the national Women and Manual Trades (WAMT) network. The MSC – with the ITBs – started *Women and Training News* in 1980, a year which saw the first courses sponsored by the MSC for women returning to work 'after a career break'.

This build-up of pressure ensured that the MSC began the 1980s with the objective of equal opportunity, but very much a policy stance rather than a programme of action. This results in token paragraphs in the Annual Report and arms-length phrases like 'the MSC seeks to encourage women into non-traditional areas'. This glosses over enormous practical and political issues, many relating directly to the Conservative government, whose policies the MSC was now required to implement regardless of actual training needs.

Conservative government training policy

By weakening statutory mechanisms and giving employers control, and certainly by using the MSC since 1979 to develop and deliver its labour market policy, the Conservative government has hindered opportunities for women.

The abolition of 16 of the 22 ITBs and the return of the remaining six to industry control was significant. It meant pressure from employers to keep training costs at a minimum was immediate, leading to reluctance to allow these Boards to fund even limited initiatives for women. This led to redundancy among staff working on women's training – for example, in the Hotel and Catering ITB – at the same time as the MSC was starting initiatives for women, astoundingly engaging ex-ITB staff to deliver schemes, though on a subcontract basis. Of the ITBs abolished, several served key industries for women like the Distributive ITB. Others, like Food, Drink and Tobacco, and Printing and Publishing, had done pioneering work in promotional training for lower-graded women, in single-sex management and assertiveness training, and in women's approach to learning through self-development. The Inter-Board Liaison Group of Training Opportunities had provided many of the ideas and much of the work seen in the MSC's women-only provision, but this was severely curtailed after the ITBs went – only two years after it had been set up. The patchy nature of the remaining work is given apparent credibility by the MSC's continuing to publish the group's paper, *Women and Training News* and supporting its remaining limited network.

But the key development has been the adoption of the New Training Initiative (NTI) in 1981 – to be delivered through the MSC. As a policy, it complements the Conservative ideology of catering to employers' short-term needs. Its strategy base of 'letting employers decide' represents no way forward for women, since employers themselves operate the labour market's discrimination against women! The NTI's supported aims of no barriers on account of age, and flexible access through mechanisms like Open Tech, may sound ideal, especially for older women, but even the EOC has pointed out that for women to benefit there must first be positive action schemes, financial incentives to train in non-traditional skills and, crucially, childcare facilities. Resources for none of these have been forthcoming.

The Adult Training Strategy (ATS) of 1983 only mentioned women in passing in a single paragraph about helping 'groups such as women, ethnic minorities and disabled people with some disadvantage in the labour market [who] would continue to receive special attention'.[10] MSC papers on adult training in 1984 and 1985 did not even mention women. Nor did the regular progress reports to the Commission on YTS. Nor did the white paper, *Training for Jobs*, of January 1984. Nor did the two white papers of 1985, *Employment – Challenge to the Nation* or *Education and Training for Young People*. Women can hardly feel included in the statement that 'training . . . is a necessity for all'.[11]

Along with the aim of increasing employer control of training and so of the labour market, and the parallel development of MSC programmes like YTS, CP, TOPS, ATS projects like Open Tech, and smaller programmes like the Voluntary Projects Programme (VPP) – women-only activities have remained. They act as buffers for the MSC's public stand of equal opportunities and ensure that scrutiny from the EEC can be absorbed. Meanwhile, the 'new vocationalism' pushes women towards a jobs future even more limited, unstable and lower paid than the status quo, reinforced by the cumulative effects of other government policies in health, housing and social services which force women out of work and into the home.

Before we look at the impact of the MSC's programmes on women in and out of work, there are observations to be made about the way the MSC is structured – not to mention its name, 'manpower', which barely conceals its intended role.

On the Commission itself, there was until January 1985 but one woman member out of nine commissioners, representing the CBI. Now there are none, for she has since been replaced by a man, a change that passed without comment in public life. Youth training matters are dealt with by the Youth Training Board (YTB) which has only two women members out of 14, one from the TUC and another from the voluntary sector. This lack of representation stems in part from the discrimination already described (since senior officers in industry, trade unions or local authorities are unlikely to be women) but also from the fact that the MSC does not see its role as including any responsibility for changing matters relating to past discrimination.

A similar situation exists on Area Manpower Boards (AMBs).

There is no pressure for women members from the MSC or from Boards themselves, and even the non-voting co-option of women has been low. By March 1984 only 10 of the 54 AMBs had such members. When this became known, the response to the MSC's Review of AMBs[12] led to many calls for membership with voting rights for women's representatives.

Structures for delivering MSC programmes are no more reassuring. The rise of the 'managing agent', operating in the marketplace, fosters the reproduction of discriminatory recruitment and assumptions in training for women, and also ensures that any cases of discrimination which are brought will not involve the MSC itself. The Skillcentre Training Agency (STA) has no women centre managers. The very few women instructors there, are in 'female' trades, almost all in catering, office work and hairdressing. In fact, many such instructors are men, since women tend to work in colleges rather than in the male-dominated Skillcentres.

Within the MSC there are inevitably few senior women, with most being in the lowest grades. No executive reporting directly to the Director is a woman. There is no general policy against sexual harassment except among employees exclusively, no childcare provision, and no requirement for staff training in equal opportunities. Corporate monitoring of the equal opportunity policy by the MSC seems to consist of a two-person unit (most recent incumbents both male) and the keeping of trainee records by sex and ethnic group, although this is done in such a way as to preclude data on black and ethnic minority women.

This then is the corporate context within which MSC practice pursuing equal opportunity for women must be seen – and judged.

Special measures for women: at the margins

Although certain groups have used funding from MSC programmes to start projects of value to women, these are extremely marginal. They included funds from the Special Temporary Employment Programme (STEP) and the Community Enterprise Programme (CEP) which helped set up initiatives like Women's Employment Projects Network, based in Merseyside to provide a national focus for local projects, and from VPP to set up a women's training workshop in Bristol, giving introductory training in a range of manual skills. After the MSC stopped CEP, however, programmes under its successor, the Community Programme (CP), were much less flexible and were opposed by much of the trade union movement. VPP is even worse resourced and more 'voluntary' (unpaid) than before. Using MSC money for creative community use is increasingly difficult, and never was reliable anyway, due to its short, 12-month funding period, with its lack of continuity and potential waste of effort and resources.

The MSC has not funded any women-only vocational skills training, its women-only measures being limited to work preparation, involving only a tiny number of women nationally[13]. Its Wider Opportunities for Women (WOW) has a mere 550 women.[14] Nationally organized programmes also include a few for women already in employment, especially in managerial grades. These show significant pitfalls and demonstrate the need for further development of attitude training for male managers, and trainee-responsive methods – like case studies – which ought to be developed further. Even within the MSC's limited women-only provision there are no childcare facilities and no flexible hours to promote access by women with children. In fact, the MSC assumes women will always leave work to care for children by concentrating on issues like 'managing the career break' – useful for a few women, but not tackling the problems of the vast majority.

The European Social Fund also supports some of the women-only programmes of the MSC. Not only does the MSC use the ESF as a significant resource for its programmes, but local government and the voluntary sector have more recently begun doing the same. All this permits the MSC to be vocal in Europe through CEDEFOP, the EEC's training body. But when this is accomplished through all-male, expenses-paid delegations from the UK – as was the case in 1984 – it hardly signals that women's training is being taken seriously here.

By contrast, attitudes in Brussels have been more progressive in relation to women, especially in non-traditional trades. Although there is always pressure to revise women out of the criteria, there are now at least a dozen substantial non-MSC women's training projects in the UK using ESF funding, including six in London, two in Leeds and others in Wales, Merseyside and Newcastle. The majority offer vocational skills training, and rejection of applications for yearly renewal is rare. Unfortunately, the largest share of ESF money coming to the UK goes to the MSC and it is important to impress on Brussels that the MSC represents neither the totality, nor the best practice, in women's training initiatives.

Given the importance of schooling and of 'subject choice' on women's subsequent employment and training, the MSC's Technical and Vocational Initiative (TVEI) in schools bears special examination. It aims to give employer-defined training to the 14-plus age group to 'prepare them for work'. As such it tends to add to the stereotyping of work for girls and limits skill levels generally. There are grounds for fear that its 'streaming' effect will discriminate especially against black young people.

Its impact on young women so far has been largely negative in that schemes which embrace traditionally male subjects, such as craft and design, have had difficulty in attracting girls who have tended to participate more fully in stereotypical subjects like clerical work, hairdressing or community care. Experience in Coventry, Leicester and elsewhere has indicated that TVEI is not countering the traditional school push to stereotypical employment.[15] The few positive effects it has had in areas trying hard to make TVEI compatible with equal opportunities, have been in equipping girls' schools for technology, as in Hertford, and in starting taster courses for various skills, as in Shropshire. These are pointers for development but not enough to counter the disadvantages girls face from 'the new vocationalism'.

YTS and TVEI reinforce divisions

The YOP programme started out in 1978 with 50 per cent girls, but when it ended in 1983 this was down to 46 per cent – a drop of 8 per cent in the original number of girls. It was assumed that YTS would result in even fewer girls receiving integrated training and work experience and that at best opportunities would be limited to narrow jobs traditionally considered 'women's preserve'. The first few years of YTS have confirmed these fears.

The distribution of the sexes within the nine occupational training 'families' (OTFs) shows gross imbalances for both sexes. In 1984, for example, a staggering 64 per cent of girls on YTS were in administrative/clerical or sales/personnel service work.[16] These places tend to be in the large employer-based schemes, the traditional employers of low-paid, unorganized female workforces, where 'high street' distribution and other non-union workplaces predominate. On current showing the YTS merely reinforces this 'market' division and employers' expectations, which are made nicely explicit by the restriction of young women's places in the Armed Forces YTS to switchboard operators, postal and courier operators, grooms and kennel maids.

Non-traditional options for girls are inevitably limited and found mostly in Mode B schemes, where in general girls must perform better than boys to get accepted. In work placements employers decide what work is appropriate: girls on electronics training are limited to keyboarding, girls in mechanics training to the parts department. In MSC training workshops girls are outnumbered; and in Information and Technology Centres (ITECs) in particular they are less than 3 per cent of trainees.[17] Even among those who do make it to the controversial ITECs programmes, girls tend to be ghettoized in word-processing and keyboard work, while young men move into electronics, programming and servicing. An exception is the ITEC in Sheffield, which is managed by a woman.

Despite its faults and the cuts it experiences, Mode B does offer a chance to develop wider opportunities for girls and to implement positive action. Such schemes as the GLC's 'Splintergroup' and Denham Court residential scheme, or Wolverhampton Trades Council's women-only scheme (of which YTS has only one other) have all operated successfully a positive-action programme for staff and trainee recruitment into non-traditional areas for women. Significantly, the two last have now been closed by the MSC and the first cut by half and likely to close after the abolition of the GLC.

Follow-up of young women after YTS shows it has made no difference to their disadvantaged position and narrow options at work. A full 74 per cent of those lucky enough to get jobs went into clerical or sales/service work.[18] Significantly, more girls than boys gained employment with those who had given them 'work experience', showing the power of the initial stereotying by occupation. Moreover, once in jobs, girls were less likely to get further training than boys,[19] the pattern of more expensive off-the-job training denied to girls being repeated.

Those looking for gender breakdown in MSC figures often find it is not available. Similarly, MSC reports on YTS fail to refer to issues specifically affecting young women. For these reasons the national pressure group, Women in Youth Training, has been gathering support from groups and individual women to put such issues on the MSC's agenda. Conversely, in a limited way the MSC has responded on race issues, receiving reports and commissioning research on equal opportunities (see Chapter 9), including reports from the Commission for Racial Equality (CRE) and the TUC. None, however, makes specific reference to ethnic monitoring by sex, nor to issues specific to young black women. Another example is the MSC's failure to introduce any measures to combat sexual harassment on training schemes, despite the evidence it has received. The staff structure of schemes (most training staff are on 12-month contracts rather than permanently employed) militates against tackling harassment and any continuing supportive policy. It also works against innovations from staff, such as women-only schemes. The MSC fosters the view that women-only schemes are not possible, which results in YTS schemes where many young women (and all young mothers) are invisible.

The Community Programme: disadvantaging older women

The CP – as the CEP before it – was devised in response to mass unemployment in a similar way to YOP and YTS, and this is reflected (perhaps more honestly than YTS) by its location in the Employment Division of the MSC. Its alleged aim is work 'useful to the community' without substituting for existing jobs.

Training has never been a reality inside CP, since no resources are given to it, although the MSC now claims CP is offering training. Closer examination, however, reveals this to be 'work preparation' instead – of the kind that the majority get on YTS: 'basic' education, 'social' skills, and job-search techniques – not real vocational skill training. And even this is only voluntary, depending on whether CP providers decide to include it. Currently, only 25 per cent of CP participants are undertaking it, and outside working hours at that.[20] That the government calls this an 'expansion' in training can be termed the most misleading and devaluing approach to training yet, as well as putting the blame for unemployment firmly on the unemployed.

The CP has not catered for women. In view of its wage-cutting, exploitative and casualization effects on the unemployed generally, this could be a blessing in disguise in the long term. But in the short term – where CP can sometimes offer relevant experience of work, an employer reference and employment advice – the figures show gross inequality in placements, for 77 per cent of CP places are taken by men. Moreover, 68 per cent are taken by single people, showing the CP to be largely a scheme for young unemployed males.[21] Work is concentrated in 'male' areas like the construction trades, while projects involving full-time 'caring' work or administration are being correspondingly squeezed or made merely part-time. Thus women are further marginalized within the CP by being concentrated, as they are, in these part-time places. There is a complete lack of any positive action to involve women in the programme.

As if all this were not bad enough, the government has given women a new disadvantage by the announcement in 1984 – without warning – that eligibility for participating in CP would be limited to those receiving unemployment or supplementary benefit. Thousands of women were thus excluded although those receiving benefit through their partners are still eligible. Many unemployed married women do not pay full national insurance. Also excluded are unemployed people (most often women) whose partners are working. These rules led to a great outcry on behalf of women, and the EOC challenged them at once under the SDA – as obvious, indirect discrimination against women.

Further discrimination is evident in the government's statements that it is 'fair' that women are only 20 per cent of CP participants because this is their level of representation in the target group of the unemployed, an approach that blatantly ignores the fact that women have always been underrepresented in unemployment statistics. This has been made worse now that 'receipt of benefit' has been made the basis of these statistics, so that women's particular relationship to the social security system aggravates their existing underrepresentation. Women do not make up only 20 per cent of the longer-term unemployed and their exclusion from CP on that false premise is fundamentally inequitable.

The government's Adult Training Strategy (ATS) has involved a cutback in provision for women through a cutback in the old Training Opportunities Programme (TOPS) run in colleges and Skillcentres as well as through private agencies and voluntary organizations. TOPS is important because, along with the CP, it is the MSC's key programme for adults – those over 18. The government's decision to let 'market forces' decide, and to make Skillcentres compete through the Skillcentre Training Agency along with other providers of training on a 'cost recovery' basis – rather than retain the Skillcentre network as a publicly sponsored agency to help adults train – has meant cutbacks. Equally there have been cuts in training courses offered in the clerical and secretarial fields by colleges. Since these fields claim three-quarters of all women on TOPS courses (the remaining quarter being in catering or hairdressing), such a decision obviously disadvantages women. The figures show it clearly: in 1980 women were 43 per cent of TOPS trainees, but by 1984 only 30 per cent.[22]

In addition women form less than 20 per cent of trainees on TOPS management courses, only 8 per cent in training for science and technology, only 2 per cent and 0.5 per cent respectively in carpentry and welding construction. As the TUC quaintly put it, 'Quite clearly women are not being encouraged to train for a future that is not job-segregated.'[23]

There is a particularly spectacular gap in the field of training for women in information technology, for office work courses involve no direct new skill. This fails women especially, for this is the area of work highly vulnerable to technological advance. Courses in this area are being cut back and not replaced with new skills training, even at the inadequate level offered by Information and Technology Centres. Nor is there any explicit provision in the MSC's long-term plan to tackle this crucial area of training for women. Less than a third of those entering Skillcentre Technology Access Schemes are women.

Since women's involvement in Skillcentres is less than 3 per cent nationally, a national campaign was started in 1984 to lobby for change in Skillcentre training for women. This percentage reflects the dominance of traditionally male trades and jobs in Skillcentres and their concentration of training support for skills in the construction, engineering and motor mechanics trades. In London's six Skillcentres only two courses are offered in 'female' trades – hairdressing and tailoring.

These Skillcentre courses are important, for they represent virtually the only route for women into recognized training which can lead to 'improverships', a term often applied to adults (and meaning apprentice training beyond the initial year or two). Improverships are important for they lead eventually to full craft status, crucial for women in breaking into hitherto male fields, but also important because they mean a chance to train for jobs with better pay, stability and more labour market power. The decision in 1985 to close down one-third of the national Skillcentre network will limit women's chances to press for their own better provision there.

Another barrier women now face is the trend to lower-grade 'assessment' and 'work preparation' courses in the Skillcentres that remain, combined with a tight screening process in Jobcentres beforehand. Entrance 'tests' in technical know-how are used to exclude women even from applying for Skillcentre training, after which Jobcentres assert that their education and experience is not up to the mark. In some cases women have not even been allowed to take the tests. Women who have been barred in this way by Jobcentres in as many different places as Bristol, Wales and many parts of London have taken part in a women's motor mechanics project in south London. One who went on to a Skillcentre was told that since she had the project's 'help' in passing their tests, it was no real indication of her abilities!

More ways to discriminate

Discrimination takes many forms, one of which is a failure to inform women of opportunities open to them. Although a report from the MSC itself on women in Skillcentres found that nearly half the women questioned believed such centres were for men only,[24] and, further, that lack of publicity, and course criteria, were obstacles to women, the MSC has taken no action to address these problems.

Once inside Skillcentres women face further problems and pressures. Firstly, their location is almost always inhospitable to public transport upon which more women than men have to rely. They provide absolutely no childcare facilities and start at 8 a.m., an hour which presents insuperable difficulties in arranging for childcare. The regime in centres is inflexibly male-defined and requires very short initial assessments which favour men's generally higher level of knowledge about 'male' subjects. Constant testing in this atmosphere does not cater for building the confidence of trainees of either sex, but is especially hard for what is often the only woman in a group.

Sexual harassment is also a problem at Skillcentres, although not as big a one, according to WAMT, as women face on CP schemes.[25]

The MSC has no policy for dealing with it. Where women have had to leave training courses because of it, some have pursued the matter through industrial tribunals, and the EOC has backed up two of the strongest cases. However, the EOC did not take up the case of a woman in Enfield in 1984 who alleged physical assault, which occurred during a period when an unusually large number of women were on a course at the local centre.[12] A similar case occurred in Deptford, also when an unusually large number of women were in training. Clearly women in strength are perceived by men as a direct threat.

Continuing reports of sexual harassment in MSC schemes has lead WAMT, together with the Electrical, Electronic and Plumbing Trade Union (EEPTU), to tackle this issue through meeting MSC and Skillcentre Training Agency staff themselves. Such action takes the pressure off women who are vulnerable in centres or during action on particular cases, and one result has been a circular to Skillcentre managers about harassment between trainees. However, it probably has not been seen by most instructors, who continue to be aware only of the existing Department of Employment policy which relates only to staff harassing colleagues. Thus staff harassing trainees remains unacknowledged and untackled by the MSC.

WAMT has developed useful material to be used for instructors, including a case study. This is presented through discussion of a case by a trainee, an instructor and a centre manager, and is an example of flexible teaching of procedure as well as dealing with attitudes which lead to 'blaming the victim'. WAMT is now engaged in convincing the STA's instructor-training centre at Bletchworth that it needs courses in this matter, and in pressing for racial and sexual harassment in TOPS rules to be given the same banned status as fighting and gambling. But so far without success.

While Skillcentres remain part of the training infrastructure in Britain, women must continue to campaign for access on equal terms. Some direct initiatives have begun – like the taster course in Deptford's Skillcentre, and the establishment of a creche. That the Minister of State had to become directly involved in this creche[26] – and gave permission only so long as no MSC cash or support in kind was given – shows the absurdly close control from the top that women's training gets. It barely masks the ideological opposition to women expanding their employment opportunities which were all too obvious in the Minister's letters.

Each year the situation gets worse. For example, as a result of the dispersal and privatization in Skillcentre training, all adult trainees must be employed and employer-sponsored to get on any Skillcentre course. How many women plumbers will emerge from this new system?

Preconditions for change?

The situation inherited by the MSC is redolent with the deepest issues surrounding sex roles and the sexual division of labour in our society. If a training strategy were to deal with these issues instead of ignoring them, it would open up the whole employment arena, exposing assumptions and throwing up the conflict essential to force change.

Women's jobs cannot be seen in isolation, nor can training be the isolated response. We know women's limited choices can be traced back to education and the family. Yet training is increasingly the only route to paid employment for women who want work that brings decent pay and rewards. Women need this work for inescapable financial reasons, since so many support themselves, often with children. Only 18 per cent of male workers at any time fit the archetypal profile of a man supporting a woman and children. Only pure prejudice can deny women recognition for their traditional skills or access to new ones. But current employment patterns, childrearing and domestic demands, mean women's containment and lack of power to control their lives is evident.

While 'market forces' are allowed to decide employment prospects – and the MSC continues as a body chained to market forces – such prejudice will continue. There will only be change when such policies are turned around completely, both nationally and locally. But what in that event are the questions to pose now, the preconditions for progressive change?

Striving for equality of opportunity for women turns on who decides and who implements training, in what skills, for which women, trained where and by whom, with what resources as well as whether women can afford it and whether there is childcare. Such striving means training and education that acknowledges and reflects women's experience and aspirations, and ensures a relaxed and supportive environment for all women through positive action to combat sexism, racism and anti-lesbianism, and deal with sexual harassment.

There is substantial debate among women about what skills women want or need. Whether skill is a male construct or not, some women want to acquire 'male' skills for better pay and prospects, while others want recognition and proper reward for women's traditional skills, and still others want to train to control and manage resources more generally, given women's exclusion from decision-making and policy formulation in society. White culture values traditional male skills and white women's campaigns for a fair share in this training can exclude black women and their aspirations. Women in work need skills to progress further in the same way that women who want to enter or re-enter paid work do. Women also want the opportunity to return to education, whether the courses or qualifications they pursue are for work or purely for self-development or their own interest. This adds up to an enormous, and so far unexpressed, demand for education and training resources. But the outlines of this demand are evident and one example is the overwhelming response to the training which has been set up by local authorities outside the mainstream provision. Their direct publicity and outreach work with women shows what can already be done.

Several local areas have pioneered women-only training courses, despite the MSC's lack of interest; and the GLC's expenditure on such projects alone equals the MSC's entire spending on women-only initiatives. The GLC and other local authorities like Leeds, Sheffield and Merseyside are spending money on women-only vocational training, which the MSC refuses to do at all. These projects enable progress to be made on specific problems like training trainers themselves in awareness of women's issues, training women to be trainers, and meeting the need for sensitive course structures. Equality of access alone evades the real point of conflict for training institutions.

Considerable research and experience in the UK, USA and Europe has pointed to the value of women-only provision,[27] particularly where women are training in 'non-traditional' options, where they are in an extreme minority, or where they are likely to suffer disadvantage. Especially positive results have been experienced by single-sex training for management, in the new technology, in manual trades, and in training to build confidence. This last has been shown to be crucial for women returning to work after childrearing.

Girls and women training or studying in technology fields have very different experiences when they are on their own. The key issues observed by one researcher comparing the process and organization of such a course were the girls' felt lack of pre-knowledge, their lack of confidence with tools and the way that conflicting social and course demands affected their behaviour and personal image.[28] All link back to the instructors, the presence of male trainees and the male ethos of a workshop environment. Women and girls in mainstream training often experience dismissive and discouraging attitudes from instructors and trainees alike.

In this case, when girls on their own were trained in the same process – processing plastic in an oven – they experienced no difficulty in learning, but when girls were trained with boys, they all asked the boys to take their plastic out of the ovens for them (despite the similarities to a domestic oven with which they were probably more familiar than the boys).

The importance of women-only provision for women's advance is reflected (and matched only) by resistance to it from mainstream providers. There is evidence that men, regardless of age, appear to progress equally well in either mixed or single-sex settings,[29] thus strengthening the case for women-only provision. Since a survey sponsored by the EOC and SSRC showed that 45 per cent of women work in totally segregated jobs where there are no men at all, it is odd to hear the argument that women-only training is uncommon or unnatural or unhealthy – all standard reactions to the idea.

Pressure on the MSC for women-only courses – and for resources for trainer training and proper monitoring – should be applied, particularly from the colleges, where representations from a wider range of groups is more likely to reach the MSC. Only day-to-day action by everyone involved in preparing women for work can ensure that women have a safe and rewarding work environment which respects parental responsibilities and does not exploit their sexuality. Women have a right to this and must demand it.

There must also be demand for childcare provision. Half of mothers with dependent children are currently working, but unlike other countries, including many EEC countries, Britain has few workplace nurseries. Local authority provision is at best patchy, at worst nonexistent, and what there is is under attack by public expenditure cuts and ratecapping. Although childminding is poorly paid, it is still beyond the means of many women, who increasingly ask, can women afford to train? Mainstream provision, including the MSC's, makes no arrangements for childcare, providing no creches and no allowances.

What is more, the supplementary benefit system and TOPS allowances are structured so that they actually penalize single parents (who are women) who undertake courses. Childcare expenses effectively halve their trainee income. Organizations which have taken this up with the government – like the National Council for One Parent Families and the National Childcare Campaign – find social security (DHSS) ministers and Department of Employment ministers each saying that it is to the other that complaint should be made, although in any case numbers are too small to bother with action. This is belied by the long waiting lists for training projects that do give priority to single parents with children.

In Newham in 1985 a single course enrolled 15 women who had 48 children between them for which the project arranged childcare. This suggests that provision for childcare facilities by local authorities is completely out of step with women's needs, especially those wishing to work. Their range is too limited as well, for the need is for school-age children's care as well as for the under-fives. It was these needs which led to the injection of resources by the GLC through its Women's Committee – up to £5 million a year – for community childcare in boroughs unable or unwilling to make this provision.

All these issues require massive efforts and work by many organizations trying to achieve institutional change to overcome past discrimination and provide equal opportunity. They attest to the slow and painful nature of the process. Yet such is the violent opposition to change, including that promoted by the GLC's Women's Committee and its Ethnic Minorities Unit, that the former has received constant criticism from the Conservative mass media and the latter was fire-bombed in the spring of 1985.

The experience of the GLC's own training board, together with voluntary groups, is that developing group and individual commitment to equality and setting up sizeable institutions from scratch along model equality lines, like the Charlton Training Centre in London, takes a long time – in this case over two years. The struggle is often made more difficult because it is tackling discrimination in all areas at once: sex, race, disability, sexuality and class. But the experience is that unless there is action on all fronts simultaneously there is a limit on what can be achieved. For example, tackling issues of sex without race will leave black women largely unaffected, as will tackling race without confronting sexism. Or either without taking on class. Nor should sexuality or disability be marginalized.

A new structure of accountability

Making equality a specific objective demands national level policy frameworks and targets with equality as an integral component, as well as the structures to reflect that policy. Integral also must be the allocation nationally of resources sufficient to implement action for equality, and equally important, to monitor results.

Within that policy framework, however, structures (and courage!) are needed to devolve and share responsibility locally. The national centralized MSC is poorly placed for such a response and despite efforts of its area offices, major policy always comes from the centre. Until the MSC – or whatever replaces it – devolves more decisions and power to localities by funding institutions and centres as a whole, instead of funding a constantly shifting range of 'activities' in a constantly shifting set of venues, women's aspirations will not be reflected in training provision. Nor will accountability be possible. At present there is no way of knowing how national resources, like ESF money, is used for women: how much or where it went. Without information there is no accountability. If funding were decided locally there could be direct accountability and the chance to develop locally based work – important for women, whose lives are so dependent on public transport and so tied to schools, shops and childcare facilities.

Alternative structures also presuppose a link between education and training policy which harmonizes with labour market policy in ways that reinforce equality in society. This requires a basic reassessment of labour divisions, the value of work, women's role in society and in the home – all issues felt by individual women as having intense, personal impact on their lives. Changes which women achieve are often different from the 'success criteria' normally applied to 'getting a job in your trade' or moving up your profession, forcing women to overcome pressures, often in isolation. Such 'pioneer' women are not a solution to inequality any more than training alone is a solution to progress. Simultaneous activity on employment policy, organizational structures, job design and pay is needed too.

Policy makers need to recognize that 'real work' is not what is done by white males alone, with no childcare responsibilities, and that equality for women does not mean encouraging them into traditionally male work in terms of the status quo. It requires major shifts of policy in many areas to enable them to arrive on the labour market already in a condition of equality. Thus highest on the list of preconditions is reorganizing work itself so that parents of either gender may be employed, and consequent on that, a massive increase in resources for publicly funded childcare in the local community or at the workplace.

It also means moving on from old attitudes. There is still the implicit assumption that women will continue to break their paid employment to take on childcare in society, and a principal training adviser with the MSC recently wrote that women and girls do not give sufficient thought to career development prospects for themselves and that sexual harassment is an 'unfortunate fact of life'.[30] The MSC's solution to women's training as well as to the labour market is restricted entirely to the narrow employer-based approach favoured by the Conservative government and monetarist ideology. This carries the same approach to women as to the unemployed, especially the young: your situation is your fault.

The government's public face is personified by its Secretary of State for Employment who told a women's audience that 'Britain cannot afford the economic waste involved if women do not seize the opportunities offered by new jobs and new industries',[31] once more emphasizing that the only way forward to be allowed is through Conservative economic policy, with competitive 'opportunities' restricted to the few. For women in general this means minimal training with no positive action on equality, no childcare, no end to stereotyped work and no respite from limited prospects and rewards. The male blueprint of a 'real worker' remains.

1. MSC, 'National Training Survey (1975–6): A Report', *Employment Gazette*, November 1980.
2. *Training for Jobs*, Cmnd 9135, HMSO, January 1984.
3. IFF Research Ltd, 'A Study for the EOC and SSRC, 1979', *Employment Gazette*, November 1980.
4. See, for example, Dale Spender, *Invisible Women*, WPRC, 1982; *Learning to Lose*, Dale Spender and Jane Sarah (eds.), Women's Press, London, 1980; papers from the Collective for the Education of Women and Girls in *Socialism and Education*, Vol 9, No 2, 1983, and *New Socialist*, June 1984.
5. Brown, Hilda *et al.*, *Class of 84*, The Fawcett Society and the National Joint Committee of Working Women's Organizations, January 1985.
6. Such women are now at training centres in Bristol, Leeds, London, Cardiff and Sheffield.
7. DES Statistical Bulletin and Welsh Office Figures, 1981/2.
8. DES Statistical Bulletins and Welsh Office Figures, 1982/3.
9. Article 4.2(a); and 84/C5/O2.
10. Proposals for Action, December 1983.
11. *Towards an Adult Training Strategy*, MSC, 1983.
12. *Review of Area Manpower Boards*, MSC, January 1985.
13. Hansard, House of Commons, Peter Morrison's reply to question from Tony Banks, 3 December 1984.
14. MSC, *Annual Report*, 1983/4.
15. Val Millman, *The New Vocationalism in Schools*, Coventry Local Education Authority, 1984; Birmingham Trades Council, *Report on TVEI* in *Comprehensive Education* No 48, 1984.
16. Youth Training Board, *Report on YTS Leavers Survey*, MSC, October 1984.
17. MSC, *YTS Progress Report*, (YTB/85/5), January 1985.
18. Youth Training Board, *Report on YTS Leavers*, October, 1985.
19. *Ibid.*
20. Estimates only; given by Tom King, House of Commons, July 1984.
21. 1984 figures, quoted in Greater London Training Board, *Community Programme*, GLC Report TB333.
22. MSC, *Annual Report*, 1983/4.
23. TUC, *Women in the Labour Market*, March 1983.
24. Michael Nicod, *Women in Skillcentres*, MSC 1984.
25. WAMT keep records of discussion with their workers and from women who contact them.
26. Peter Morrison, Correspondence with the London Borough of Lewisham and Lewisham Women's Training Group, 1983,1984.
27. E.g. WAMT, Report on USA Conference, *Women in the Trades*, 1983.

28. Val Millman, *Teaching Technology to Girls*, Elm Bank Teachers Centre, Coventry, 1984.

29. *Ibid.*

30. David Lisle, Principal Training Adviser, MSC, 'Training of Women and Girls – A MSC View', *Training and Development*, September 1984.

31. Tom King, speech to Women's National Commission, March 1984.

9. The MSC and Ethnic Minorities

Anna Pollert

'Young people are not worth much when they leave school, although their worth increases with the right training. But they have no God-given right to a good wage,' said David Young, one of the main architects of the MSC, as he explained on behalf of the Conservative government the virtues of deregulation.[1]

Even without formal compulsion, the government's legislative strategy is to make it virtually impossible for the young unemployed to avoid government job schemes like the Youth Training Scheme (YTS). This includes changes in social security board and lodging provision – despite a 1985 court ruling that one was illegal – which has created a roving band of homeless young unemployed, sleeping rough and forced out of cities. The scene is set for a return to poor laws, workhouses, and 'Victorian values' – with a new generation of workers denied the experience of collective organization and trade unionism.

There is also the Community Programme (CP), the MSC's second largest, taking a quarter of its budget. Even though it aims to recycle the long-term unemployed, and is a cheap labour scheme with an average wage of less than £60 a week, it is an important option for many. Yet places are scarce, demand high and recruitment highly selective.

With these as the main options in a current economic and labour market strategy that oppresses young and old alike, how can we hold out hope for 'equal opportunities' for anyone, much less those already oppressed by race, gender or physical disability? Any examination of the MSC's equal opportunities' policy and practice of what black people get – or don't get – out of the MSC's training and work programmes, will dispel any remaining illusions which the public, including the trade unions, might still be holding. More positively, for both black and white people, it might add to useful knowledge that will help in the struggle against a racist society, and help inform a new radical strategy for jobs, education and training.

How real is the MSC's 'equal opportunities' policy?

Following the inner city riots of 1981, public concern about 'equal opportunities' for black minorities gained prominence, and the MSC responded with the YTS. This was to be a major initiative to counter discrimination which the MSC stressed would deal with 'equal opportunities for ethnic minorities [which] all too often may not be a reality in working life, [and] YTS should not replicate that inequality', going on to add that equal opportunity policy needed to be 'tackled as an integral part of YTS' and not tackled as an afterthought or as a token requirement.[2]

In its early declarations, before YTS even began, the MSC announced what presumably still remains its policy, that

> YTS will, of course, be open to all young people within the range of eligibility regardless of race, sex or disability . . . and the Board will look to all parties involved in the preparation and delivery of individual programmes, and in the recruitment of young people to avoid discrimination and to accept the principle of equal opportunitity for all.[3]

Even more, the MSC's Youth Training Board, reviewing the first few years of YTS, later proposed ways by which 'more might be done' – through increased publicity, more monitoring to 'assess the relevance and impact of non-discrimination policies', and, lastly, to 'review the pattern of placement within YTS' in areas with high proportions of ethnic minorities.[4]

This may be the 'policy', but what is the reality? Managing agents of YTS are not given anything more than a token sheet, A4 size, stating that YTS is an equal opportunities scheme. The Commission for Racial Equality's (CRE) longer and better checklist is not routinely distributed[5] (although mounting pressure is forcing the MSC to increase its circulation), nor does available information suggest that MSC staff are given any education in racism or sexism awareness. Indeed, there is evidence that staff at MSC training centres consider that such a 'head-on' approach would put training staff and employers on the defensive.[6]

As far as monitoring is concerned, the practice is unequal, and scarcely satisfactory. Not all Area Manpower Boards (AMBs) by any means have set up equal opportunities subcommittees, and those that have – like Birmingham – meet continued difficulty, despite insistence that regular scheme-by-scheme monitoring to show ethnic, gender and disability breakdowns, is the way to proceed. The MSC is regularly unable to provide these figures, and is not anxious to discuss such policy. When the Birmingham/Solihull AMB decided to invite the public to discuss equal opportunities, the MSC confined publicity about this to telephone inquirers. Not until the Trades Council printed and circulated the invitation was it distributed in any wider way.

The facts of AMB membership nationally make it unlikely that a great deal of 'local action' on the racial discrimination issue would take place, since only 1 per cent of AMB members with full voting rights are themselves from an ethnic minority.[7] And the MSC has refused direct contact with organizations designed to increase awareness – like the Campaign for Racial Equality on MSC Programmes (CREMP) and Racial Equality in Training Schemes (REITS).[8]

The real test came when research, including the MSC's own, began to show discrimination in schemes. Far from the MSC pulling out the stops (including 'confidential' figures) to combat the trend, its earlier public firm stand began to weaken, so that by 1985 it was saying, 'discrimination exists in society and in employment and YTS experience is reflecting that . . . it would be wrong to look to training schemes of any kind to solve more widespread problems of discrimination in employment'.[9]

By this time just about all that the 'equal opportunities' policy was good for was 'the chance it offers employers to come into contact with ethnic minority young people on a scale which might not otherwise happen'[10] – a euphemism for giving employers the chance to taste the fruits of cheap or free labour from ethnic minorities.

Even the most elementary exploration of action shows that the MSC's commitment to 'equal opportunities' is both unclear and superficial. Despite two early reports that argued the case for special, and in some circumstances separate, training for ethnic minorities and women,[11] the MSC has never in actual practice adopted a 'positive action' approach. Indeed, hostility to black-only schemes by MSC staff has been noted in the MSC's own research.[12] The MSC's official policy remains one of mixed training offering 'open access' to all applicants, but it is based on the model of 'open contest' where everyone, regardless of how unequal their starting points, is theoretically equally able to 'have a go'. Behind the words, it is a patronizing attitude that offers nothing to combating the roots of inequality. Worse, it avoids acknowledging them at all.

For the MSC the policy is only to note that many people fall down in the race. At this point, it steps in to 'help' failures and inadequates with its 'special needs' formula. This formula is the other side of the open access coin, and instead of promoting equality of opportunity, has the opposite effect.

'Special needs' equals 'less opportunity'

The 'special needs' formulation regarding ethnic minorities has to be set in its context of post-imperialist racism, where black people are regarded as 'cultural problems' in need of the white missionary's 'help'. This gives the MSC's concept of 'special needs' an interpretation it shares with other state agencies concerned with training and the labour market, including the Careers Service. It also blends with the broad political strategy of substituting alleged individual deficiences – whether wrong attitudes or lack of skills – for what is really the failure of our social and economic system to provide jobs.

The MSC's 'special needs' formula has a crude, circular logic that starts with a variety of human categories who have tripped up on the way to 'open access' – women, ethnic minorities, ex-offenders, and the disabled – whose common symptom is disadvantage in the labour market. This is translated to a common cause, an individual pathology called 'special need', which in turn requires 'special measures' like 'work preparation' to make these individuals more employable. In other words, the unemployed are not unemployed because there are no jobs, but because they are 'unemployable'.

The MSC's 'special needs' programmes started in the early days of rising unemployment when young black people were disproportionately affected. Hence it was not surprising that black school leavers became overrepresented on the early Youth Opportunities Programme (YOP) and that this in turn 'confirmed' for the MSC that since the programme was set up for the least 'able' and 'employable', young black people were inadequate and in need of work preparation.

When, however, the YOP added to its remedial programme a

broader job experience scheme, young blacks did not spread with it. The MSC's own studies showed that 'non-whites' were almost three times as likely to be on the remedial or work preparation courses compared to other forms of training like Work Experience on Employers' Premises (WEEP).[13] Other research confirmed this, showing that only 35 per cent of black and Asian school leavers in Birmingham entered employers' work experience schemes compared to 65 per cent of whites and others.[14] This directly deprived blacks of job opportunities and increased their likelihood of unemployment as, once again, MSC research revealed: for of similarly qualified YOP leavers, only 15 per cent of blacks got jobs compared to 31 per cent of whites.[15]

Racial disadvantage reinforced

The effect of the 'special needs' formula in depressing the opportunites for blacks is clear and well known to the MSC, whose own research has to confirm it. So too are other factors affecting the chances of ethnic groups in education and the job market – which the CRE and Lord Scarman's investigations into the Brixton Riots of 1981 both confirmed – like the connection between the proportionate increase in black school leavers and the rise of black youth unemployment. There is also research, like that from the Home Office, to show 'continuing . . . discrimination against minorities on a large scale, particularly against minorities perceived as "coloured" '.[16]

Equally important, there is evidence to show that the problem is not, as alleged, shortage of skills but often *over*qualification in terms of labour market demand. In a study of Asian and black school leavers with the same qualifications as white school leavers, and the same desire for craft or technician apprenticeships, only 18 per cent and 17 per cent respectively were successful in getting apprenticeships compared to 57 per cent of whites.[17] The point is driven home further in a study showing that although black youth, especially girls, tend to leave school better qualified than local whites, they were more likely to be unemployed.[18] Later in life, it is the same story. Half the employed black adult men in 1981 were skilled manual workers compared to only 38 per cent of white men, but high concentrations of ethnic minority workers in 'shrinking' industries contributes to an overall higher unemployment rate.[19]

Although the MSC's Special Programmes Division, together with the CRE, prepared a special report on race discrimination and argued the case for positive action under the Race Relations Act,[20] the MSC ignored its recommendations and proceeded with its policy of referring ethnic minorities to remedial and preparatory courses within a frame of reference limited to training and local labour market needs.[21]

There is no policy to encourage ethnic minority entry into skilled, technical, professional and managerial sectors of the labour market. In MSC research and general publications, the 'special needs formula' has been used to connect ethnic minorities with needs for 'work preparation' programmes but not with skill training, new technology or professional jobs. In MSC documents ethnic minorities, along with women and the disabled, are marginalized towards the end of the texts. In 1982 it was a section charged with policy on 'work preparation, race relations and industrial language training' (later called SG2), while in the 1984–8 MSC plan it was a section at the end of the chapter on 'Training and Preparation for Work' which talked still of 'equal access' but only of 'offering special provision designed to meet particular needs where it is appropriate to do so . . . and appropriate special provision to all young people regardless of race, sex and disability.'

The MSC decides what is 'appropriate' for groups, and it should be noted that positive action is indeed envisaged for one lucky group: adult women aspiring to management and the professions. For this small number, the MSC will ensure that they get 'new training courses [and] . . . specific help . . . to encourage [them] into occupations of economic importance, such as management and technical occupations.' Ethnic minorities, however, – even a token elite among them – are omitted from consideration in this field, without any apparent awareness that this amounts to systematic denigration of black people's abilities and ambitions.

Within the MSC's programmes, particularly YTS, the patronizing 'special needs' approach continues to function as convenient social control, deflecting attention from the social causes of job disadvantage. It appears to be about 'doing something' for ethnic minorities and other politically sensitive groups, but in reality it is about keeping them in their place, the very reverse of positive action.

Hidden hierarchy inside MSC schemes

To understand fully the discrimination in training experienced by black people, it is important to understand the divisive nature of the schemes themselves.

In YTS, for example, the division appears to be quite simple: Mode A schemes for large employers, and Mode B schemes run largely by voluntary bodies and local authorities. This is totally misleading. A large number of local authorities operate under the more cheaply funded Mode A (£2,000 a place as opposed to Mode B at £3,000). Even more significant are the large number of divisions within Mode A itself, not least the fundamental one between mere 'work preparation' schemes and schemes which provide genuine skill training. After this comes the division between employer-based schemes, where young people are trained on the premises, and those schemes where the managing agent is a college or a private training agency (PTA). The latter were never part of the original design but now account for between a quarter and a half of all Mode A schemes, depending on the region.[22] To make it even more complicated, a third administrative category was added half way through, the Large Companies Unit (LCU), which often provides the most prestigious training of all, and is, significantly, not required to submit to monitoring by local Boards.

In short, YTS is a two-tier system with at least four further sectors cutting across the official division. Since most YTS schemes are Mode A, the mode favoured by the MSC, its divisions and their relationship to equal opportunities, are particularly significant.

The assignment of the majority to 'work preparation' is particularly striking. This is wrapped up in all the jargon of 'broad-based', 'transferable' and 'core' skills, for what started as a temporary stopgap under YOP has now been elaborated into a 'new training philosophy' (see Chapters 3 and 5). This aims to produce a generation of cheap, flexible and disposable workers trained not to expect a 'job for life'. But there is also provision for a small elite of skilled workers in Mode A, and more particularly, a small stratum of technical and managerial workers – although the continuing drain of highly skilled workers out of Britain suggests that even for this the government is not prepared to allocate the support necessary.

This two-tier system was planned from the start. In the New

Training Initiative of 1981 there were two quite different objectives. Objective 1 talks of developing 'skill training, including apprenticeship'; Objective 2 only of giving all people under 18 not in full-time education a period of 'planned work experience combined with work-related training and education.' The dualism is traditional British elitism transferred to training, and was clearly expressed later by David Young, the MSC's Director at the time, talking of YTS trainees:

> At the top end . . . they will go through information technology centres . . . [or] centres sponsored by [the engineering and construction industries] Board [s] where they will be able to enjoy some basic modules of knowledge and experience . . .
>
> At the lower end . . . I hope by making some advance in numeracy and problem solving and the discipline of work, they will come out of the programme very much more employable.[23]

Also planned from the start of YTS was the restriction of vocational training (as opposed to vocational 'preparation') to around 10 per cent only of all YTS places,[24] although the latest surveys show it to be about 12 per cent.[25] This may be small in terms of YTS provision, but it covers about half of all long-term apprentice training in England and Wales, and as such is a sought-after route for school leavers. Since this route also leads to a higher chance of getting permanent jobs,[26] more education off the job and topped-up allowances – YTS apprentices got £41 a week in 1984 compared to the standard YTS wage of £26.50[27] – employers can and do 'cream off' candidates highly selectively.

Despite assertions that the two year-scheme will give all trainees the chance 'to seek recognized vocational qualifications', there is no indication of any plans to increase skill training or expenditure upon them, other than by exhorting employers to shoulder more of the cost.[28] Owing to the objectionable nature of this whole elitist and inegalitarian training system, the chances of entering prime schemes of YTS are very narrow, but narrower still for those suffering racial discrimination.

The distinction within Mode A between training and work preparation is not the end of the story. There is also a division between schemes run by employers themselves and those run by training organizations, be they local authority colleges or private training agencies. Obviously the employer-run schemes include all apprentice training, but they also include some 'broad-based' occupational experience which has become a privileged sector in itself, often in national firms with 'high street outlets'.

Although the MSC now refuses to recognize the distinction, in the early planning stage of YTS there was discussion of an elite mode A1, all other schemes being A2. The latter includes those where training organizations have had to subcontract trainees to sources of outside work experience, reviving in many cases the same small sweatshop schemes condemned under YOP. Indeed, the MSC Survey of YTS Providers shows that the average size of a work experience establishment is 25 workers or below which suggests that many are much smaller. Many PTAs have as many work placements as they have trainees, and with hundreds of placements to visit, agencies with only two field officers – a common situation – can hardly be doing any effective checking. The unsavoury aspects of privatized training have been well catalogued, and the shady side revealed by publications as disparate as *Youthaid Bulletin* and *Private Eye*.

Employer-led racism

Private training agencies, and some colleges, need large numbers of trainees and offer places to most applicants, including blacks. But they also need large numbers of work experience placements, and it is in the managing agents' interest to keep on the right side of employers they use for placing trainees. Collusion with racist employers is one of the worst examples of corruption which has arisen inside YTS, and it has opened a minefield of racial discrimination.

Matters are made worse because most subcontracted work-experience placements are in the service sector, with 40 per cent in the part that covers work in shops, garages, hotels, warehouses and restaurants, and another 22 per cent in services which include hairdressing and the social services.[29] These are precisely the sectors where racial discrimination is rife.

The employer-led Mode A schemes, alongside their upper echelon of apprentice-type schemes, are highly selective. But while their quality undoubtedly varies, they control their own work experience on their own premises, and their general training record is far superior to the schemes which trade in training. They also on average spend £550 a year of their own money on each trainee and are thus likely to be more committed to taking them on afterwards. Most such employers also run large organizations, which are more likely to be unionized and thus with more direct accountability expected from trainers, supervisors and the MSC.

Since we know that in YTS overall more than half the trainees don't get jobs when they leave, and only 19 per cent of YTS trainees get them with employers where they trained,[30] gaining access to an A1 scheme is like getting a year-long job interview. Not that all employers have a good record. Some, including some large companies, want an annual supply of cheap workers in preference to workers to train. In some sectors of work this has led to a situation where the ratio of part-time workers to full-time workers prevailing before YTS, has reversed itself. The shopworkers' union, USDAW, for example, found that 60 per cent of workers are now part-time compared to 40 per cent before YTS, and when one of its officials challenged a Woolworth's manager about cheap labour, the retort was, 'It's not cheap YTS labour – we are not paying for them.'

Neither the government nor the MSC have wanted to publicize the wide differences within the Mode A section of YTS, and they are also reluctant to give figures. Figures that claim only 28 per cent of all Mode A trainees under private agencies are suspected of being gross underestimates.[31] But they are well aware that young people are voting with their feet and not joining poor quality schemes, and that the latest figures reveal a shortfall of 10 per cent in Mode A entrants over original plans, and 'a large number of unfilled Mode A places'.[32] However, nothing is mentioned about making Mode A more acceptable by raising the quality of its many bad schemes to the level of its few good ones. The complex and differential hierarchy within YTS is obviously a perfectly acceptable situation for a government bent on oiling the wheels of cut-throat competition.

Racial discrimination: the evidence

Not surprisingly, in view of the divided nature of MSC programmes and the MSC's failure to accept any obligation to deal with inequality, evidence about both direct and indirect discrimination piles up.

In the field of ethnic minorites, major studies by both the CRE and the MSC itself – as well as others – show that employers discriminate in schemes they run, Careers Service workers collude with such practices, and agents charged with monitoring discrimination fail to do so. From information supplied to the CRE from employers and agents, it was found that ethnic minorities were not well represented on employer-based schemes,[33] being worst represented in private sector companies and best (but still inadequately) on local authority schemes. One of the most disturbing features was the low number of black youngsters accepted on LCU schemes, the big organizations with outlets on the 'high streets'.

Indirect discrimination was found in practices like the reluctance of the Careers Service to refer black trainees to schemes that required travelling, even to inform them about them. And while there is evidence that black young people are being concentrated into Mode B schemes in their areas of residence, there is also evidence that even when there are Mode A schemes in these areas, they are often filled with whites from outside the area and, as a study of YTS in London's Southwark area showed, whites from outside the area who were also predominantly middle class.[34]

Other findings were that very few managing agents had monitored the destination of YTS leavers, and of those who had, none found any black trainees who had obtained jobs. Few agents had taken any steps to issue guidelines for recruitment or for selection to promote equal opportunities, and there was almost no training for staff in race equality. Over all, it is clear that the twin processes of employers' selective recruitment and Careers Service channeling, combine to depress ethnic minorities' opportunities.

The MSC's own research confirms the problems, showing that from the start of YTS white youth were more often on Mode A schemes than black, and that on Mode B schemes it was the reverse; 41 per cent of non-whites were on Mode B compared to only 29 per cent of whites.[35] A majority of black males attended Mode B, compared with less than one in five white girls.[35]

Further MSC-commissioned research from Bristol University's School for Advanced Urban Studies (SAUS) concentrated particularly on the 'special needs' approach to black people. It confirms the better deal for white trainees over black in entry to 'better' schemes, notes that MSC statistics omit the important processes of referral to and rejection from schemes, and overestimate the proportions of black trainees in schemes, and concludes, most significantly, that the main practice responsible for unequal allocation is the hierarchical ranking of Modes (and schemes within Modes) by the MSC staff themselves. This is linked with discriminatory attitudes, revealed by one of many typical statements by YTS managing agents: 'Mode B provision is needed for those with special needs . . . the emotionally disturbed and ethnic minorities'. Another crude example is, 'We've saved her from Mode B and she can still be with normal people.'[37]

The ranking of young people goes along with the ranking of schemes. Most YTS agents and employers claimed academic qualifications and motivation were their main 'selection' criteria (a process we might also want to query for other reasons), but SAUS found them riddled with racial prejudice as well, including the observation from one that 'so many Asians are lazy and West Indians are happy-go-lucky, you have to accept it.' These views, and the conviction that work preparation improved their attitude to work and helped them to 'play whitey', were found especially in the private sector.

Labelling was common, but more so in 'creaming off' schemes, where there was use of tests, educational qualifications and motivation criteria for selection. Most 'open access' attitudes claimed to be 'colour blind' – 'I don't care if they are black, brown, green or pink' – but 'open access/sifting out' was common for those not speaking English well or not thought to be motivated.

Certain schemes, like those run by NACRO, FULLemploy and those offering English Language Training (ELT) were geared to identifying those who had discrete and specific needs. But the authors also found indiscriminate use of the 'needs' notion, where some Careers Service workers regarded all ethnic minorites as having 'special needs' and diverted them all to Mode B. They also found that providers were either unaware of, or hostile to, the very idea of equal opportunities wherever it involved blacks.

The SAUS researchers put their main focus on stereotyping but they also looked at prejudice, where they found that some subcontracted firms 'refuse young people on grounds of race and that managing agents are sometimes reluctant to report this situation to the MSC'. Some racism is overt – 'Don't send me any blacks'; some covert – blacks are constantly rejected. Firms contacted denied they were racist but justified their position by saying their customers did not want physical contact with blacks. Because agents needed the employers for the training places they offered, there was reluctance to challenge these attitudes. On the other hand, black young people showed their feelings about relegation to schemes with fewer opportunities by their very high dropout rates, particularly in workshops and community projects.

On the whole, SAUS researchers would only recommend changes within the bounds of attitudes and ideas about YTS, not changes in the scheme itself. Many ethnic minority organizations were angered that it concluded that racial discrimination was 'not widespread'.

But what is really wrong with the report is that it fails to raise the fundamental issues of the ideology and structure of YTS as a scheme tied to the free market, and thus unable to function if the structure necessary to implement equal opportunities were created. Unless the scheme is transformed it cannot work.

While an objective hierarchy remains (largely unacknowledged) and black people are systematically excluded from its upper reaches, no amount of 'reranking' schemes will alter the nature of YTS as a scheme entrenching the labour market disadvantage of black people. The removal of racist stereotyping of trainees would be a step in the right direction, of course, but without being tied to positive action, little more than 'racism awareness' will be achieved. The SAUS team attempts to resolve this dilemma by arguing for mixed ability recruitment and training across the board in YTS, which sounds attractive but would demand the sympathy and extremely rigorous monitoring of the MSC and the Careers Service. It is claimed that the independent SAUS researchers really wanted their most important recommendation to be that the 'MSC should tackle racism within the private sector'[38], but obviously an MSC under the thumb of a Conservative government did not include this in the final report.

If YTS can be criticized for being highly selective, the Community Programme, also introduced in 1982, is even more so. Designed to provide short-term spells of work for the long-term unemployed, it is taking an increasing share of MSC funding, and some of its placements now include a training element.

Independent research, however, shows that there is an extremely low participation rate from ethnic minorities.[39] Placements are 92 per cent while, only 5 per cent Afro-Caribbean and 3 per cent

Asian, while scheme supervisors are 97 per cent white, with no Asians at all. It is ironic that the need to serve those in greatest need was the excuse given for restricting eligibility to the programme to those actually claiming benefit personally (a 1984 ruling that disqualifies many women for whom benefit is claimed by the husband, and which has been challenged by the EOC as indirect discrimination under the Sex Discrimination Act) because it is clear that many in greatest need, are not receiving equal opportunities to join the Community Programme.

Countering racism in MSC schemes

In looking at initiatives that have been taken to deal with racism in practice, the West Midlands offers itself as a good case study. It covers an area with many ethnic minorities and many types of employment, where organizations like the Campaign for Racial Equality on MSC Programmes (CREMP), Racial Equality in Training Schemes (REITS) or Birmingham AMB Equal Opportunities Subcommittee, and the Midlands Commission for Racial Equality have been able to provide a focus for activity on equality, particularly for ethnic minorities. In addition, the research centre in ethnic relations at two local universities, Aston and Warwick, has contributed related research.[40] The Trades Council in Birmingham has been concerned about abuses on MSC schemes from the start, and together with West Midlands County Council, its pressure led to the West Midlands YTS Research Project that turned its attention specifically to racial discrimination, and despite difficulty in getting statistics from the MSC, produced a report that shocked local and national opinion, and convinced the County Council to monitor the problem.[41]

What the project showed in its scheme-by-scheme survey was the systematic exclusion of ethnic minorities from the 'cream' of Mode A, the employer-based schemes and those in large companies in the area. These two were overwhelmingly white – 95 per cent and 92 per cent respectively – in an area where in 1984 ethnic minority young people formed 20 per cent of the fifth-year school leavers in Birmingham and 15 per cent in Coventry. If Sight and Sound, which takes large numbers of black trainees, and is currently classed as a large company, was reclassified, as many believe it should be, as a private training agency instead, the Large Companies

Unit percentage comes up as 95 per cent white.

Out of 39 Mode A private employers in the Birmingham/Solihull area taking trainees under the scheme, 26 took only white trainees, among them Jaguar, Land Rover, Lucas Aerospace and Safeway Foodstores. Large companies with outlets in the area taking only whites included Burtons, Dixons, Finefare, Mothercare, The National Bus Company, Foster Menswear and Marks & Spencer. In Coventry a REITS survey found a similar picture: out of 52 private employers offering YTS places, 39 took only white trainees, among them being Sainsbury, the police, Rolls Royce, Massey Ferguson, Boots and Marks & Spencer.

Figures from the Careers Service[42] showed that in Birmingham white youngsters were three times as likely as Afro-Caribbeans and two and a half times as Asians, to get jobs. Were it not for Asian businesses in Coventry, a REITS report, *YTS or white TS?*, said the picture would have been far worse. Nor can it be anything to do with ethnic minorities being less well qualified, for quite separate research from the University of Warwick shows black and Asian young people entering YTS had better qualifications – in terms of CSE passes – than did their white counterparts,[43] a finding that also seriously challenges some previous explanations of underemployment among ethnic minorities.

The picture was quite different with private training agencies (which take up 40 per cent of all YTS places in the Birmingham area). They must have all their places full to break even or make a profit, and have to offer an open-access policy in order to fill them. With the exception of schemes specializing in personal and retail services – like hairdressing – where there was low ethnic representation, agency schemes had ethnic representation in line with the general distribution in YTS, although among schemes with 20 per cent or more of black trainees were a handful of larger ones offering a mixture of clerical and manual 'occupational training families'. Three of these – for a combination of reasons concerning training quality and financial troubles – were discontinued as YTS managing agents.

Figures for the five college-based YTS schemes in Birmingham were also examined. As with other college-based schemes in the country, ethnic minorities are overrepresented. In Birmingham, while B1 made up 21 per cent of YTS places, it caters for 30 per cent and 28 per cent respectively of Afro-Caribbean and Asian trainees.

The West Midlands YTS Project showed the importance of scheme-by-scheme analysis, for while Mode B black overrepresentation will show up anyway, Mode A will not, unless research can separate out the college schemes and the private training agencies from the employer-based schemes. Otherwise, ethnic minority representation in Mode A looks better than it is, and the extreme disparity between scheme types is not revealed. In particular, only this kind of analysis reveals that ethnic minorities are gaining virtually nothing from the skill training that exists on YTS in the better-quality schemes.

Incredibly, scheme-by-scheme figures are not given out by the MSC – even to the MSC's own Area Board, although the Chairperson of the MSC has admitted that 'the production of such statistics would prove useful in our monitoring of each providers commitment to equal opportunities.'[44] However, he also mentions problems of 'confidentiality and misinterpretation and reliability', the old excuses for failing to provide what is readily available. Even YTS providers themselves express surprise that such statistics are not publicly accessible when the MSC appears to have no trouble giving out the much more difficult and unreliable statistic: how many YTS leavers find jobs.

Experience of racial discrimination

Fighting to get statistical proof of discrimination is vital, but the grass roots experiences count as well, if only to characterize the nature of the racism which black and Asian trainees face in MSC schemes.

At present few reports come directly from trainees themselves – although a lot of the cartoons are theirs and express clearly what they feel, and certain filmed records are available which show how articulate young people on schemes are.[45] But generally the young are isolated, as are the long-term unemployed, and unorganized. Few know their rights or have the confidence to complain. The carrot of a possible job at the end of schemes tells them to keep their heads down. In addition, racial discrimination operates in insidious ways, and in the referral and recruitment process trainees do not know whether or how they are being stereotyped and discriminated against. It isn't always verbal abuse, it can be as intangible as waiting around for weeks for a placement without being told why.

In the Birmingham area it was not until the CRE initiated an investigation into Birmingham City Council's own college-based Youth Training Units, that even a start was made to report incidents of discrimination which up to now have remained 'in house' between the MSC and the Careers Service. There are no national guidelines for reporting discrimination in the workings of MSC schemes, particularly discrimination involving informal remarks or requests, and in many areas it appears that considerations of racism or sexism are expensive luxuries that those working at the scheme-face readily disregard. Thus a white Careers Officer had no qualms in saying to the predominantly black audience at the inaugural meeting of CREMP, 'We do not submit the names of blacks to sponsors of Mode A schemes.'

Careers Officers and MSC workers are, however, slowly coming forward with evidence of racism they encounter, which they will often give 'off the record' to researchers in the field, even if not publicly. Thus several private training agency workers, in well-known PTAs, told Careers or YTS placement officers that many black young people on their schemes have had to wait weeks before being found work placements. The degree of racism in the labour market is a shock, they have said, even to them.

Often the racism is purely pragmatic. An administrator from a Chamber of Trade and Commerce YTS told CRE she saw nothing wrong with mentioning ethnic origins to sponsors 'because the scheme did not like sending black young people to employers likely to reject them'. A YTS co-ordinator at a further education college admitted he advised lecturers not to reject discriminatory work placement instructions, because it was a matter of 'horses for courses'. Every college from the Birmingham College Group scheme admitted receiving discriminatory instructions from work sponsors – i.e. no blacks. The CRE commenced proceedings against Brooklyn College in 1984 when a lecturer offered to find a garage work placement for one of the CRE's own trainees on condition he was white, but the lecturer won his case on the grounds that he had not intended to discriminate. It is 'they' who do.

What 'they' in the labour market say is now being collected by the CRE, the West Midlands YTS Research Project, REITS, CREMP and the universities' researchers in the area. Their pooled collection includes:

- a snack bar manager to a college YTS officer, 'You do realize that we only want white girls behind the counter?'

- a small building firm to a college scheme, 'It's not possible to arrange an interview because we don't want a black trainee. The customers do not like blacks in their houses.'

- a hairdresser to a Mode B scheme, 'There's no way I'm having coloureds here. It's not that I regard myself as particularly prejudiced . . . Quite honestly, I think I would lose an awful lot of custom.'

What is clear is that employers in turn blame the wider public and rarely admit discrimination even when they practice it. Solihull Careers Service tells of two Afro-Caribbean young men sent for an advertised YTS vacancy in a well-known men's clothing store only to be turned away, one with the excuse that there were no application forms, the other that there was no vacancy. The Careers Office then discovered that another officer had sent a white boy to the same shop, and he was instantly recruited. Careers Officers reported the incident to the CRE, since they felt they had been pressurized into colluding, but the two young men were not told of their right to complain.

The victim of discrimination can use the complaints procedure under Section 13 of the Race Relations Act of 1976. Successful tribunals have been held against Snips Hairdressers in Wolverhampton and Aigburgh Glass Centre in Liverpool, but otherwise very little use has been made of this provision. One reason is lack of knowledge, but another may be that the Act restricts complaints to discrimination only on entering or leaving schemes. It does not cover matters like harassment and racist remarks during training, although it may soon be possible to widen the definition to do this.

The West Midlands pool of evidence includes many examples of on-the-job harassment, including provocative remarks about immigration being too high and 'These people shouldn't be here' from a Wimpey supervisor to a black trainee who was trying to transfer from bricklaying to carpentry. The youth reported the incidents to the managing agent and the supervisor admitted what he had said, but the managing agent merely asked the trainee to put up with it. Another case reported to the CRE involved black trainees on a Mode B scheme taunted with 'nignogs' and 'too slow' and 'too thick', a matter which parents took up in this case, but they were unaware that once it had been reported to the scheme manager, and he or she had failed to stop it, the matter could have been taken further under the Race Relations Act. Had there been a trainee council or union, there is a much better chance that the issue would have been caught.

A union did not help initially in the case of an Afro-Caribbean young man – of frail build, incidentally – who was tied up by workers at the metal work factory where he was training, and put in a box with a lid on – to shouts of, 'Get back to the trees!' He kicked himself out some time later, but said nothing, only to find that a few days later he was trussed up by hands and feet and hoisted in midair over a beam. When he was let down he ran away and it was not until his mother reported him missing that the incidents came to light. It also came to light that the YTS placement officer had only ever visited this factory once. Legislation can only go so far. Harassment in the workplace is a trade union issue and unless individual unions act on the spot, and unless the labour movement as a whole takes on the wider issue of racism, it will not go away.

All that said, it is significant that the largest volume of complaints about MSC programmes from ethnic minorities received by the CRE (to whom minorities go in preference to the MSC itself, it seems) do not concern harassment. They concern the lack of quality on MSC schemes.

Will the MSC learn to respond to these criticisms, and to the finding from so much research, particularly about discrimination and lack of quality in its schemes? Detailed recommendations in reports to it – like that from Bristol's School for Advanced Urban Studies (SAUS) – include anti-racist training for MSC staff, a more visible commitment to equal opportunities in recruitment, appointments of black and Asian supervisors and trainers, and the creation of a climate at MSC office level which would allow managing agents who discover racism to feel confident in reporting it.

A paper on racial discrimination from the MSC's Youth Training Directorate in 1985[46] listed five areas for further work and improvement: monitoring arrangements, recruitment, guidance to providers and marketing, meeting 'special needs' and dealing with discrimination. It is important that black organizations and trade unions exert pressure to sharpen them into useful practice, particularly as the paper reiterates the need for guidance to AMBs 'on how to approach the question of ethnic minority participation in schemes in the context of scheme approval or renewal'.

But hopes should not be set too high, for the MSC still refuses to make any clear statement about public money being used to demonstrate a commitment to equal opportunities; it rejects the CRE recommendation to involve trainees in the process of monitoring; it hedges over discriminatory stereotyping by the Careers Service, and in the 'special needs' section unsuccessfully tries to extricate itself from its own stereotyping by stating that for most ethnic minority people, their only 'disadvantage is the colour of their skin'. The MSC does not seem able to recognize disadvantage that is social and not internal to the individual. Lastly, and quite incredibly, in view of the abundant evidence showing how easy it is to produce figures for ethnic representation in any part of any MSC scheme, it rules out positive action because it would be too hard to demonstrate that a particular racial group is 'underrepresented in a particular area of work'!

Probably the strongest statement from the MSC is the one that refers to AMB powers of approval and renewal of schemes – 'ultimately a readiness to withdraw from the use of providers who are unwilling to take steps to remove discrimination where it clearly exists, and to make it clear that this is MSC policy'.

This sentence should be pinned up at every area Board.

Conclusion

For all its talk of equal opportunities, the MSC has not implemented any policies which will break the mould of racial inequality or seriously challenge racial discrimination. All evidence suggest that YTS is not only entrenching but may be widening racial inequality, and information on the Community Programme suggests the same may be happening here.

Action by black and Asian organizations and the labour movement is urgently needed. Despite the fact that the TUC has produced a policy statement on equal opportunities,[47] it remains locked in MSC assumptions about equal opportunity policy itself, and its recommendations are neither specific nor rigorous enough.

There is much more hope in the clear demands which local pressure groups have not put forward – like REITS in Coventry. They involve excluding all workplaces which practice discrimination from all MSC schemes and money, the creation of an effective equal opportunities policy for every scheme as a condition of its contract, assessment of performance on equality at each monitoring visit, the appointment of equality officers by the MSC to assist schemes to implement equality policies, open and public access to all statistics the MSC possesses, a review by the MSC of its own equal opportunities policy as an employer, and elected representatives from every major black and Asian community on Area Boards.

With agreement on minimum programmes of this kind, which can be pressed locally as well as nationally, we will be in a stronger position to open up on the wider and deeper aspects of racism and discrimination in society at large.

1. *Guardian*, 26 March 1985.
2. MSC, 'Training Division's Special Groups', unpublished paper to Youth Training Board, April 1983.
3. MSC press statement, January 1983, available as an abstract in CRE, 'Equal Opportunities and the Youth Training Scheme', 1983.
4. MSC, The Youth Training Board, *Review of YTS*, 1984.
5. Its contents were once printed in the MSC's *Youth Training News*.
6. Based on author's interview with Co-ordinator of Birmingham Accredited Centre, together with other reports received by the author.
7. This was the percentage given in the House of Commons, Written Answers, 20 March, 1985. In addition, there were 22 co-opted members from ethnic minorities, three with a vote and the rest without.
8. CREMP was founded in Birmingham in 1984 (can be contacted c/o Stanier House, 4th Floor, 10 Holliday St, Birmingham B1 1TQ). REITS was founded in 1984 (can be contacted c/o Coventry Workshop, 38 Binley Road, Coventry CV3 UA).
9. MSC, Youth Training Board, *Ethnic Minorities and the Youth Training Schemes*, February 1985.
10. *Ibid.*
11. MSC and CRE, *Special Programmes, Special Needs: Ethnic Minorities and the Special Programmes for the Unemployed*, 1979; and *Give us a Break: Widening Opportunities for young Women within YOP/YTS*, MSC Research and Development Series No. 11, 1983.
12. R. Stares *et al.*, 'Ethnic Minorities, Their Involvement in MSC

Special Programmes', MSC, Research and Development Series No. 6, 1982; and B. Sheppard, 'Training and Ethnic Minorities: Case Studies in Three Areas', MSC, Manpower Intelligence and Planning, 1983.

13. G. Courtenay, 'Analysis of Data from the Survey of 1980–81 YOP Entrants', unpublished Paper, London, SCPR, 1983.

14. M. Cross et al., 'Ethnic Minorities – Their Experience on YOP', MSC, Special Programmes Occasional Paper No. 5, 1985.

15. T. Bedeman and G. Courtenay, 'One in Three – the Second National Survey of Young People on YOP', MSC, Research and Development Series No. 13, 1983.

16. HMSO, Fields et al., Ethnic Minorities in Britain: a Study of Trends in their Position Since 1961, Home Office Research Unit Report No. 68, 1981.

17. G. Lee and J. Wrench, Skill Seekers: Black Youth Apprenticeships and Disadvantage, National Youth Bureau, Studies in Research, 1983.

18. K. Roberts, et al., 'Racial Disadvantage in Youth Labour Markets', in L. Barton and S. Walker (eds), Race, Class and Education, Croom Helm, London, 1983.

19. Office of Population Census and Surveys, 1983; Labour Force Survey, 'County of Births and Ethnic Origin', OPCS Monitor, 1981.

20. MSC and CRE, Special Programmes, Special Needs: Ethnic Minorities and the Special Programmes for the Unemployed, 1979.

21. B. Sheppard, 'Training and Ethnic Minorities: Case Studies in Three Areas, MSC Manpower Intelligence and Planning, 1983.

22. Research by the West Midlands YTS Research Project shows 60 per cent of all Mode A schemes in Birmingham/Solihull to be private training agencies. Figures in a Parliamentary written answer from the Secretary of State for Employment (31 January 1985) for the end of December 1984 (and almost certainly gross underestimates) are in rounded percentage figures: Birmingham 35, Greater Manchester 21, Coventry and Warwickshire 38, London North 29, London Northeast 28, London Southeast 50, London Southwest 2).

23. David Young, Evidence to the Select Committee on Employment, House of Commons, 20 April 1983.

24. MSC, Task Group Report on YTS, 1982.

25. Youth Training Board, Survey of YTS Providers, March 1985.

26. Ibid.

27. Ibid. Just under one-third get £50 a week or more.

28 HMSO, 'Education and Training for Young People', Cmnd 9482, April 1984, MSC, Corporate Plan, 1984–1988.

29. Figures from MSC, Youth Training Board, Survey of YTS Providers, March 1985.

30. Report, Youth Training Board, June 1985.

31. Parliamentary answer, 31 January 1985; and West Midlands YTS

Project figures, given in note 22 above.

32. Secretary of State for Employment, Letter to MSC Chairperson, 8 March 1985.

33. CRE, *Racial Equality and the Youth Training Scheme*, October 1984.

34. CRE, briefing paper, 'Equal Opportunities and YTS', October 1984; YTS Study, Southwark, reported *Times Higher Education Supplement*, 17 August 1984.

35. MSC, Youth Training Board, Sample Survey of YTS Start Certificates, November 1983; and MSC, unpublished statistics, 1984, giving cumulative totals, in 'YTS Starters by Mode and Race', 1984.

36. Fenton *et al.*, *Ethnic Minorities and the Youth Training Scheme*, MSC, Research and Development Series No. 20, September 1984.

37. *Ibid.*

38. Reported in the *Reporter*, National Council for Voluntary Organizations, February 1985.

39. MSC, Social and Community Planning Research Report, Survey of Community Programme Participants, 1983. It covered 172 schemes.

40. Relevant research (in addition to that already mentioned) includes J. R. Austen, 'Black Girls in the Youth Training Scheme', M.Sc. thesis, unpublished, Research Unit for Ethnic Relations (RUER), University of Aston, 1984; M. Cross and J. Edmonds, *Training Opportunities for Ethnic Minorities in the UK*, ESRC, RUER, 1982; M. Cross, *The Training Situation of Ethnic Minority Young People in Britain*, CEDEFOP, Berlin, 1985, G. Lee and J. Wrench, *In Search of a Skill, Ethnic Minority Youth and Apprenticeships, A Summary with Recommendations*, CRE, 1981; R. Jenkins, 'Managers, Recruitment Procedures and Black Workers', Working Papers on Ethnic Relations, No. 18, RUER, 1982; J. Wrench, 'Ethnic Minorities and the Youth Training Scheme: Impressions of Unequal Opportunity', unpublished paper, RUER, 1983.

41. A. Pollert, *Racial Discrimination and the Youth Training Scheme*, West Midlands YTS Research Project, for West Midlands County Council Economic Development Committee, Birmingham, 1984.

42. These figures come from the monthly figures (to which the author had access). Only these give the breakdown comparing white school leavers with Asian and Afro-Caribbean ones. Official reports only provide breakdowns comparing all school leavers and ethnic minority leavers' destinations (as in *Facing Decline and Change: A Study of the Destinations of Birmingham School and College Leavers in 1984*, Birmingham Careers Service, March 1984).

43. M. Cross, 'Who Goes Where: YTS Allocations by Race', in M. Cross and D. Smith, *YTS and Racial Minorities: Equality or Inequality?*, National Youth Bureau, 1985.

44. Letter from Geoffrey Holland to Clare Short, MP, 28 May 1985.

45. The 'Rights – Wot Rights?' Video from TURC in Birmingham; the

BBC series on YTS.
46. MSC, Youth Training Directorate, *Ethnic Minorities and the Youth Training Scheme*, February 1985.
47. 'Equal Opportunities in the Youth Training Scheme: Note for the MSC Youth Training Board', no date, no author, but printed in Appendix 5, *Ethnic Minorities and the Youth Training Scheme*, MSC, 1985.

10. Trade Union Responses to the MSC

John Eversley

When the Conservative government was elected in 1979, trade union reaction was to defend the role of the Manpower Services Commission. The expectation that the MSC programmes might be under threat was not without foundation: the government had made much of its criticism of high-spending quangos; the MSC itself and its special programmes could be seen as a response to trade union pressure, and it was certainly unpopular on the Tory back benches; within a few months of taking office, the government cut back on, for instance, the Community Enterprise Programme. Trade unions were rapidly put on the defensive.

Since 1979, however, evidence has steadily accumulated to indicate that in fact the MSC is being used as an instrument central to the economic policy of a new kind of conservatisim – the 'New Right' or 'Thatcherite' version. Its central assertion is that 'inefficiencies' in the labour market cause persistent mass unemployment. The 1985 white paper on Employment[1] describes the labour market as 'the weak link in the economy'. Transforming this market becomes a key project of the government, consisting of a determined drive against the 'inefficiencies' which prevent wages falling fast enough to help people 'price themselves into jobs'. In March 1985, Peter Morrison (the government minister responsible for labour market policy) explained his view of the causes of youth unemployment by likening this to consumer reluctance to purchase doughnuts which are too highly priced. The white paper points to the key areas of labour costs, worker flexibility and labour quality. All of these require radical treatment in pursuit of the New Right's dream of a 'free' labour market unfettered by trade unions, wages councils, protective legislation or greedy school leavers.

The statements and the action in pursuit of the free market goal have become more explicit and crude in the years since 1979 but the ideology has been there from the early days of Norman Tebbit's 'on yer bike' comments and the 1980 Think Tank report on 'Education, Training and Industrial Performance'.[2]

The Manpower Services Commission has been a highly effective weapon in the Thatcher government's labour market policy. It has been possible to use the MSC in this way because of the TUC's strong loyalty to the MSC; because of what individual unions have thought they could get out of the MSC; and because trade unionists have seen the MSC programmes as 'doing something' for the young unemployed.

The TUC commitment to the MSC was strong. Not only was it centrally involved in MSC tripartism, it has also played a major part in framing the 1973 Act which set up the MSC. Even if the MSC appeared to be falling under the corrupting influence of monetarism, the TUC would be most unlikely to abandon its progeny. As long as the TUC remained loyal to the institution, so too would the majority of affiliated unions, for most of them did not regard training as important, and were happy to follow wherever the TUC led.

These early realizations by government strategists undoubtedly saved the MSC, for in 1979 Tory backbenchers were baying for its blood. When its future was secured, MSC's senior officials set about the task of skilfully winning labour movement support for MSC proposals. The MSC offered something to everyone. Education unions were offered cash, jobs and schemes described as comprehensive. The large general unions were presented with programmes which seemed to be capable of democratizing training and opening up the privileges of skilled status to their members. The smaller craft unions were offered youth programmes which seemed to defend apprenticeship. Trade unionists in their capacity as parents, sisters and brothers were told of schemes based on compassion for the unemployed.

Experience has shown all these claims to be untrue, but they remained credible long enough to build a huge bandwagon of support for the New Training Initiative (NTI) and the Youth Training Scheme. The emergence of flaws in the programmes did not itself change things. As the unions had climbed aboard for different reasons, it was difficult to reach agreement that the bandwagon was out of control, let alone on what to do about it.

This chapter looks at the origins and the nature of the trade union response to the MSC and at what some of the elements in an alternative strategy could be.

The fragmented response of unions

Despite the objective of destroying trade union power and influence, Thatcher's government needed union co-operation to pursue interventions in the labour market. No government can implement mass work experience programmes like YTS and CP without a degree of trade union co-operation. Even in areas where most YTS projects are not in with the union-organized sectors of the economy, the union's blessing is important to the legitimacy of the intervention. Early on Thatcher's government lacked the self-confidence and the level of preparation needed directly to confront organized labour. In 1981 it backed off from confrontation with the miners. It sought limited co-operation as a short-term tactic until the overthrow of consensual tripartism could be effected. Early on in the NTI, this limited co-operation was vital to the rapid provision of a large-scale YTS. The risks of this co-operation to the government were slight, as the nature of the MSC's work experience programmes could be relied upon to fragment the trade union response.

MSC officials did not divide the labour movement any more than did rightwing leadership or the lack of strategy. The officials did their bit by playing up policy variations between unions and by exploiting these differences. Individual unions have widely varying relationships to the labour market, to their unemployed members, and to the organizing and recruiting of school leavers. Some, notably craft, unions seemed to have a lot to lose from mass training programmes. They were (mostly) talked out of their hostility and won to support the YTS by MSC officials, and to a certain extent by the TUC. Others, notably education unions which appeared to have a lot to gain by jumping in with both feet, did so. The movement was divided from the start, primarily because each was rightly trying to defend its members' interests and these varied widely.

Just as unions have different policy approaches to wages, conditions and work itself, so they were bound to develop different responses to unemployed programmes based on work experience in office and factory.

The features of MSC programmes, and YTS in particular, were always likely to cause major headaches for the trade union movement. At a time when the TUC and many individual unions were beginning to campaign for an Alternative Economic Strategy based on controlled expansion of the economy, MSC schemes raised an ideological controversy. Schemes like YOP, YTS and CP imply that unemployment is very much an individual's problem arising from lack of skill, lack of work experience, etc., rather than a social problem of a depressed economy. In these terms, the solution is an individualized 'training' opportunity, and not a new type of economic strategy.

The YTS takes place primarily in the workplace where trainees gain 'work' experience, often through performing real work, for which wages were previously paid. There was always likely to be widespread substitution of trainees for waged workers, especially as the TUC did not press for adequate monitoring of the scheme. The MSC's own survey suggests that in 1984, 25 per cent of YTS trainees were occupying jobs previously held by young people, 7 per cent had been recruited in preference to adult workers, and about 18 per cent had been taken on as 'apprentices'. This suggests a very high displacement effect. Research on the YTS in Dundee and Renfrew suggests that the rate may be even higher. In over 90 per cent of cases where employers thought it a feasible option, YTS trainees were taken on to fill vacant posts.[3]

Trainees are not supposed to receive work-related training. YTS is supposed to be broad-based and non-vocational; an approach justified by the MSC ideology of occupational training families (OTFs) which group together very diverse activities which are claimed to have common features. The nebulous nature of YTS raises doubts in every multi-union workplace over which union should be consulted and asked to give approval. MSC officials have fully exploited this confusion, carving out the line of least resistance.

In the workplace the task of selling trade unionism to trainees is Herculean. The YTS traineeship is for only 12 months, and trainees competing with each other to be 'kept on' have strong incentives to keep their noses clean and avoid showing signs of militancy. Training contracts are with the MSC, the allowance is fixed in faraway London, and much protective labour legislation does not apply to YTS. It is hardly surprising that despite the efforts of many stewards and officials, the mass of youth trainees are not being organized by unions. Trade unions which were losing members through factory closures and public spending cuts found MSC programmes cutting away at the possibilities of recruiting young people.

In this confusing and novel situation trade unions and active members looked to the TUC for guidance. Lacking its own independent policies and concerned to protect the MSC from possible Tory attacks, the TUC was pushed into a position of delivering the fruits of MSC tripartism. Within the MSC the TUC failed to achieve important concessions and safeguards on vital issues like job substitution, health and safety, anti-racism and anti-sexism. Although Thatcher's early need for co-operation left the TUC some power, this does not seem to have been realized or utilized. No efforts at all went into formulating alternative labour movement policies. After six years of Thatcherism no new policies and precious few substantive criticisms of MSC have emerged from Congress House. In this situation, individual unions have tried to find their own way through the confusing maze of MSC schemes and guidelines, or have simply followed the TUC's recommendations.

A look at the policies of major trade unions on the YTS illustrates the range of trade union attitudes. Most major unions (i.e. those with a membership of over 100,000 members) have a written policy on the YTS. Often in practice the unions' attitudes are less straightforward than conference decisions would suggest. It is necessary first to look at the diversity of individual union responses in the face of a coherent attack by the government in order to understand the central role played by the TUC: a role not merely of co-ordination or interpretation of trade union responses but a determined force in itself.

The response of the public sector unions

All the public sector unions have one fundamental problem in common: the government is ultimately responsible for their numbers, pay and conditions. That means that the government can and does attempt to control their recruitment and training policies. The public service unions have resisted the government's attempts to channel entry to the sector through YTS but it is certain that this is what they will go on trying to do. A second problem that many public sector unions share is that their members are involved in running MSC programmes as civil servants or local government employees (teachers, careers staff, etc.). This means that the programmes are a source of jobs and because of the nature of the present government, a threat to jobs.

Opposition in the civil service has been particularly strong. Within the civil service, the Society of Civil and Public Servants (SCPS) has been openly critical of the role played by the MSC in Thatcher's strategy. In 1982 the SCPS gave an important signal to other unions by publishing its own alternative plan for the MSC.[4] The union opposed the introduction of YTS in the civil service. The Civil and Public Services' Association (CPSA) also opposed the introduction of YTS in the civil service. The CPSA has a large membership among clerical grades, many of whom enter as school leavers. The clear risk of job substitution in the context of public spending cuts brought the union into opposition to YTS in its area of organization. The smaller Inland Revenue Staffs Federation, with a more professional, older and better-qualified membership, did not perceive the same threats to its position, and gave support to the YTS.

However, this aspect should not be overemphasized. Particularly in the case of the differences in the policies of the CPSA and Civil Service Union (CSU), industrial factors have to be taken into account. The CPSA has a large membership among clerical officers in the civil service. Their jobs have been under threat for some time from cuts in government expenditure, the introduction of new technology, etc. The Civil Service Union on the other hand has a big membership among trainees in the MSC whose future to some extent has seemed to lie with extending training programmes. Some members of both unions work directly on YTS but that is less significant than the more general observations about their membership.

For the Civil Service Union it is important to note that the government's Adult Training Strategy is seen critically. In 1984–85 the union campaigned against the planned closure of a third of the Skillcentres and the encouragement of private training agencies in that field. It has not however generated the same degree of cross-union support as for example the 'Save our Skills' campaign mounted by a number of unions in opposition to the closure of the Industrial Training Boards.

Branches of APEX and ASTMS, the unions which represent ITB

staff, jointly campaigned against the closure of most ITBs under the Tory legislation of 1981. Under the slogan 'Save our Skills' they lobbied the TUC and parliament, with some success. During the parliamentary closure debates, labour speakers promised that a labour government would restore statutory training arrangements.

In local government the response of the National and Local Government Officers' Association (NALGO) was crucial. YOP had been heavily dependent on local authority schemes. In 1981, for example, Strathclyde Regional Council directly sponsored nearly 10,000 YOP places. YTS was intended to be more based on private-sector employers, but nevertheless local authorities would be very important, particularly in those areas where the private sector had collapsed during the recession, and for those young people not wanted by private employers.

NALGO organizes local authority Careers officers who played an important role in YOP and place most of the trainees entering Mode B of the YTS. Early in the development of the YTS it became clear that the MSC scheme would be used to completely change the role of the service. Peter Morrison talked of the service being 'on trial', making it clear that employers would have to be provided with the service they wanted. YTS arrived with a very clear threat to a section of NALGO's members.

NALGO has developed one of the more critical national policies on YTS, though this has gone through a number of important changes. The 1983 conference demand for the 'rate for the job' for trainees proved unhelpful as a negotiating stance at local level, in large part because of confusion over which area of work was most closely related to any particular 'broad-based' YTS place. This policy also failed properly to take account of the fact that the union organized many supervisors on Mode B schemes. A strict enforcement of the policy could have placed the jobs of these NALGO members in jeopardy. The 1984 conference debated YTS in the light of the scheme's first full year, and called on the TUC 'to seek immediate improvements and if unsuccessful to consult affiliated unions with a view to withdrawing support from YTS . . .' NALGO put this policy forward at the 1984 TUC in Brighton. NALGO is one of a number of unions where any return by government to the 1981 proposals to conscript young people into YTS would be likely to provoke a conference response of outright opposition.

At local level, NALGO's experience has varied widely. In local authorities which support radical criticisms of the YTS, many of the union's objectives have been easily met. Good quality training, equal opportunity policies and the 'rate for the job' have proved possible where the authority has been willing to devote additional resources. In some authorities, there have been examples of other unions being asked to give approval to schemes so that the employing authority and MSC officials could avoid potential opposition from NALGO.

The response of the further education lecturers' union, NATFHE, was also crucial to the development of MSC programmes under Thatcher. NATFHE had a long tradition of developing policy on vocational training. Indeed, one of NATFHE's problems has been the theft by the MSC of some of the union's language to legitimize unacceptable goals and activities (the MSC is adept at appropriating and redefining the labour movement's own slogans and policies). Documents on the New Training Initiative (NTI) and YTS appeared to promise much on many of NATFHE's most cherished objectives, e.g. education for all school leavers, an extension of comprehensive principles, the opening up of training to adults, the break-up of restrictive and exclusive apprenticeships training, and equal opportunities. Undoubtedly unions lacking NATFHE's tradition looked to them for a lead when they were trying to sort out their own response to the MSC. In addition to this central role in the movement's policy, NATFHE's membership also had a key role in the delivery of the off-the-job parts of MSC schemes.

When NTI and YTS appeared as proposals, NATFHE was under pressure from the impact of education cuts and a government-inspired drive to worsen conditions of service throughout education. While it was odious to NATFHE in many respects, Norman Tebbit's white paper of 1981 pointed to 'perhaps 80,000' full-time equivalent places in FE colleges as a consequence of YTS. The MSC seemed to offer jobs and resources to a sector which was being slowly starved of both. In reality, of course, the college-based YTS activity was not developed on the promised scale.

The MSC now controls the purse strings for over a quarter of non-advanced further education (NAFE). At a time when other resources for education and training are being cut back, the MSC offers work. On the other hand, the conditions of service are significantly worse for teachers than previously – larger classes, shorter holidays, temporary and part-time posts, more outside control of the curriculum, inadequate backup and so on. The MSC has been open in its favour of privatization of education. They have had considerable success in their attempt to do so. In written parliamentary answers, Peter Morrison has stated that in southeast London on Mode A over half the training places are provided by private training agencies. For Cheshire the figures is nearly two-thirds (64.5 per cent). Far from securing jobs for NATFHE members, MSC programmes have brought conditions characteristic of unstable parts of the labour market into what was previously a stable, 'core' area of employment. In this way, while participation in YTS sustains many jobs, it also carries threats to the terms and conditions of all FE workers. Many in NATFHE were very aware of the risks that YTS carried. Nevertheless, the pressures on FE and the dangers of isolation for a union trying to fight education cuts made outright opposition a non-starter.

The 1985 NATFHE conference voted 'to oppose' the YTS, despite the opposition of the union's hierarchy. However, the contradictions facing union members in the colleges may make this simple response of conference inoperable.

Among school teachers' unions, although there has been concern about YTS there has understandably been more concern about the MSC's increasing involvement in schools. Within the largest school teachers' union, the NUT, there has been concern about the impact YTS has had on education in schools, but much more anxiety over the introduction of the Technical and Vocational Education Initiative (TVEI) for 14–18-year-olds. The TVEI met with some hostility because it was introduced without any consultation with unions. In particular, concern has been expressed at the 'streaming' effect of TVEI on schools – young people being separated into quite different curricula at the age of 14 through 18 within the same schools or education authority. This is seen as a new form of technical/secondary modern/grammar school split. The 1985 budget announcement of a £25 million programme of MSC-controlled teacher training related to TVEI, quickly followed by white papers on employment and education calling for greater involvement by schools in work-related education, did not reassure teachers.

However, as with NATFHE and the YTS, the availability of TVEI and its resources in a period of general spending cuts has made the programme impossible to resist. In some parts of the country an anti-comprehensive drift towards a narrow, streamed vocationalism was already in evidence in schools prior to TVEI. It is typical of MSC that its interventions make opposition difficult by backing trends which have already appeared, and so acquiring the cloak of progress and modernism.

Trade unions and apprenticeship

Trade unions with a craft apprentice tradition can be found on both extremes of the YTS debate. This is not surprising given what the MSC has meant for apprenticeship in different industries and sectors.

The issue of apprenticeship shows clearly that the MSC, ostensibly an embryonic 'national training agency', is performing an important role in the government's attempts to transform industrial relations by destroying union power.

Apprenticeship had been on the decline through the 1970s. Deindustrialization played its part. As industries contracted there were fewer skilled jobs to train for. New technology contributed by displacing skilled and semiskilled labour. Most important though was the traditional reluctance of Britain's employers to invest in skill. The Heath government's Act of 1973 had stripped the ITBs of the powers they needed to make employers take their training responsibilities seriously. In the 10 years to 1983, manufacturing apprenticeships in London fell by 50 per cent, for example.

The Thatcher government came to power with a deep hostility to any trade union influence, including the influence over training which apprenticeship arrangements and the ITB system permit. The 1980 Think Tank report reflected this hostility. The report argued that apprenticeship was a 'restrictive practice' which must be swept aside by any government concerned to modernize the labour market. Union-regulated apprenticeships, even the very modern ones with ITB approval, should be replaced with a system of lower-level, employer-defined 'competences'. In this context the YTS acquired a new strategic usefulness for the Tories, in that it could be used to transform the conditions of entry to work and directly undermine recruitment to craft unions at the same time as it functioned as 'a response' to youth unemployment.

During the early development of YTS, MSC officials were covertly advising employers to abandon apprenticeship and move over to YTS. Trade unions were being told by officials that YTS would help save apprenticeship, and that displacement could be avoided through careful monitoring. In April 1983 the TUC told the Commons Select Committee on Employment: 'The TUC sees a sound YTS and a strong apprenticeship system developing hand in hand in future years. It is not a choice between one or the other; the country needs them both.'[5]

With the arrival of YTS and the slack approach of MSC officials to risks of job displacement, employers were offered a clear choice. They could continue to recruit apprentices on proper, negotiated rates of pay, with full employment rights. In some sectors this meant a full year in off-the-job training and a strong moral responsibility to finish the apprenticeship. Alternatively, they could recruit through YTS, and get their young people on a free 12-month trial. The 'trainees' could be used in production work for up to nine months, they were not fully covered by employment protection laws and there was less chance of trade union interference. At the end of the period the employer was free carefully to select any 'worth' retaining. Not surprisingly the YTS made rapid inroads into previously apprenticed areas. In construction, road transport, hotels and electrical contracting, YTS has displaced the first year of apprenticeship. In the first three of these some protection of standards is maintained through the surviving ITBs. However, in all these sectors the MSC scheme has brought about a lowering of pay, security and training quality, which is bound, in the long term, to weaken the unions. In the short term it is often true that there is much less contact at local level between trade unionists and YTS trainees, because of the short-stay nature of the scheme, than characterized the relatively stable arrangements of apprenticeship.

Out of those unions directly concerned with apprenticeship, the print union, the National Graphical Association (NGA) has been the most outspoken critic of the YTS at the annual TUC. At the 1983 Congress, Brenda Philbin described the YTS as a 'cynical rerun of YOP', and predicted (correctly) that it would produce a pool of low-skill, cheap labour. The NGA is of course in the front line of employer attempts to smash trade union organization through the introduction of new technology. In this context a mass, broad-based work experience programme like YTS is bound to be seen as an attack on trade union influence properly exercised through structured standards-based apprenticeship.

The YTS was seen as a dangerous initiative by a Tory government in the wake of the closure of the statutory ITB for the print industry, an ITB which had been an effective agent of modernization and on good terms with print unions. On the other hand, another print union, SOGAT 82, particularly in the person of Bill Keys its General Secretary, took a less hostile view. As Chair of the TUC's Employment Policy and Organization Committee (EPOC) and a Commissioner on the MSC, Keys was a staunch defender of the YTS.

In the building industry the main union, UCATT, faced a very different situation. Apprentice training had collapsed particularly quickly in the sector during the 1970s and early 1980s. Employers in the private sector slashed their training programmes as recession bit hard, and local authority direct labour faced new legislation which discouraged training. The government retained a statutory ITB for this industry where traditionally many employers do not even feign a commitment to training. In this context, UCATT felt that so long as the ITB ran the programme, support for YTS might be a way to save some aspects of apprenticeship.

The new national agreements in construction officially replaced the first year of apprentice training with YTS, the whole scheme being centrally run by the Construction Industry Training Board. The YTS intake is streamed into low-skill and 'craft' programmes, with most young people being kept on after their YTS year, at least in the early years of the YTS programme. Lothian in Scotland has the highest job placement rate. In 1983, prior to YTS in the industry, there were only 314 apprentices in the region. In 1984 twice this number were taken on after YTS had been introduced, with 90 per cent of all trainees being offered proper apprenticeships at the end of their YTS.

The union takes the view that it has acted to save the skillbase of the industry, to protect its own membership base, and in the interests of young people. Opposition to the YTS would have been difficult, and would have contributed nothing to raising the level of training and school leaver entry in the industry. The employers and the government would have been presented with a huge propaganda weapon had the union adopted an 'oppositionist' stance. However, the price paid by the union's compliance with the YTS has been high. Apprentice wages have been halved, and it remains to be seen whether the complicated formulae for recouping wages lost in subsequent years of training will work. Trainees do not have full employment rights. The quality of training in the first year is much reduced to conform with the low standards permitted on the YTS. The fact that the ITB functions as a central managing agent and deals with the MSC Large Companies Unit means that there is virtually no contact between construction YTS and trade union representatives on local Area Manpower Boards. The main success of the scheme in job placement is unlikely to persist beyond a couple of years unless there is increased public spending on construction, but first-year apprenticeship and union influence over it have been given up.

UCATT – the Union of Construction, Allied Trades and Technicians – is the largest union in the building industry and is able to influence the entry and training of craft workers in the industry. Other unions in construction such as the Transport and General Workers Union take a more critical view. The TGWU membership includes workers in occupations not traditionally apprenticed. As well as the craft YTS schemes, there are also YTS schemes for general building operatives. These have a much worse record in job placement, for example, than the craft schemes.

It is also clear that the construction unions generally dislike the Community Programme much more than YTS. This is not surprising given that the majority of CP projects involve 'environmental landscaping, building, construction and decorating', according to an MSC survey. These jobs are usually paid well below union rates and are frequently in poor conditions with inadequate and unskilled supervision doing work which could be done by a proper, permanent workforce.

In the engineering industry we also find sharp controversy around the apprenticeship issue, and a divided union response to the YTS. Engineering had perhaps the most modern apprentice arrangements to be found in Britain. The Engineering ITB (EITB) had begun the move away from 'time-serving' to standards-based training as early as 1968. The first year of apprenticeship was made off the job and to recognized standards. Reaching recognized craft levels required the acquisition of two EITB modules after this first year. The EITB's revolution in engineering training had reduced the time taken to qualify as a craft worker from five or six years to an average three-and-a-half-year period. On most of the EITB reforms the unions had welcomed the changes and co-operated fully, though along with some employers the unions had opposed a two-year apprenticeship.

During the 1970s and early 1980s the level of apprentice training fell. Deindustrialization, new technology and employers' reluctance to invest all contributed to the decline. The EITB had had its wings clipped by the 1973 Act and could do little to overcome employers' attitudes. The board increasingly resorted to providing publicly-funded first-year apprentices (generally on lower rates of pay than those privately recruited). However, the board stuck with a narrow interpretation of its statutory remit to 'meet the needs of its industry' and refused to acknowledge any broader social responsibility to unemployed youth, though union pressure had sustained some positive action in favour of young women.

In this context a scheme like YTS, which was apparently social in its objectives, was bound to cause confusion and controversy. Employers were uncertain about its ability to meet their requirements, except in deskilled parts of electronics where it seemed ideal. Some employers' organizations supported the YTS because it helped in their industrial objectives. The analysis of the situation made by the Engineering Employers Federation is revealing: they do not see the New Training Initiative (NTI) as a social programme, but as part of the government's overall policy of reducing the wages of young people and breaking down the barriers to entry into skilled status. For them all aspects of the NTI are industrial relations issues.[6] The EITB was uncertain how to respond, at least until Sir Richard O'Brien was moved over from the MSC to head the board. The trade unions were divided amongst themselves.

The Amalgamated Union of Engineering Workers has been critical of both the nature of the YTS and the scheme's encroachment on apprenticeship. The union's 1985 conference in Eastbourne heard a Scottish delegate complain of YTS trainees being 'smuggled like contraband' into apprentice programmes. Other delegates criticized both the TUC and the umbrella union organization, the Confederation of Shipbuilding and Engineering Unions (CSEU) for their uncritical approach to the YTS. The AUEW conference rejected a motion calling for withdrawal from the scheme, but approved a very critical motion from the union's youth section. This instructed the executive to insist on proper rates of pay for YTS trainees, no job substitution, full benefit entitlement for trainees, and a much stronger union involvement in YTS training programmes. The motion also called on the executive to seek an increase in proper apprentice training.

The engineering union TASS was succinct in its view: 'The Youth Training Scheme may be' 'work preparation for all'. It is certainly not real training for all, which will have to be developed on the basis of YTS experience.' The CSEU has been very active in supporting YTS and its general secretary has been a chair of an Area Manpower Board.

Diversity in union responses

From the discussion of trade union responses to YTS so far it can be seen that they range from total opposition to schemes in general to strong support for particular schemes. There are unions which however much they do not like YTS have accepted it, – for example, because it means jobs for their members. There are unions for which YTS is the major MSC programme of concern. For others, the Community Programme or TVEI are more central. In the case of the CSU, cuts in the TOPS programme are more significant than developments in youth training.

In between the unions which have endorsed YTS and those which are opposed are a number of major unions which have adopted a 'conditional approval' approach. These are generally unions which lack a tradition of developing training policy, or which organize such a diverse range of workers as to make a general policy response impossible. The approach is to approve schemes on an individual basis if they meet certain criteria. Unions taking this view include the General, Muncipal, Boilermakers and Allied Trade Union (GMBATU), the National Union of Public Employees (NUPE), Shop Workers (USDAW), the Transport and General Workers Union (TGWU) and the Association of Scientific Technical and Managerial Staff (ASTMS).

The 'conditions' these unions lay down cover a number of specific areas, for example:
1. Terms and conditions, e.g. holidays, grievance procedures and fringe benefits should be the same for trainees and employees. A number of unions underline their opposition to any form of compulsion.
2. Topping up of the allowance or the rate for the job.
3. Equal opportunities for young women and ethnic minorities.

4. Trade union involvement and membership.
5. Safeguards against the substitution of permanent employees by YTS trainees.
6. Minimum standards for training.
7. Specific procedures for approval and monitoring schemes.

While this seems the most rational and coherent approach, and the one most likely to benefit those on MSC schemes, it is fraught with difficulties. Unions interpret the criteria differently, or rank them in different scales of importance. Within the same union the criteria may be pursued with more vigour in some areas than in others. The success of this approach hinges on the ability and commitment of representatives in the workplace. At local level trade unionists are already overburdened with work, and often cannot take on an extra load of MSC-related work. Making the criteria stick requires an expertise in training matters which it will take a long time to achieve, particularly when trade unions cannot provide resource/research/backup, and appropriate education programmes, and there is a lack of effective joint negotiating machinery.

Diversity of approach is of course a common feature of British trade unionism. However, with MSC schemes being used consciously to restructure the conditions of labour, this diversity allows the MSC officials and managing agents to pick their union for the purposes of approving schemes, to pilot projects where unions are weak, and generally to 'divide and rule'.

Differences within unions

Sometimes the differences within unions are as significant as those between unions. There are geographical differences: the outlook for trade unionists in Scotland or the northeast of England may not be the same as that for trade unionists in the southeast of England. Differences reflect industrial or political circumstances. For instance, where there are sympathetic local authorities, trade unionists on Area Manpower Boards may be much more effective than where the local authority representatives are hostile. There are major differences in the experience that trade unionists have had of the MSC machinery. Another major difference is between the perceptions of ordinary members, activists and lay officials and paid officials. Work carried out on the Youth Opportunities

Programme (by the William Temple Foundation) illustrates this.[7] The study looked at the attitudes of Area Manpower Board members (mostly full-time officials at the time) and at shop stewards' attitudes.

Shop stewards knew less about YOP than Area Board members, not surprisingly, and were more suspicious. Their attitude was summed up as a 'static set of fears and dynamic understanding of what is happening in the labour market'. They could see what is happening to jobs both in their workplaces and in general, and they could see that YOP would not improve these situations and might make matters worse. There is no reason to expect that the introduction of YTS has changed views very much. It is worth noting that three-quarters of the stewards interviewed were between the ages of 31 and 60; over 90 per cent were men and nearly 60 per cent of them were in skilled manual or professional and technical occupations. This means many are in the age group of parents of 16–year-olds, seeing things from a parent's point of view; many are men who have been through periods of vocational training themselves, most likely apprenticeships. These factors will strongly influence perceptions of MSC schemes.

The factors influencing trade union response

The above review of trade union responses illustrates the main reasons for differences in trade union responses, and shows that these are rooted in the nature of the unions themselves:

1. Differences in industrial circumstances, e.g. between public sector unions and construction unions.
2. Differences in what structures already exist or survive for training and the degree to which a union influences entry to an industry. At one extreme there are unions in industries where the ITBs survive, on the other, e.g. clerical, sales and distribution occupations where entry is virtually unfettered and without a coherent training policy.
3. There are differences between unions about how much YTS actually affects them – from NATFHE which is very dependent on YTS through to the printing industry which can attempt to ignore it.
4. The dominant political influences within unions certainly contribute to how YTS is perceived – though this factor may be

exaggerated: NALGO's suspicion of YTS is much more industrial than political.

5. Finally, the regional variations and the differences in knowledge and perception of different levels in the union are influential.

To these factors relating to the internal organization of trade unions must be added the characteristics of the Youth Training Scheme itself. Three features are particularly significant in amplifying the differences between unions. Firstly, the sheer size of the Youth Training Scheme would stretch the resources of the trade union movement, even if places were evenly spread across industries and unions. The fact that YTS is concentrated in particular industries compounds the pressure on particular unions such as those in local government and most particularly distribution. Where schemes are not firmly located in a particular occupation there can also be another problem: the nebulous nature of some schemes means that it is often not clear which union is appropriate on the basis of the limited information available. Finally, there is the problem of where trade unions can most effectively intervene. The nature of the YTS means that trade union intervention may be at the level of the workplace, the Managing Agency, the Area Manpower Board or national level in the case of Large Companies Unit Schemes. Even at the workplace, negotiation or approval of schemes may not be the exclusive responsibility of one union.

It is in the context of the coherence of the government's strategy, the implications of the structure of YTS and the fragmentation of individual unions' response that the TUC is put in an important position of influence.

The TUC's response

Although the TUC has been able to defend its response to the MSC at successive congresses, it has been under increasing pressure within the labour movement. Among trade union lay activists – represented by Trades Councils for instance – criticism has been persistent. Within the Labour Party, Party conferences and the Labour Party Young Socialists have been critical. Criticism from the Labour Party/TUC Liaison Committee has also been growing. From the Left of the labour movement there has been a consistent demand for 'withdrawal' from the MSC tripartite structures.[8] Anger and frustration at the TUC's apparently uncritical support of the MSC is now a major issue which must be taken into account in formulating alternative strategies.

The TUC's support for the MSC needs to be viewed against four factors: a labour movement which, as we have seen, is sharply divided on the main issues; the TUC's own long and consistent involvement in labour market policy; TUC fears about the social and political consequences of mass youth unemployment; and the ability of Thatcher's ministers to divert debate and outmanoeuvre the TUC.

The TUC has not been in a position to ignore or heal the divisions in the labour movement. The divisions are too fundamental for either of those options. What it has done, however, is to advance its own policies which neither address the divisions nor provide a basis for any kind of unity either temporary or permanent: centralization has been adopted as a strategy and as the only basis for unification. The question is whether that centralization works or not. While it may have worked when training was seen as a marginal issue and youth unemployment a temporary phenomenon, it will not work now when youth training and employment have become of much greater concern to a wider range of interests.

The history of TUC policies on the labour market also leads it to considerable loyalty to the MSC. The TUC has been in favour of a strong centralized labour market planning agency since at least the 1960s. When Heath's Conservative government set up the MSC in 1973, the TUC had its criticisms but believed that the MSC represented a significant step towards its long-term objective. Commitment to MSC tripartism was considerably strengthened during the social contract period under Labour in the 1970s. In this period TUC pressure led to the MSC being transformed into a vehicle for unemployment palliatives like the YOP and the STEP (Special Temporary Employment Programme) for adults. The YOP was started up in this period because the TUC pressed Labour 'to do something' in response to rising youth unemployment. The TUC's preference was for a short scheme combining work experience with some off-the-job education/training. The TUC has difficulty now criticizing schemes like YTS which in a sense have evolved out of earlier schemes initiated by the TUC itself.

The TUC commitment to the MSC as an agency is, however, the most important point. In 1979 the TUC feared that Tory backbench pressure would lead to abolition of the MSC itself. There is a sense in which the TUC responded to this threat by defending the institution first and worrying about policy as an afterthought. Within the labour movement the TUC frowned on criticism of the MSC, seeing this as weakening the fight to defend the Commission. The TUC continually presented the MSC as 'our agency' to which the whole movement should show loyalty. At the 1983 Congress, Bill Keys of the print union SOGAT 82 put the view of the TUC General Council saying 'the MSC was the concept of the Congress and indeed we fought for it and we got it'. Trade unions had a duty to stay committed to the MSC, and, through it, to defend the interests of the unemployed. Without TUC involvement, it was argued, the MSC would be hijacked by employers and the Thatcher government. Now, in so far as criticisms of MSC are acknowledged by the TUC, they are blamed on the government which is held to be excessively 'interfering' in the programmes of 'our MSC'. Recent documents like the TUC/Labour 'Plan for Training'[9] concentrate on restoring the MSC's alleged former independence and innocence; loyalty diverts attention away from the need radically to transform MSC functions and programmes. The government is seen as the sole villain with the MSC as a rather helpless, passive victim. The criticisms ignore the extent to which Thatcher's labour market policies actually originate from MSC civil servants, and particularly the way that appointments to the Commission (especially the successive chairs, David Young and Bryan Nicholson) and the Youth Training Board have been arranged.

The TUC does of course criticize the MSC publicly and privately. However, the language of that criticism is 'anger' and 'disappoint-ment' rather than a more critical, distanced view which might suggest that the TUC sees its role as negotiating with the MSC rather than planning or collaboration. The threat of withdrawal when it has been made by the TUC has been in relation to government action not MSC action; for example, in 1984 when MSC was given control of 25 per cent of non-advanced further education in England and Wales, and in 1985 when decisions were taken to reduce the Skillcentre network. Only rarely has the TUC strongly and publicly criticized MSC decisions.

The TUC acts to discourage and dampen criticisms of the MSC. Within the labour movement this increases confusion at local level where the defects of the scheme are often plain to see, and where trade unionists are grappling with the contradictions of MSC programmes. Activists often feel equally frustrated by the TUC and the MSC. The anger and sense of 'being conned' held by many trade unionists does not find its way into the debates at the annual TUC. Nor does it always find expression on the local tripartite Area Manpower Boards, where trade unionists sit to represent TUC policy rather than local feeling. The result is a growing gulf between those on the ground who are expected to negotiate around training and police MSC schemes, and those at the centre who are expected to set the policy lead for the whole movement. In the long term this must undermine the power and authority of the TUC itself in a vital policy area. The authority of the TUC is further undermined by the TUC's passivity in relation to information about the MSC. The TUC neither collects nor distributes information relating to the MSC from independent or trade union sources. This often leaves Area Manpower Board members in the dark. Even information about what TUC representatives are saying on the Commission or the Youth Training Board is not circulated. This reliance on MSC information and secrecy must seriously weaken the TUC's ability to encourage support for its policies among trade unions.

Since the late 1970s the TUC has been afraid of the social consequences of rising youth unemployment. These fears were heightened by the urban riots of 1981, and have been exploited skilfully by Thatcher's government. The TUC demanded the expansion of YOP and welcomed its transformation into the more permanent, structured YTS. In taking this approach, the TUC partly moved away from its traditional concept of the MSC as a strong labour market planning agency, towards strengthening the MSC role in social policy, particularly the amelioration of unemployment. It helped to shift the debate from policies for job creation and industrial regeneration to MSC and unemployment palliatives which were incorrectly described as 'training' policies. It is not that the TUC in any sense actively and consciously collaborated with Thatcherism. It is that the Tories, and particularly Norman Tebbit as Employment Secretary, saw the contradictions in the TUC position and carefully exploited them. The TUC had not thought through the way in which a determined government could use aspects of TUC policy against the movement. Consequently there was no real attempt to counter the Tory offensive by encouraging local debate, initiative and resistance. Where local authorities like the GLC tried this approach the TUC attitude was distinctly cool. Similarly the TUC has effectively discouraged young people's criticisms of the Youth Training Scheme. In 1985 the forthright condemnation by Norman Willis and Neil Kinnock of the Youth Trade Union Rights' Campaign was a highly publicized example of this general stance, seen earlier during the 'Jobs for Youth' campaign.

The government's skill in getting its own way has been shown repeatedly since 1979. One strategy has been to advance with a stick in one hand and a carrot in the other. Perhaps the clearest example of all, has been Norman Tebbit's white paper on the NTI issued in December 1981.[10] At this time the TUC was supporting MSC proposals for a 12-month YTS on the grounds that it would be significantly better than the discredited YOP, particularly in terms of training quality, the level of allowances and the attractiveness of the scheme to young people. Tebbit's white paper proposed slashing the allowance and industrial conscription of young people. TUC fury (which was shared by most unions, education, the voluntary sector and some employers) merely achieved a restoration of the terms and conditions which had characterized YOP, and which were felt to be unsatisfactory throughout the labour movement. Tebbit's eventual climb-down was hailed as a victory, even though the spectre of coercion quickly reappeared on the agenda. The white paper did its job in deflecting the TUC from the important task of ensuring that the YTS was from the outset significantly better than the YOP. In fact what has happened is that not all the recommendations of the Task Group were implemented and the actual YTS in 1985–86 is nearer to Norman Tebbit's proposals than the Task Group's. On the proposal for a two-year YTS once again the TUC was outmanoeuvred. It was presented as a move towards a TUC goal though in fact it was not a proposal for more training but more 'work experience'. Once more the TUC favoured a 'task-group' style response – this time an ad hoc group dominated by the CBI, TUC and MSC. Where the government cannot get the MSC's support for its policies it can simply go ahead with its plans through the Department of Employment, taking any funds necessary from the MSC's budget, as happened with the Armed Services YTS and Young Workers' Schemes.

It is important to note that within the labour movement the division is not a simple one between 'radical grassroots' and 'conservative TUC'. The reality is much more complex. At local level there is much discontent with the common perception of the TUC's role. However, the discontent and anger is as yet confused. Worked-out alternatives do not yet exist. It is to the possibilities of an alternative strategy that this chapter now turns.

Towards an alternative policy

The problems facing the trade union movement in responding to the MSC and developing alternatives are complex, just as they are for others trying to come to terms with Thatcher's labour market policies. The diversity of interests and experience in the movement precludes simplistic approaches. Differences between areas and localities probably rule out highly-centralized solutions. While many activists and young people would undoubtedly welcome a TUC withdrawal from the MSC, on its own this is unlikely to change very much. It would certainly not create any unity in a divided movement. What is needed is an approach which recognises the needs of all levels in the movement, and helps to build bridges between trade unions and those who are on MSC programmes.

Despite the TUC's apparently very low-key approach within MSC structures, there is evidence that where TUC commissioners dig in their heels, limited successes are possible even in the present political climate. The failure and eventual withdrawal of the wage-cutting Young Workers Scheme is due in large part to the TUC's absolute refusal to go along with it, and its ability to win over a majority of the tripartite Commission to oppose the YWS.

This suggests that some improvements could be won if the TUC were to dig in more often and more deeply, starting perhaps with a more rigorous approach to existing criteria for trade union satisfaction with schemes. These are all the aspects where trade unions have clear ideas of good practice which go far beyond the MSC's minimum criteria of acceptability. A more combative and open approach, within which the TUC was willing publicly to criticize the MSC, would give a great boost to grassroots campaigns and to the beleaguered TUC representatives in local AMBs. It would also help to raise the stock of the labour movement in the eyes of those on MSC programmes.

The present role of the TUC is a centralized and managerial one. It includes offering general endorsement of programmes with specific endorsements where there is a recognized and appropriate union. This generalized, centralized endorsement is unnecessary and undesirable.

The 'managerial' role of the TUC includes the participation of the TUC in the Youth Training Board and Area Manpower Boards. An alternative would be to use and establish where it does not already exist, joint trade union negotiating machinery. In many industries such machinery already exists – especially in the public sector.

The general endorsement given by the TUC to MSC programmes is a major headache to trade unionists actually working with young people or being asked to approve specific schemes. Young people hold the trade unions responsible for the defects they experience in schemes and this makes it much more difficult for trade unionists to convince them that they have anything to offer. The implication of general endorsement is that an 'MSC scheme is good unless proved bad'. Other contributions in this book suggest that it is the other way round – MSC schemes are bad unless proved good.

It is becoming a bigger and bigger problem to find trade unionists willing and able to serve on Area Manpower Boards. The job they are asked to do on Boards frequently involves them in making decisions about sectors about which they know little or nothing. A sector-based approach would enable trade unions to draw on their experience, expertise and interests much more effectively.

To begin with, an industry-based approach would draw on the best experience of the Industrial Training Boards. It would also lay the foundations for effectively linking training to economic planning and the creation of permanent jobs. As well as the links to industrial planning, it is necessary to have a regional structure to take account of the need for regional economic planning. The TUC already has embryonic industry-based regional structures in so far as regional TUC's often have sector committees such as public services, construction, transport and so on. These committees could be enhanced to link up with trade unionists working in education and local trade unionists (through Trades Councils) to provide a coherent response to Youth Training Schemes.

In order to be effective, trade unionists need resources for monitoring. As a condition of continued involvement the TUC could demand resources for monitoring from the MSC. Even if the existing Area Manpower Board structures were maintained, one researcher for each of the 54 Boards and the Large Companies Unit would be a small outlay compared with the MSC's £2 billion budget. The regional TUCs could also play an active part in supporting local authority and trust-funded monitoring projects. These already exist in London, Birmingham, Newcastle and Manchester, for instance. The Labour Movement Inquiry into Youth Unemployment and Training provides an important forum for the exchange of information, ideas and experiences of trade unionists involved in issues arising from the MSC. The inquiry was initiated by Trades Councils and local authorities and has won support and respect at all levels of the labour movement. As it grows, it is increasingly a major source of new thinking on policy approaches to youth unemployment and training.

A number of Labour-controlled local authorities – the GLC, West Midlands County Council, Sheffield, Hackney, Birmingham and others – have tried in conjunction with the local labour movement to implement alternatives to MSC programmes. They have worked to develop training linked to job creation, and schemes which challenge racism and sexism in the labour market. They have also funded projects which monitor MSC activities and provide information useful to those campaigning for improvements. It is to these innovations rather than to the centre that we should look in the construction of alternative policies. They show that even in the least promising economic and political climate progress is possible. They also reflect the fact that training is an issue which is of concern to local authorities and electors, that it is a political issue and should be subject to the kind of accountability that education is, for instance. There is a growing demand for programmes which recognize the needs of particular industries and communities and for institutions which have the statutory power to make employers invest in training but are also locally accountable. Opinion polls in Scotland show that over 70 per cent are in favour of job and training programmes being controlled by an elected Assembly.[11]

The current range of responses to the MSC, and the degree of frustration experienced at local level, strongly suggest that the TUC should move beyond its commitment to a 1960s-style centralized planning agency.

These issues of devolution of responsibility, accountability, resources for monitoring and building on the experience and organization of trade unions are only a starting point. A central weakness of the trade unions' approach to youth unemployment and training is that while it claims to have formulated policies in the name of young people and in their interests, trade union mechanisms for finding out what young people want are in many cases limited and in some cases nonexistent. If young people are not to be completely dislocated from the labour movement, much more energy has to go into promoting collective organization and action by young people. This calls for a new approach by unions. It is unlikely to be effective if it is only scheme-centred or workplace-centred (even in a two-year scheme the time spent on the schemes is often too short). Trade unions will have to get involved with young people on a broad range of issues affecting their participation in society – the right to independent income or housing; the experience of discrimination as young people, as women or black people, for instance. The TUC's role should be to encourage the expression of views, to amplify what is being said and to put its weight behind young people, not merely to stand as their guardian.

1. Department of Employment, *Employment: the Challenge for the Nation*, Cmnd 9474, HMSO, London, 1985.
2. Central Policy Review Staff, *Education Training and Industrial Performance*, HMSO, London, 1980.
3. Scottish Council Development and Industry, *Youth Training and Beyond – An Appraisal*, Edinburgh, 1985.
4. Society of Civil and Public Servants, *Back to Work – An Alternative Strategy for the MSC*, London, 1982.
5. Employment Committee of the House of Commons, 1982–83, *The Youth Training Scheme*, HC 335-i, HMSO, London, 1983.
6. H. Rainbird and W. Grant, *Employers Associations and Training Policy*, Institute for Employment Research, University of Warwick, 1985.
7. D. Gregory and C. Edgar, *Youth Employment and MSC Special Programmes: Trade Union Responses for Wales and the North West of England*, William Temple Foundation, Manchester, 1980.
8. E. Jacques *et al.*, *Youth Training – The Tories' Poisoned Apple*, Independent Labour Publications, Leeds, 1983.
9. Trades Union Congress/Labour Party Liaison Committee, *Plan for*

Training, London, July 1984.

10. Department of Employment, *A New Training Initiative, A Programme for Action*, Cmnd 8455, HMSO, London, 1981.

11. *Radical Scotland*, December 1984.

11. The MSC and the Local Community

Leisha Fullick

Introduction

An MSC publicity video produced shortly after the 1985 budget which announced the creation of the two-year Youth Training Scheme stated that the MSC 'had now assumed enormous importance in British society'. On the face of it this was an extraordinary declaration to make about an organization concerned with training, traditionally a marginal issue on the British political scene. From the Left's point of view the analysis was entirely correct. The Thatcher Tories since 1979 have pursued policies which have been highly centralizing and interventionist on behalf of market capitalism. The MSC has been a conscious agent in this process. Not only has it been a very effective means of maintaining control in the labour market but it has played a key role in pursuing other objectives in the Thatcherite political project for British society. It has sought to undermine local government and erode the autonomy of local education authorities, it now controls the future of large sections of the voluntary sector, it has created new forms of 'consultation' and 'participation' which are in effect an attack on local democracy, and it has played a key role in attempting to reshape values in our society, particularly around the right to education and the right to jobs.

The Thatcher government's economic policies since 1979 have been characterized as 'neo-liberal' in that they seek to promote a strong state in the interests of a free market.[1] In this context the MSC has had a strategic role to play. As an organization concerned with labour market policies its role has been to free the labour market from traditional constraints. The Tory commitment to the MSC's New Training Initiative can be seen in the context of the drive to restructure traditional labour markets and to lower wages,

particularly youth wages.[2] Few could have predicted this role for
the MSC when it was set up under the 1973 Employment and
Training Act. The TUC heavily influenced the final shape of the
Act and the corporate semi-independent structure of the MSC was
as much a reflection of the traditionally consensual approach to
training policy since 1945 as of any belief that a free-standing
agency would be better placed to significantly alter the nature of
workplace relations, let alone play a major transformative role in
the operation of the local state. While the genesis of the MSC was in
the tripartite approach to planning characteristic of the Heath,
Wilson and Callaghan governments of the 1970s, and its corporate
structure could hardly have been expected to find favour with the
new Tory administration post-1979, this was clearly of less
importance to the Tories than its semi-independent status. This has
offered advantages not only in the promotion of potentially
controversial training policies, but also in pursuit of other political
objectives which have required a greater degree of centralization
and control than that traditionally available to central government
in our society.

Since 1979 there has been a conscious attempt by the Tories to
create a new agenda for public policy in Britain. This agenda
contains a clear commitment to dismantling large parts of the
welfare state and handing over responsibility for the provision of
services to the private sector or to the 'family and community' –
often of course a euphemism for women. In effect the commitment
is to the reintroduction of selective access to health care, social
services and educational opportunity based upon class and wealth.
This attack on the 'social wage' of most people, particularly
working-class people, has gone side by side with an attack on real
wages and the promotion of competition, market forces and the
rights of capital in order to break up the existing economic
structure in the hope of creating a more dynamic and profitable
capitalist economy. But while this policy is anti-statist in publicly
declared intent, the Thatcherites had in fact had to create and use a
strong central state to enforce their vision of society and the
economy. In its most extreme form this has been manifested in the
scenes of police violence against communities during the miners'
strike. The law also has been used to break the power of the trade
unions in a whole range of other ways, to promote the interests of
other groups in society that the Tories deem 'friendly' (e.g. parents

as 'consumers' in education) and to threaten other sites of political activity like the Labour-controlled metropolitan and inner-city borough councils.

The Thatcherite Tories' second term of office has been particularly characterized by an attack on local government. It has become increasingly clear that this onslaught is being mounted not only because of the necessity of reducing government spending, but also because in its second term the government is bent on consolidating the consensus around economic 'realism' and authoritarian populism that was supposedly such a winning formula from 1979–83. Economic 'realism' demands an individualistic 'self-help' approach to social needs and problems. Embodied within the very meaning and tradition of local government is the collective provision of services for the safety and wellbeing of local communities. While it would be an exaggeration to say that local government has very often been a liberating political force, there is no doubt that many of the most successful and creative ideological challenges to the Thatcherite vision have emerged from Labour-controlled local authorities like Sheffield, the GLC, and some inner London boroughs. These authorities have not only reasserted values of collective state provision but have developed new ways of ensuring that that provision is controlled by and responsive to the needs of communities. They have done this by attempting to develop new forms of representation for 'excluded' groups – black people, women, disabled people. They have grant-aided voluntary groups to enable them to define their own needs and run their own services. They have attempted to provide a community base for certain services previously locked up in town hall bureaucracies. They have tried to practice positive discrimination in the allocation of funds. They have set up employment and training committees to develop opportunities for local people.

Such practical alternatives to the Thatcherite vision have proved very unpopular with Tory ministers who have clearly wished to see the promotion of their own alternatives as quickly as possible. Clearly the total privatization of all government services is not on the agenda. What is possible is the use of quangos like the MSC, or the creation of new ones like the joint boards set up to run services in the wake of the abolition of the GLC and Metropolitan Counties. Such organs are far more susceptible to government control because of the government's ability to make political appointments to them and because they are more amenable to rapid reorganization in the face of changing objectives. Attempts to change the nature of decision-making and control have been most clearly marked in the health service. John Hoskyns, head of Margaret Thatcher's Policy Unit from 1979–1982, is perhaps unusual in his *public* advocacy of the transfer of the health service to the private sector as soon as possible and for control of the demand for health care on the basis of price.[3] The Thatcher governments themselves have recognized that it has not been politically feasible to overtly shift most aspects of medical care back into the market. Instead they have encouraged the growth of the private sector while cutting expenditure on the NHS and reorganizing it in such a way as to alter the balance of forces within the health service decision-making structure. The input of high-ranking businessmen and professionals has been strengthened while that of local government, the community and non-professional staff has been weakened.[4]

Of course training is a highly marginal activity compared to the delivery of health care. (Although even in training the Thatcherites clearly feel the need to universally impose their own vision. The Department of Employment publicly attacked the GLC's training 'alternative' – the Greater London Training Board – via a press release in 1984.) But the importance of the MSC as a centralizing force now goes well beyond training. This chapter will argue that the growth of the MSC as a major institution for the delivery of social policy has led to the same kind of process at work in relation to local government. Central government, unable directly to dismantle services previously provided collectively, and to some extent redistributively, has indirectly sought to undermine these services by altering the balance of forces at local level through expenditure cuts, privatization and by bypassing traditional notions of local representation and accountability. Its chosen instrument has been the MSC. The process has been particularly marked in education, the major local government service, but the operation of the various MSC programmes for the unemployed has also had a marked effect on a range of other services provided by the local state.

The MSC in the local community

It was the massive growth of the MSC as an agent for social policy in the late 1970s and the divorce of training from economic planning which started the process whereby the MSC began to have a major impact on local communities. As the economic crisis deepened after 1974 and as youth unemployment became a central political issue, the MSC took on the important new task of providing special temporary measures to combat the worst effects of unemployment amongst young people. For the first time since the 1930s training became an instrument for the social control of youth. These developments coincided with the abandonment of any pretence of an industrial strategy by the 1974–9 Labour government. After Tony Benn was dismissed from the Department of Industry in 1975 following the EEC referendum campaign, such progressive elements as there had been in the 1975 Industry Bill were allowed to atrophy. This included proposals for planning agreements with major industries, and industrial democracy. However minimalist these proposals may have been (following the mangling of the Bill at committee stage), Benn and his group had started to pursue an economic strategy that contained within it the notion of planning industry in accordance with the needs of consumers and workers. This could have had very important implications for training policy and the development of the MSC. But the MSC was not asked to undertake the task of promoting real training opportunities linked to socialized economic development. It never developed structures for the planning of training which had as their perspective the need to eliminate inequalities between individuals and regions in the labour market. The MSC was not linked to a strategy for jobs and democracy but to one of employment, poverty and 'special programmes'. The consultative structures which the MSC developed for these special programmes became the paradigm for the delivery of training programmes which were to be an important instrument of the New Right's political and economic project after 1979.

On the face of it the special programmes heralded a significant breakthrough in terms of local involvement in local labour market policy-making which traditionally had never concerned itself with more than the limited number of young people, overwhelmingly male, who had access to apprenticeships. Early in its life the MSC had replaced the old Local Employment Committees (set up as a result of trade union pressure after the First World War) by a network of 88 District Manpower Committees which were supposed to develop plans for training to meet the needs of their local areas. The DMCs exerted little influence over important manpower and training matters affecting their communities, and the MSC largely developed its training plans in the 1970s without reference to the DMCs.

But the high political profile accorded to the Youth Opportunities Programme (YOP), which the MSC was asked to launch following the Holland Report in 1977, meant that the issue of local consultation had to be taken more seriously. Both YOP and the Special Temporary Employment Programme (STEP) for the adult unemployed needed to use the commitment of local people in order to offer a strong platform from which the quite major interventions in the local labour market that they implied could be launched. Such people could, through their local contacts, provide places on the programme. Because of their standing in the community they could also lend legitimacy to the whole enterprise. Accordingly 28 Special Programmes Area Boards (SPABs) were set up in 1978 containing representation from employees, trade unionists, educationalists, local authorities and voluntary organizations.

The Area Boards, through identifying places for young people in local firms and projects and through approving schemes, became a significant part of an extremely flexible and versatile system which launched a major new social programme which was able to incorporate an enormous number of young people very quickly in the late 1970s and early 1980s. In these few years a network of regional and area offices was established by the MSC which rapidly drafted in large numbers of staff to co-ordinate and develop the programmes. This meant the introduction of whole new layers of bureaucratic cadres into the local scene – civil servants, often better trained, better paid, more experienced than the local authority staff with whom they had to deal. They also had money to spend when local authority services were being cut. The Special Programmes Boards played an important role in bringing these staff into direct contact with local communities for the first time, and in providing a gloss of accountability for their activities.

Increasingly, of course, the Area Board structure became unsteady as it failed to operate effective controls at local level over YOP schemes. In the end the Boards were unable to limit the promotion by the MSC of poor-quality and exploitative schemes for the young or to mobilize locally for good-quality training.

Trade unionists and community organizations motivated by a desire to 'do something' about the rapidly deteriorating plight of young people found themselves caught up in a structure in which they were powerless to do little more than legitimize the massaging of the unemployment figures.

The MSC and the control of training

Despite government hostility to tripartism, the MSC set up a new local tripartite consultative structure for the Youth Training Scheme (YTS) in 1982. Fifty-four Area Manpower Boards were created which were to combine the co-ordinating and planning functions which in theory had been accorded to the now defunct DMCs with the special project approval and monitoring functions of the SPABs. This commitment to consultation and involvement with the local community over YTS was all the more surprising because in Tory theory (though certainly not in practice) YTS is not a make-work programme for the young unemployed. Both YTS and the new Adult Training Strategy are promoted as employer-led training schemes whose character will be determined by the operation of market forces. New Right economic theorists see no need for the planning and co-ordination of training and no need to intervene in the market to ensure that future training needs either of the individual or industry are met. Certainly the Tory governments since 1979 have had no interest in interventions at local level to provide either jobs or training. The reverse has been true – they have been willing to see whole communities go to waste in pursuit of their macro-economic policies.

Despite this there has been little attempt, on the surface at least, to undermine the corporate tripartite nature of the MSC or to prevent the MSC from developing a local delivery structure which pays lip service to planning training according to local needs. Undoubtedly the AMB structure has been useful, even for hard-line Tory ministers, in providing a gloss of accountability to potentionally controversial local schemes. But a closer examination of the operation of the MSC at local level since 1982 and the use to which the MSC's consultative structures have been put locally all point to a more political project. The MSC has had considerable impact on the way services are delivered through the local state. It has been capable of effecting radical change untrammelled by convention and traditional consultative procedures. Through the MSC the government has been able to effect direct interventions into local services which have been traditionally impervious to implementing centrally determined objectives. It is arguable that the MSC's consultative machinery at local level is intended as some kind of 'model' for local participation in the planning of education and training designed to cut across and undermine other units of local government. And because the MSC's special programmes are now such an important element in the delivery of social policy locally the influence of the Area Boards extends well beyond education and training.

The structure and operation of the Boards themselves point to a particular approach to local planning that accords well with the developing features of the Thatcherite state. In essence the Boards are part of a centralizing and undemocratic system. For a start the network of 54 Area Manpower Boards established in 1983 were not 'local' in any real sense at all. There is little evidence that serious consideration was given to what would be the most sensible geographical units for local economic and manpower planning. Some areas were made co-terminus with local authority boundries, others were not. The necessity to fit into the MSC's regional planning structure was more important than working with established local units. This was particularly evident in the Greater London Area which was arbitrarily divided into four quadrants. This of course occurred just prior to the Tory campaign for the GLC's abolition. It effectively undermined the Inner London Education Authority and outer London borough structures (particularly the Careers Services) at a time when their ability to plan adequate education services according to local need was coming under increasing attack. Since the Tory government does not have policies geared to combatting the special impact of unemployment and inequality of opportunity, it is hardly surprising that the Boards were not set up in a way that would help develop a meaningful local perspective on the planning of training.

While in theory the Boards had a classic tripartite structure, this representation was so constituted as to make the ability of particular groups to relate effectively to their constituencies very limited. Employees and employers had five representatives each. This was organized through the TUC and CBI at regional level. This centralization of representation made it difficult for nominees to be accountable downwards, as well as upwards to the regional nominating body. The sheer range of schemes and the numbers of industries covered by one Board and the regional nature of the representation effectively distanced the membership of particular unions from developments affecting them. This contrasts with the District Manpower Committees which had local trade unionists nominated by the Trades Council or even the area committee of individual unions.

This distancing effect was equally marked with local authority and education representatives. Where the Boards were not co-terminus with local authority boundaries, councillors and officers found themselves 'representing' the interests of areas of which they were not part and in which a different political party could be in power. Above all, no effort was made to make the Boards representative of the community in any wider sense. The Boards contained only one voluntary organization representative. There was no way that the black community or women could be adequately represented. Both women and black people have of course been excluded from training opportunities in the past and while the MSC on paper pays lip service to equal opportunities, nothing was done to extend this to the planning of training. As early as 1977 the Social Services and Employment Subcommittee of the House of Commons Expenditure Committee had recommended that the MSC make efforts to appoint more women as chairpeople and members of its Area Boards.[5] The Area Manpower Boards however continue to reflect and promote the interests of the dominant white male power group in society. Lack of voluntary sector representation was also profoundly unsatisfactory in that in many inner-city areas the MSC's 'employer-led' YTS scheme was a fiction rather than a reality. Without the voluntary sector contribution in many areas YTS would have collapsed in the first year. The Boards also advised on the development of the Community Programme which is equally highly dependent upon the voluntary sector and community groups. This contribution of community groups to training was given virtually no recognition in the Board structure.

Other kinds of access to the operation of the Boards by community groups or trade unions has of course not been developed by the MSC. There is little evidence that many Boards used their powers of co-option to involve the community more. In any case co-optees were not given voting rights or rights of veto over schemes. No help has been given to Board members to enable them to report back to their constituencies or to publicize the activities of the Boards. Indeed, some Boards were advised that individual members should not speak to the press, and publicity and information distribution has been usually carefully handled by Board officials or other civil servants. Lists of Board members have been made very hard to come by, and in general the MSC does not widely publicize the existence, activities or membership of the Boards in areas in which they are operating.

The Boards' terms of reference ask members to advise on the planning and delivery of MSC employment and training programmes in their area and to advise on the allocation of resources to particular kinds of training and other opportunities. In theory this should have given the Boards a fairly wide-ranging brief to enable them to develop labour market plans for their areas in consultation with a variety of interested parties. In fact it has been made impossible for the Boards to operate according to those terms of reference. From its inception the MSC has operated a highly centralized planning system. Its local networks are all pursuing objectives determined at the highest level. Its officers function according to the most precise instructions and guidelines issued from the MSC's headquarters at Sheffield. This lack of autonomy extends to even the most banal and routine aspects of the MSC's operations. There have been numerous examples of interventions – some coming from as high as ministerial level – which have shown a political determination to shape the nature and content of the services the MSC can deliver. The most notorious of these were the MSC's various directives on the social and life skills aspect of the training curriculum and the vetoing of the discussion of 'political' issues by those engaged in the training of youth on YOPs and YTS schemes. Ministerial interventions have gone so far as to embrace seemingly trivial issues like the banning of mural painting as a legitimate occupation for those engaged in community programme schemes.

In this context the rhetoric of planning training in accordance with local community needs, which has been a feature of MSC public utterances since the early 1980s takes on a somewhat hollow ring. There has been widespread frustration and cynicism about the Commission's advisory machinery at local level. It is not clear that the Boards fit into any recognizable decision making structures that exist within the MSC. The Boards have no formal contact with representative members on the Commission. The Boards' opinions and decisions about local matters have been systematically disregarded and ignored when referred 'upwards' to Sheffield. This has even happened when the Boards' opinions have been sought – as in 1984 when the MSC decided to cut the number of Mode B1 YTS places. Although the Boards are supposed to 'advise on the allocation of resources to particular kinds of training', those Boards which tried to oppose the MSC's decision on the grounds that Mode B1 was an appropriate type of opportunity for their area were simply overruled. Area managers told the Boards they could make the cuts anyway on instruction from Sheffield.

In 1984 the AMB for Fife tried to oppose the privatization of education which was taking place through YTS. It was overruled by the MSC. This prompted John Pollock, General Secretary of the Education Union, the Educational Institute of Scotland (EIS), to publicly question the usefulness of the AMB system.[6] The MSC has cut the employment service and reduced the number of Skillcentres in a similar fashion: announcement with no local consultation. In 1985 plans to close Skillcentres ignored the advice of the Boards on the damaging effects that the reorganization would have on support for the long-term unemployed.

Not only has consultation been a farce on major national issues. Board members have found it very difficult to get local officers to regard themselves as in any way accountable to the local consultative machinery. Information has not been made available to the Boards to enable them even to do a proper advisory job. The Boards do not enjoy the services of a proper research facility which would enable them to obtain a clear picture of local labour market needs. (In the Board on which I served members were told we 'would not want to be bothered with' detailed local labour market information.) And even when routine statistical information has been made available, Boards have not been able to get MSC officials to do other kinds of research and 'outreach work' both in the community and local industry to enable a proper planning job to be done, despite their brief to promote these links. Board meetings were structured in such a way that the major item on the agenda was always the approval of YTS places – clearly seen by the MSC as the primary function of the Boards. No attempt has been made to place the frantic search to find and fill YTS places in the context of real local economic needs. Once the places were on offer, regardless of their context in the local economy, the pressure was on Boards to 'approve' them. Hence thousands of hairdressing and other service sector YTS places have been approved with no reference to their relevance to the development of the local economy. This has produced a training scheme that is simply for the young unemployed and is not linked to industrial regeneration and permanent employment.[7]

The MSC under Thatcher clearly wants its local representative structure to do as little as possible. It has been difficult for Boards to develop their monitoring and assessing functions also. Progress reports and assessments have usually only been made available in the context of approval or renewal of schemes. The Boards did not develop a system to enable members to really take stock of what was going on in training locally. Needless to say, trainees themselves were given no means of reporting back to the Boards. Many Board members have described how visits to schemes have been carefully controlled and policed by MSC officials, thus preventing any meaningful contact with trainees.

Given the limitation of their sphere of influence, it would be a mistake to claim that the actual operation of the Boards was of major importance in undermining structures of local accountability. Nevertheless, it is significant that the MSC did set up local planning arrangements and that they have developed the particular anti-democratic features that they have. These local planning arrangements have had, and will probably continue to have, an important role to play in the context of the other mechanisms and funding arrangements which the government, in its attack on local services has chosen to operate through the MSC.

The MSC and the attack on local delivery of services

Such mechanisms have been especially marked in education where control has traditionally been highly devolved and surrounded by a range of democratic conventions. The precise impact of the MSC on education is discussed in Chapters 4, 5 and 6 of this book. What is of interest here is the success the government has had through the MSC that would have been very difficult to achieve through the Department of Education and Science. Traditions of consultation and participation have always been very strong in education and have operated at all levels of the system. Since 1944 education has generally been run according to notions of 'partnership'. This partnership has at various times and in various guises included the government, the local authorities, the teachers and latterly parents.[8] It was at its height in the days of educational optimism and expansion during the 1960s when educational policy-making was most susceptible to input from those committed to expansion and greater equality of opportunity at all levels of the system.

It has been argued with good effect that this system was highly elitist in that policy was under the control of a relatively small group of politicians, academics and educational professionals. Because of a lack of truly popular involvement in education, the whole service was highly vulnerable to cuts and attacks from the Right which occurred with the breakdown of the progressive consensus around education in the late 1970s.[9] Even so this does not detract from the fact that there are many loci of power within the education system and very strong decentralizing traditions. Notions of partnership and participation have mediated national control of education and legitimized, however weakly, notions of community control via the local education authorities' governing bodies and educational interest groups. This has been as true of Tory-controlled LEAs as Labour ones. Thatcherite Tories are relatively thin on the ground in local education politics.

While the DES has itself developed a more centralizing approach to education,[10] it is through the MSC that the government has most effectively developed its own alternative model for educational policy-making. The government's approach has been to simply bypass the existing and previously powerful structures for educational decision-making and to develop alternative mechanisms for funding education which mean that the level and type of provision in schools and colleges, once very much a matter for local negotiation, can be centrally determined. This has been done most spectacularly through the Technical and Vocational Education Initiative (TVEI) which now, through the money it can command, exercises a major influence on the curriculum in local education authorities. MSC control of funding has also been extended to teaching training for TVEI-type initiatives in the schools.

In further and adult education the ideological and financial attack on local accountability has been even fiercer. Following the

1984 white paper *Training for Jobs*,[11] control of 25 per cent of funding for courses in further education which are 'non-advanced' will have passed into MSC hands by 1986. If local authorities refuse to co-operate they will lose a similar amount from their Rate Support Grant. Clearly this is a controlling stake in the further education system for the MSC. The ability of LEAs, college staff and governing bodies to make their own decisions about college courses in the light of locally determined needs and priorities is well on the way to being destroyed. YTS has already threatened wages and conditions in further education and made its funding insecure. By taking existing provision away from further education and putting it under the MSC the government is now saying clearly that it intends to put a significant slice of education under the control of employers and market forces and beyond the control of local communities. By seeking to privatize further education through the MSC the government is offering a clear challenge to notions of opportunity inherent in all educational developments since 1944. Whatever its faults, further education has traditionally provided a second chance for many students who had been denied access to educational opportunity. Its potential for meeting the needs of working-class students, black people and women is undoubtedly there, and has been put to good effect by committed local authorities. The government is clearly determined to control who will get access to education and training. Both the MSC's Adult Training Strategy and the government's own Adult Loans scheme are clearly directed at particular groups – those with an already fairly well developed level of training and earning potential. The 'Training for Jobs' proposals are part of the drive to ensure that educational opportunity goes the same way. This will never happen as long as education decision-making is as susceptible as it is to public opinion, progressive pressure groups and councillors accountable to local electorates who can, however imperfectly, keep alive the notions of universality of opportunity. Hence the government's reliance on the MSC to change the ideological and decision-making framework.

While the drive towards privatization through the MSC has been less obvious in the provision of other local services, its impact has nevertheless been quite profound. The Community Programme (CP) has been the latest in a long line of make-work schemes for the long-term unemployed. These schemes have progressively adopted more and more dimensions of the Thatcherite vision described elsewhere in this chapter. The Community Programme is quite explicitly a low-wage programme, which through its complicated funding formulae encourages part-time work. Until recently it provided no training, and what it is likely to offer in the future will be minimal and offered only under the MSC's own Adult Training Strategy. The eligibility rules mean it is restricted to the long-term unemployed in receipt of supplementary or unemployment benefit. This of course excludes women who have been paying the married women's national insurance contribution or who have husbands who are working. The MSC has typically instituted changes in CP several times without consultation. The eligibility rule described above was one such example. It has instituted recruitment freezes which have caused considerable disruption locally. Schemes have been closed down on political grounds. Prohibitions have been placed on the display of posters and pamphlets in schemes which question government policy – a state of affairs which it would be hard to imagine being tolerated by many staff in central or local government.

The Community Programme is supposed to provide jobs in projects of benefit to the community which are not being undertaken elsewhere in the local state. It has become a major source of funding for the voluntary sector, particularly those bits concerned with 'caring'. As a result of CP there has been a growth in voluntary sector activity in this area, while the statutory sector has been cut. Mainstream welfare services like daycare centres for the elderly are being provided increasingly by the voluntary sector via the MSC. In this way services can be provided on the cheap and the organizational implications accord very well with government strategies for the welfare state. Local government has since 1945 built up an expensive infrastructure of capital investment and trained staff for the provision of welfare services. Clearly this is not to the Tories' liking and they are attempting to undermine it not only by rate-capping and cuts in funding but also via programmes like CP. Hence the schemes are short-term; it is not possible to build on good practice or develop long-term plans and funding can be switched very quickly according to changing central political imperatives.

All this has meant the transfer of financial responsibility from local government to a central agency on quite a large scale, but the issue is not only financial. The MSC is not accountable as a social service body locally. Nor has it any expertise in managing social services. In Barnet, Margaret Thatcher's constituency, CP schemes have been set up to provide after-school play centres which over the border in ratecapped and threatened ILEA are run by trained and supervised staff able to act in *loco parentis*. (Attempts by local Area Board members to turn this scheme down on political grounds were overruled.) Numerous other examples abound. It is possible to argue that the deprofessionalization of some social services may be desirable, in so far as that might lead to greater participation and control by 'clients'. But what we are seeing here is the deprofessionalization of those services in the interests of saving money, undermining local accountability and centralizing financial and political control. Professional control is being taken away from educators and social workers accountable to elected authorities and placed in the hands of employment training 'experts' accountable ultimately to central government.

The privatization of welfare through MSC projects is taken one step further by the Voluntary Projects Programme. The VPP is a small MSC programme the aim of which is to provide unemployed people with 'constructive activity'. The Programme provides a means of putting unemployed people in touch with a variety of voluntary projects, of training for volunteers, and is a source of voluntary work which is supposed to be of benefit to the wider community. While only a small scheme, the VPP clearly promotes the ideology of welfare services as something that should be provided by individual voluntary effect. There is no doubt that this scheme represents a government response to the lobby within the Tory Party for compulsory community service and to shifting of responsibility for provision for statutory to voluntary bodies. As such it reflects Mrs Thatcher's own views presented to the Women's Voluntary Service in late 1981 that the voluntary sector should be the main provider and the state should offer backup. Or as William Rees Davies, a former Tory chairperson of the House of Commons Select Committee, enthusiastically put it – 'There is a lot of unskilled work in the health service that could be done by volunteers. I hope that because the scheme may harm two or three trade unions we are not going to go cap in hand to their leaders.'[12]

What must also be of concern is the success the MSC is having not only in promoting the New Right's welfare ideology in local communities but also the way it is changing the nature of the voluntary sector itself. Since the 1960s the voluntary sector has become increasingly radicalized under the influence of the anti-bureaucratic community policies of the libertarian Left which got involved in issues like tenants' and squatters' rights. Latterly the women's movement and black activists have been increasingly involved with community groups and campaigns at local level. Community activists have developed an increased confidence to take on local bureaucracies and to mobilize dispossessed groups. The charity-dispensing image of the voluntary sector has changed and it has come to have increasingly significant influence on local politics. By and large this has been a liberating and positive influence on many local Labour Parties and Labour-controlled local authorities who have learned to deal with different groups on their own terms. With the cut-off of central government funding to local government, many of these groups have become increasingly dependent on the MSC to keep their activities going. This is transforming the voluntary sector into something different again.

Voluntary groups that may have identified particular needs in consultation with clients are being forced to modify their response in order to obtain MSC funding. In effect the MSC is defining what is of benefit to the community. The strength of the voluntary sector lay in its ability to develop democratic and participatory ways of operating locally. Funding via the MSC can be very insecure. Projects which are forced to go to the MSC for funding when other sources are cut off find that conditions are imposed which will transform the nature of a project which may have built up in a particular way over a long period of time. This has had the effect of undermining the democratic operations of whole chunks of the voluntary sector. Management committees have become increasingly financially oriented, to the detriment of their other functions. That, coupled with the uncertain future of other sources of funding like the Urban Programme, points to the transformation of voluntary action in the inner cities along depressingly conformist lines.

The role of the MSC as an increasingly significant instrument for implementing government policy at local level shows no sign of being modified. 1985 saw proposals to make YTS a two-year scheme for 16-year-olds and to increase the size of the Community Programme. It also saw a review of the Area Manpower Boards. There is little likelihood, given the state of the youth labour market and the government's commitment to an employer-led scheme with no increase in state financing, that the new YTS will provide any more real opportunities than the old. The government itself conceded that the build-up of an extra 100,000 places on the Community Programme by 1986 will increase the inequality of opportunity between regions as schemes become even more 'market led'.

The contradictions at local level

There is no doubt that the MSC has been remarkably successful in pushing forward the frontiers of the Thatcherite state. But this development has also helped to bring into sharper focus a number of issues that should be of central importance to the Left. The MSC itself has engaged through the Area Manpower Boards with notions of planning training according to local needs. This has created spaces for the development of new notions of training which can productively be linked to the economic and political aspirations of local communities. Training has never been an important idea for the Left and indeed the issue has been traditionally colonized by the Right in the Labour Party and certain trade unions. While there were and are very good reasons for training to be linked into collective bargaining issues, and while the unions have not been as conservative and exclusive over training as conventional wisdom would allow, it is only recently that the idea of 'training for social advance' has gained ground within the labour movement. Training is about access to knowledge and skill, and to power within the labour market. Above all, it is linked to employment, which still remains fundamental to full citizenship in our society. Full citizenship has always been denied in significant ways to women, to black people, to disabled people. It is now being denied to whole communities. Ironically the use made by the Tories of the MSC as a way to intensify its attack on local communities has put training very much on the agenda of local government and community policies. By making unemployment a social policy issue the Tories have created the basis for a collective local response.

In confronting the MSC trade unionists, councillors, local government workers and the voluntary sector have had to raise issues about the links between training opportunity and the kind of work they want to see in their local communities. The MSC has not always been able to prevent these discussions at Area Board level. Local councillors and voluntary sector representatives have often for the first time been able to obtain a sharper focus on the activities of certain firms in their localities through working with trade unionists on AMBs. In the Glasgow AMB trade unionists have, by working with these other groups, been able to ensure that 70 per cent of its YTS places were in organized firms. On the Northeast London Area Manpower Board, Trade Council representatives and community groups met regularly with Board members to brief them on community and trade union needs, and the Board was able to actively promote the training needs of the Bengali community in that area. Local struggles around MSC activities have meant that not only has training developed a much higher profile in communities but it has also become clear that training can now provide an important bridge between people's experience at work and in the wider community. To struggle for access to training resources is to struggle for a share in the character and organization of work. As traditional employment opportunities collapse, communities are already developing their own definitions of what is or is not worthwhile 'work', and campaigning around training will be an important part of this process.

Such notions link in well with the new theoretical framework being developed by some Marxists which emphasize the necessity for transforming production as well as controlling the market in the creation of a socialist economy. Robin Murray [13] has argued for direct planning of labour within a public economy in a way which will attack inequalities within production which feed back into income equalities and inequality between men and women and black and white people. He argues that local government initiatives in economic policy since 1979, most notably those of the GLC, West Midlands and inner-city borough councils, have worked to transform local firms and industries in the interests of labour. They have worked to enable trade unions and local organizations to determine economic development. A variety of approaches have been developed by the GLC and other local councils to enable strategic planning at the level of the locality by trade unions and local groups.

If this emphasis on the processes of production and the kinds of work that people do was ever to become the basis of new national economic and social policies by a socialist government, then training would have a key role to play as a significant part of the process of control over productive and ultimately social life. (Training is fundamental not only to controlling the job in hand but also to understanding the context of work and the work environment.) If socialist planning is to be done, as it never was in the past, training will, through popular support and local control be a fundamental part of it.

Urgent thought needs to be given now as to how people can be involved in their own learning and training needs as part of a collective local enterprise. As well as continued opposition to the worst features of YTS, to compulsory training for youth and to the accelerating trend towards the privatization of education and training, the Left needs to think about and where possible create alternative models for the delivery of training locally. So far the leadership of the TUC and the Labour Party have failed to grasp this or deal with it in any imaginative way. In 1984 the TUC-Labour Party Liaison Committee produced a plan for training which, while it was a recognition that training is achieving more political prominence, failed to link training policy to industrial and employment policy and did not even begin to address itself to any notion of community involvement in the planning of training or to positive discrimination for women and ethnic minority groups. Some local councils, again most notably the GLC, have begun to develop alternative models to the MSC. The Greater London Training Board has planned training in consultation with local groups and pushed resources towards those at the margins of the labour market. These experiments, underfunded and tentative though they may have been, will provide very important lessons for future training policy.

Constructing the alternative

The need to have a training system which is responsive to the needs of local people and local economies does not mean that we do not also need a strong national framework which will statutorily require employers to provide training and which will co-ordinate policy and provide equality between regions (see Chapter 7). We will need policies that will take into account both local and national perspectives. Properly developed spatial policies will be as necessary for training as economic planning. This has led to the argument that even under a socialist government we will need a co-ordinating body like the MSC. But there are a number of compelling reasons why any future socialist government should abolish the MSC and why the Left should be campaigning for its abolition to become part of the TUC and Labour Party policy now. This will not be easy, given the entrenched position of the TUC in particular within MSC structures, but a direct challenge to what the MSC has actually come to represent in our society is the only way that fundamental issues to do with future education training and social policies will get on to the agenda in a radical way.

There is no doubt that the MSC itself has presented a radical change to entrenched interests within the system. But in doing so it has developed a style of operating that is profoundly undemocratic and which is pursuing the class interests of the Tories. Its dynamism is the dynamism of the New Right. It is highly unlikely that institutionally it would be able to adapt to becoming an organization capable of delivering socialist training policy in the ways described above. The Left's political priority should not be to change the MSC but to find new ways of integrating training education and economic planning which will offer real opportunities to working-class people to have more control over their own lives.

People are interested in training; they do want to control it. In 1984 in an opinion poll conducted in Scotland on the future functions of a Scotland Assembly, 70 per cent put training at the top of the list. If training is to be planned democratically it will have to be done locally. This will require creative institutional reform by a future socialist government. Whatever structure is devised nationally, there will have to be an enhanced not a diminished role for local government. The integration of education and training nationally means local education and training authorities which will have to be very different bodies from local education authorities. Here the democratic shell has got to be given real content. They will have to be truly part of the local community's economic and social interests. They will have to be linked to local and regional economic planning bodies that were really attempting to undertake 'popular planning' with trade unionists and local people. The MSC's Area Manpower Boards could be replaced by local labour market consultative committees to the education and training authority. There would be representatives of all the different interests concerned with training. They would gather intelligence on local industry and undertake proper research into local labour market needs. This would entail talking with and consulting with a lot of people and community groups in a way that most local authorities don't do at the moment.

The links that have developed between social policy and training should be dismantled. The welfare state was and should be predicated on low unemployment. Measures to tackle unemployment will have a training component but that is not to say that training should be used to mitigate the worst effects of unemployment. Quite rightly this has been seen as a cynical exercise. Even worse has been the way the link has undermined the proper delivery of welfare. The limitations of social democratic welfarism have now been coupled with the appropriation of large chunks of social policy by the MSC. A new approach to the welfare state is needed to redistribute resources and status and decentralize power. There will be no place in the new style for delivering welfare services for independent centralizing agencies like the MSC. Education and community care will have to be under local control.

The creation of more democratic local structures should also help us to rethink what our education system should really be about. Of earlier periods in our history, Brian Simon has argued that our state education system has been mainly influenced by the unique characteristics of the British class structure. Education reforms needed not only for the tackling of social injustice but also for the modernization of the economy have been shelved in favour of the expansion of a system suited to the creation of a liberal academic elite. This has done profound harm to an education system which has always been institutionally and ideologically split between high-status academic and low-status vocational education and training. The MSC has enhanced this divide and is recreating class-related secondary modern schemes in our schools and colleges. The MSC has come to be an institutional embodiment of particular class divisions in our society. The institutional divide needs to be overcome and the position of vocational education and training enhanced if there is to be a radical reform of the system which gives equal respect to all kinds of knowledge. This equal respect will only come through the living experience of people who not only have increased access to education and training but also power to control it.

1. A. Gamble, 'Thatcherism and Conservative Politics', in Jacques and Hall (eds.), *The Politics of Thatcherism*, Lawrence & Wishart, London, 1983, pp. 109–31.
2. J. Fairley and J. Grahl, 'Conservative Training Policy and the Alternatives', *Socialist Economic Review*, Merlin Press, London, 1983, pp. 137–53.
3. J. Hoskyns, *The Times*, 12 February 1985.
4. S. Iliffe, 'Dismantling the Health Service', in Jacques and Hall (eds.), *The Politics of Thatcherism*, Lawrence & Wishart, London, 1983, pp. 235–52.
5. House of Commons Expenditure Committee, 1977–8, *People and Work, Prospects for Jobs and Training*, HC, 647-i, HMSO, London, 1978.
6. *Scotsman*, 22 and 23 September 1983.
7. P. Dutton, 'YTS – Training for the Future', *Public Administration*, No. 62, 1984, pp. 483–94.
8. Maurice Kogan, *The Politics of Educational Change*, Fontana, London, 1978.
9. Centre for Contemporary Cultural Studies, *Unpopular Education*, Hutchinson, London, 1981.
10. B. Salter and T. Tapper, *Education Politics and the State*, Grant McIntyre, London, 1981.
11. Department of Employment, Cmnd 9135, *Training for Jobs*, HMSO, London, 1984.
12. H. Barnard, Discussion Paper on the MSC, COHSE, July 1983.
13. Robin Murray, 'New Directions in Municipal Socialism', in B. Pimlott (ed.), *Fabian Essays in Socialist Thought*, Gower, London, 1984.

Glossary

No glossary in this increasingly complex area can hope to be fully comprehensive. We include only items used in the text or requiring explanation in the context of the book's subject matter.

ABTA Association of British Travel Agents

Accredited Training Centres network of 54 (one for each AMB area) providing training for staff of MSC-funded schemes' managing agents and sponsors on a voluntary basis; not many volunteers.

Action Plan Scotland's vocational education programme for 16–19, devised after general curriculum 'reforms'; offers low-quality narrow 'modules'. Much praised by Conservative education ministers; so closely mirrored Conservative objectives that MSC control over NAFE did not have to be extended to Scotland.

ACTT Association of Cinematograph, Television and Allied Technicians.

AFE Advanced Further Education. Work at degree level and above.

AGCS Advisory Group on Contents and Standards. Sets bare-minimum criteria for YTS schemes; one-third of all monitored schemes fail to reach these; most YTS schemes still unmonitored.

AMB Area Manpower Board. Fifty-four local tripartite boards set up in 1983 to combine the functions of the old DMCs and SPABs; proceedings not public; members not elected but appointed by their organizations; supposed to oversee YTS and CP but defeated by workload, lack of information, poor attendance, absence of powers and lack of genuinely representative structure.

APEX Association of Professional, Executive and Clerical Staffs.

Apprenticeship form of training/work experience which was the traditional means of entry to skilled manual, and other, occupations.

A/S levels shorter academic courses to balance narrow A levels, confined mainly to small group already taking A levels.

ASTMS Association of Scientific, Technical and Managerial Staff.
ATS Adult Training Strategy, covers third objective of NTI (adult training) but having almost no funds available and striving to reassert employer control has little to offer.
AUEW Amalgamated Union of Engineering Workers.
AUEW TASS technical, advisory and supervisory (white collar) section.
AUT Association of University Teachers.

Basic Skills Unit MSC-funded project at Selwyn college, Cambridge, to develop materials for vocational education.
B/TEC Business/Technical Education Council. National body controlling courses and awards in a wide range of commercial and 'new tech' fields. Employers' influence increased sharply in early 1980s.
BIFU Banking, Insurance and Finance Union.
Black paper(s) pamphlet-style publications from rightwing educationalists in the 1960s and 1970s opposing comprehensive education, egalitarian reforms and progressive teaching methods; supported grammar schools, private schools, streaming, elitism and formality of teaching styles.

Careers Service a national public service assisting young people in choice of careers, with vocational guidance and information; coerced by MSC into role of 'gatekeeper' to YTS placement process in employers' interests.
CBI Confederation of British Industry.
CBT computer-based training. MSC-backed learning 'packages' being developed to replace face to face education and skills training.
CEDEFOP European Centre for Vocational Training. EEC vocational training organization based in Berlin.
CEP Community Enterprise Programme. Replaced STEP in 1981; provided adults with work, some very valuable in itself (though an average of 80 per cent of participants were men, mostly under 35); shut down abruptly to make way for lower-level CP in 1982.
CGLI City and Guilds of London Institute. Royal charter body in London devising courses and exams for skilled and semi-skilled workers on behalf of employers; with its technical courses now moving under B/TEC, increasingly turning attention to operative-level 'vocational preparation'.

CG 365 '365' is a CGLI life skills course of prevocational preparation, consisting of three Rs education, locally based 'social studies', plus some vocational options; widely used in streamed or tracked curriculum for the 'non-academic', and in YTS for off-the-job education.

CI Community Industry. Early special programme for the young unemployed, run by MSC, limited now to over-18s, being phased out or incorporated into YTS.

CITB Construction Industry Training Board. The second largest ITB retained in 1982; largest YTS managing agent.

CNAA Council for National Academic Awards. Body awarding and validating courses at degree level and above in polytechnics and colleges of higher education.

COIC Careers and Occupation Information Centre. Publishing unit of the MSC; produces information packs and MSC bulletins and publicity, including (the old) *Special Programme News*, *Newscheck*, *Youth Training News* and *Community Programme News*; spreads good news, firmly shuts out criticism.

Common Core the minimum curriculum (or set of subjects) required in any one school of all students, often associated with 14–16 age range; taking up from 20 per cent to 80 per cent of pupils' time, options taking up the rest.

Common Curriculum a course of learning devised by a school to be experienced in common by all pupils in the group or year, and taking up most of their time.

Comprehensive education education for 5–18s in schools or colleges which serve all pupils/students in a given area and offer the full range of education normally provided for their age range; no selection by attainment at entry; no differentiation in learning opportunities within; as common a curriculum as possible up to 16, and equality of choice thereafter. Not fully available anywhere after 13-plus due to selective national examination system but increasingly influential as a criterion for measuring advances in educational practice and organization.

Core main off-the-job educational component of training (YTS) courses; not yet developed; can mean a lot or very little, depending on the scheme.

Core skills supposedly the skills common to all OTFs of YTS; theoretically defined by such phrases as 'manual dexterity' or 'problem solving'; in practice, often a combination of low-level three Rs education and attitude-shaping subjects like Communications – with computer literacy to whet new-tech hopes.

Corporate Plan MSC's five-year plans for its own long-term development and expenditure, rolled forward and modified each year; examined each year by the Select Committee on Employment.

CP Community Programme, replaced CEP as make-work scheme for adult unemployed in 1982; after 1985 expanded numbers dramatically; year-long (often part-time) places by 1986; offers places mainly to men; pays low 'wages', displaces real jobs; often used for employers 'dirty work' jobs.

CPRS Central Policy Review Staff. Government 'think tank' abolished by Mrs Thatcher.

CPSA Civil and Public Servants Association.

CPVE Certificate of Prevocational Education. Year-long course introduced in 1985 for school leavers (sometimes also called the 17-plus); for both schools and colleges; includes education, introduction to the market economy and to employers' needs. Progressive methods of teaching and assessment conflict with reactionary objectives and low level of general education offered.

CRE Commission for Racial Equality.

CREMP Campaign for Racial Equality on MSC Programmes. Pressure group fighting race, sex and other forms of discrimination within YTS and the MSC.

CSCS Centre for the Study of Comprehensive Schools. Unit housed at York University, funded jointly by DES and several large private companies; collects valuable data; encourages good practice; steers comprehensives towards employer-approved development.

CSE Certificate of Secondary Education. Subject-based qualification designed for the middle 40 per cent of school leavers at 16-plus (when schools reorganized comprehensively in 1965); being rehoused inside GCSE.

CSEU Confederation of Shipbuilding and Engineering Unions.

CSU Civil Service Union.

CSU Community Skills Unit. Set up by National Council for Voluntary Organizations to advise on CEP and CP involvement, publishes *Reporter* magazine; Wales and Scotland have equivalent bodies; some work MSC-funded.

CTF Community Task Force. Largest single sponsor of CP programmes; others are NACRO and YMCA.

DE Department of Employment. Government department which houses the MSC.

DES Department of Education and Science. Oversees work of schools and colleges and operates through decentralized, locally accountable local education authorities (LEAs); has largest stake in vocational education and training; currently deferring to MSC in both fields.

DHSS Department of Health and Social Security. Has influence on training and access to it through restrictive benefit rules and regulations.

DI Department of Industry. Has some involvement in training through regional initiatives, ITECs and microelectronics policies.

DISC Drop-in Skills Centre. MSC experiment for motivated adults to get 'taster' skill courses; small business library; never developed widely.

DMC District Manpower Committee. Eighty-seven tripartite labour market committees which advised MSC at local level. Replaced by AMBs in 1983.

DOE Department of the Environment. Influences training policy through its inner-city policy and its general restrictions on local government spending.

EEC European Economic Community (the Common Market). No clear role in training/education according to its founding treaty but issues influential directives and controls channels of communication between governments and civil servants; operates ESF.

EEF Engineering Employers Federation.

EEPTU Electrical, Electronic, and Plumbing Trade Union.

EIS Educational Institute of Scotland. Trade union for school teachers and college lecturers.

EITB Engineering Industry Training Board. The major ITB retained in 1982.

EMA Educational Maintenance Allowance. Payments to students to enable them to stay on in full-time education at school or college after 16; not yet available in Britain.

Enterprise Allowance Scheme started 1982/3, gives year's income (currently £40 a week) to unemployed individuals/firms with some capital to start own business; about half succeed.

EOC Equal Opportunities Commission.

ERC Employment Rehabilitation Centres. Twenty-seven in 1983;

train disabled people; 16 per cent got jobs (1983).

ESL English as a second language. Any course teaching the English language to the non-English-speaking.

ESF European Social Fund. EEC fund providing some training money for equal opportunity schemes; much of UK's share of ESF is swallowed up by the MSC.

FE further education. The post-compulsory sector of education offering a wide range of learning to adults of all ages; housed in local colleges varying in size, range and nature of courses on offer; traditionally offering off-the-job education to apprentices, increasingly now to YTS as well.

FEU Further Education Unit. Established within DES in 1977 to advise FE service, particularly on 16–19 education development; pioneered quality vocational preparation for young workers; thunder and resources stolen by MSC's intrusion into education with low-quality mass training schemes.

FTAT Furniture, Timber and Allied Trades Association.

Full Employ voluntary body running schemes for young people under YOP and YTS.

General education traditional free space in the off-the-job training curriculum where young workers and trainees can increase knowledge and critical capacities; being squeezed out by 'new' vocational and 'communications' courses which often limit both.

GCE General Certificate of Education. Subject-based exam designed for the grammar school era; O level taken usually at 16-plus, designed for top 20 per cent of the age group; to be rehoused in GCSE.

GCE A level Subject-based two-year exam course, qualifying students for many professions and higher education, usually taken at age 18 and comprising 90 per cent of all sixth-form work; only 15 per cent of the age group get two or more passes (the minimum needed for higher education) – one of the lowest participation rates in the advanced industrial world.

GCSE General Certificate of Secondary Education. New 'single' examination for school leavers at 16 plus; subject-based, retains separate GCE and CSE grading and segregated papers; despite more teacher involvement, essentially the old assessment system in a new dress; due for introduction before the end of the 1980s but already facing serious support problems.

GLC Greater London Council. The elected local government of London; abolished by Conservatives in 1986 primarily because of its pioneering alternatives to monetarism.

GLEB Greater London Enterprise Board. Set up by the GLC to create/save jobs and promote new forms of ownership and control; £30 million annual budget.

GLTB Greater London Training Board. GLC training agency set up to promote skill training and implement alternatives to MSC programmes; £7 million annual budget.

GMBATU General, Municipal, Boilermakers and Allied Trade Union.

Great Debate discussion launched by Labour government in 1976 following Prime Minister's speech at Ruskin College exhorting schools to make education 'relevant' to work; began the process of moulding education to employers' interests.

Health and Safety Executive like the MSC, part of the Department of Employment.

HMI Her Majesty's Inspectorate. The officials who monitor schools' and colleges' programmes, progress and provision.

HND/C Higher National Diploma/Certificate. Degree-level technical or business courses and awards, now under control of the B/TEC Council and SCOTVEC.

IDS Incomes Data Services. A company providing regular information on incomes, industrial relations and training issues.

ILEA Inner London Education Authority. Largest LEA; Conservatives defeated on attempts to abolish it in 1985.

IMF International Monetary Fund. Demanded 'cuts' policy in Britain in 1976 as condition of loan to Labour government.

Industrial Society an organisation promoting 'harmony' in industry.

IPCS Institute of Professional Civil Servants.

IRS Industrial Relations Services. A company providing regular IR information.

IRSF Inland Revenue Staff Association.

ITB Industrial Training Board. Twenty-three boards set up by the Conservative Act of 1964 with responsibility for overseeing/ modernizing training in industrial sectors. All but seven of original 23 abolished by Conservatives in 1982.

ITECs Information and Technology Centres. MSC-staffed, DI-operated centres for training the young unemployed (in YTS) in computer literacy; glossy, high-tech part of YTS; only 1 per cent of trainees get to use centres, mostly for 'keyboard'/assembly skills.

JCP Job Creation Programme. Started by Labour government in 1975; ended by it in 1978.

Jobcentre replaced old labour exchanges as local MSC centres, advertise job vacancies, mainly for age 18 and over; cut back and rationalized under Conservatives; deregistration of unemployment reduced percentage of unemployed using them still further.

LCU Large Companies Unit. Special unit for MSC, London-based, dealing with UK's big (almost all private) employers; supposed to advise on their needs; in fact used to bypass scrutiny of AMBs in arranging YTS schemes; law unto itself, keeps low profile, though formally 'overseen' by YTB.

LEA local education authority. 104 in England Wales; in Scotland, regional councils are the education authorities.

Link a private training agency working closely with MSC to organize and run YTS schemes in office and clerical fields; national network of regional companies to organize training in business firms.

LRD Labour Research Department. An independent research organization which provides the labour movement with essential information on industry and the industrial relations aspects of training.

Management Action Programme MSC-backed service run by private consultants to advise local networks of executives and managers about business development.

Managing Agent private and public employers and private training agencies (PTAs, some profit-making) paid by MSC to devise and run the majority of all YTS schemes of training; about 4,000, but being reduced in number.

MIPD Manpower Intelligence and Planning Division. MSC think-tank on economic and labour market developments; publishes *Labour Market Quarterly*; produces Corporate Plan.

Mode A YTS schemes run by employers or by managing agents on employers' premises; form of training favoured by the Conservatives;

accounted for vast majority of YTS schemes at launch, now the basis of the 'two-year YTS'.

Mode B residual, non-employer-provided schemes in YTS; run direct by MSC, colleges or voluntary organizations; sometimes more responsive to needs of special groups; but persistently cut back in favour of employer-led Mode A.

MSC Manpower Services Commission. Set up by Conservatives in 1974 to co-ordinate employment and training; originally a small body with a budget of only £250 million, ten years later its budget was nearly £2,500 billion. Peak employment numbers (before job cutting associated with privatizing its services) were over 24,000 – all civil servants, headed by a permanent Director (currently Geoffrey Holland). The MSC operates as an arm of the Department of Employment and is controlled by the Employment Secretary. He is advised by a nine-member, all-male Commission (ten counting the Chairperson), three appointed with advice from CBI, three from TUC, two from local authorities and one with an educational 'interest'.

The Chairperson's office is in London, but the Commission's main operations moved to Sheffield in 1982, where currently there are four divisions. Two are small support divisions (one for statistics and planning – MIPD – the other for finance and personnel); and two are large operational divisions: Training Division (TD) and Employment Division (ED), accounting for nearly all the MSC's budget and staffing. Under TD comes youth training (YTS), adult training, the Open Tech and until hived off, the Skillcentres. Under ED, the Community Programme (CP), Jobcentres, Voluntary Projects Programme (VPP), disabled programmes, and professional employment services (PER). There is also a small 'education unit' (based in London) running TVEI and further education. Locally the MSC operates its TD and ED work through area offices which are supposedly overseen by a network of 54 tripartite appointed and generally toothless Area Manpower Boards (AMBs).

As the Glossary shows, programmes and projects were created (or recreated under new names) increasingly from the mid-1970s – mostly due to governments using the MSC to conceal and control the extent of unemployment. Early ones – e.g. YOP, STEP, CEP – were developed by Labour governments; those after 1979 by Conservatives, who used the MSC to forward their political plans to restructure the labour market in employers' interests and to privatize as much of education and training as possible – through a controversial new strategy set out in a New Training Initiative (NTI) in 1981. NTI proposed 'conscripting' the young into compulsory, low-paid 'work experience' (later launched as the Youth Training Scheme – YTS); cut back the MSC's original skill-training operations, abolished most of the Industrial Training Boards, scrapped or cut many MSC training programmes; privatized Skillcentres in 1983, closing the 'uneconomic' ones in 1986; and changed TOPs training for adults from genuine skill training to low-quality courses and small self-employment schemes.

Hard-line Conservatives put like-minded people in to run the MSC. In 1982 David Young, merchant banker, former chair of ORT UK, former advisor to a Conservative Cabinet minister, was put in to chair the Commission through the critical launching of NTI, and especially the YTS. In 1984 he was replaced by Bryan Nicholson, seconded from Rank Xerox, supposedly 'independent' of Cabinet ministers. Under the leadership of Young and Nicholson the MSC became increasingly undemocratic and dictatorial. It expanded its empire into mainstream education to mould as much of it as possible to serve employers' interests: first the school curriculum through TVEI; next the further education colleges, taking control of 25 per cent of non-advanced further education (NAFE); and in 1986 moving into teacher training. It also vastly extended the CP and short-life, part-time 'community' make-work schemes (instead of jobs) for unemployed adults.

The MSC's operations and jargon are promoted by massive propaganda and publicity. The constant and confusing changes as MSC schemes and programmes disappear (or reappear in new dress) are justified in glossy handouts. Policy already agreed, and often being implemented, is covered by spurious 'consultative' documents. As the high-quality work and long-term planning of the MSC decreases, escalating complaints are met by public relations activity about changes planned to end old abuses, or by appearing to offer more 'work' or 'training' to wider numbers of the unemployed. In reality, most new arrangements systematically worsen pay, conditions, quality and choice of what is on offer to the majority. Only a small minority experience high-quality or innovative schemes. The MSC's much vaunted capacity to get things moving is simply funding power.

NACRO National Association for the Care and Resettlement of Offenders. A voluntary organization running YTS and CP schemes.

NAFE Non-advanced further education. Courses and programmes in colleges below degree level.

NALGO National Association of Local Government Officers.

NAS/UWT National Union of Schoolmasters/Union of Women Teachers.

NATFHE National Association of Teachers in Further and Higher Education. Main union for those who teach in further education; opposes YTS.

National Labour Movement Enquiry into Youth and Community Training independent, Sheffield-based labour movement investigation of MSC activities.

NEB National Enterprise Board. Investment/industrial restructuring agency set up by Labour government in 1975; quickly moved away from its radical intentions to become crutch for lame capitalists.

NEDC National Economic Development Council ('Neddy'). Tripartite economic planning agency set up in the early 1960s.

NEDO National Economic Development Office.

NGA National Graphical Association.

NIEC National Institute for Careers Education and Counselling. Produce MSC-commissioned reports.

NTI New Training Initiative. Launched in 1981 as MSC 'consultative document' outlining key Conservative strategy of restructuring the labour market and education to suit employers' short-term interests; NTI had three objectives, none yet successful: 1. to 'modernize' skill training in UK; 2. to equip all young people for work; and 3. to widen opportunities for adults through an Adult Training Strategy (ATS).

NUJ National Union of Journalists.

NUM National Union of Mineworkers.

NUPE National Union of Public Employees.

NUR National Union of Railway Workers.

NUS National Union of Students. Organises YTS trainees in colleges.

NUT National Union of Teachers.

Off-the-job education or training which takes place away from the work situation, at college, workplace, PTA, or elsewhere.

OND/C Ordinary National Diploma/Certificate. First-level technical and business awards for courses in business and technical fields, now under control of B/TEC Council and SCOTVEC.

Open Tech started 1982, MSC programme developing distance learning to employers' specifications; guided by Open Tech Steering Group, produced Open Tech Task Group Report, 1982; high profile, low output.

ORT Organization for Rehabilitation and Training. Private European training organization; influenced David Young, once president of its UK section.

OTF Occupational Training Family. Nine groupings of work activities within YTS, held to have similar training requirements; being used in planning the 'work' to which most vocational courses will lead; groupings are crude; two ('administration/clerical work' and 'personal service work') account for over 35 per cent of all YTS and 65 per cent of all young women in YTS. On the other hand, less than 2 per cent of either sex being trained for the OTF are called 'scientific'.

PEL Paid Educational Leave. Legislation giving workers rights during their working lives to return to education for short courses (retaining jobs and full pay meanwhile); not yet available in Britain.

PER Professional and Executive Recruitment. MSC-funded service to find jobs for unemployed middle-class professionals and managers; operated separately from Jobcentres through a separate Jobsearch Unit and Jobsearch Centres, with access to VPP funds.

PICKUP Professional, Industrial and Commercial Updating. DES unit to encourage FE and HE to provide updating courses for those already employed.

Practical Action MSC-funded appeal in 1983 to private employers for cast-off equipment and expertise to use in YTS.

Prevocational Education preparing people for work in a limited range of occupations; often offered to those deemed 'non-academic' during schooling; later, courses devised for those who 'fail' the 16-plus or who are on training schemes.

PRISE Programme for Reform in Secondary Education. A school-based campaign for innovation and good practice in comprehensive schools.

Project Trident a charity using staff seconded from large companies to 'help' schools give unpaid work experience to pupils from age 14.

PTA Private Training Agency. A private company running training schemes for the MSC.

Quality Branch MSC unit developing curriculum, assessment and trainer training; has Quality Advisors (seconded from industry and education) to oversee Programme Development team; work still rudimentary.

REITS Racial Equality in Training Schemes. A campaign concerned with ending race discrimination in YTS and CP.

REPLAN small DES initiative in response to adult unemployment, financed by cuts to other parts of the DES budget.

RICE Right to a Comprehensive Education. An umbrella group campaigning for the development of genuine comprehensive education in schools and colleges.

RSA Royal Society of Arts. Body which awards qualifications in a range of clerical skills – e.g. typing; also devises vocational courses in office skills, based on employers' needs.

SCDI Scottish Council for Development and Industry. Tripartite, independent agency set up in early 1940s.

SCOTEC and **SCOBEC** Scotland's Business and Technical Education Councils. Devised SCVS (Scottish Certificate in Vocational Studies, roughly equivalent to CPVE, running since 1983); replaced by SCOTVEC in 1985.

SCOTVEC Scottish Vocational Education Council, unified replacement of SCOTEC and SCOBEC.

SDA Scottish Development Agency. Independent investment agency which pursues training initiatives with private firms and local authorities in Scotland. Largely concerned with small firms, property and 'glossy' new-tech initiatives.

SDA Sex Discrimination Act. Law passed in 1975 making it an offence to discriminate on grounds of sex; many areas of education and training are outside it, however.

SERTUC South East Region of the TUC.

Skillcentres local workshops equipped to train people in a variety of skills (over 95 per cent of users being male); a public service being privatized under Conservatives' NTI through the STA; one-third of the centres were closed down by 1986 as 'uneconomic' – in preparation for new 'market-led' adult training.

SLS social and life skills. Courses (or components of vocational education) teaching young people how to accommodate to consumer society, the market economy and employers' needs; some scope for genuine personal development if devised independently.

SOGAT Society of Graphic and Allied Trades.

SPB Special Programmes Board. Set up in 1978 to advise MSC on YOP and STEP.

SPB and **SPABs** Special Programmes Board and 28 tripartite Special Programme Area Boards set up in 1978 to oversee YOP and STEP, replaced by AMBs in 1983.

SCPS Society of Civil and Public Servants.

Sponsors main vehicle for early Special Programmes (STEP, YOP, etc), gradually displaced by managing agents as part of NTI; still used to refer to providers of work schemes in CP.

SSRC Social Science Research Council.

STA Skillcentre Training Agency. Separated off from MSC in 1983 to run Skillcentre training commercially, paved the way for closure of 'uneconomic' Skillcentres after 1985.

STEP Special Temporary Employment Programme. Set up in 1978 for adult unemployed, forerunner of CEP and CP and the best of the MSC adult programmes in terms of conditions and quality.

Subcontractor employer with small workforce (usually under 25 and non-unionized) taking trainee(s); in schemes run by managing agents, through a consortium of linked subcontractors, or run by a PTA.

Tertiary college a further education college which provides a range of full-time and part-time courses for adults (how wide a range varies with the college) and also incorporates all local sixth-form work.

TES *Times Educational Supplement*. *Times* Group newspaper covering education and training issues.

TGWU Transport and General Workers Union.

TOPs Training Opportunities Programme. Started in 1973; main, high-quality training programmes for adults through short (up to one year) courses in Skillcentres and FE colleges; now being run down as part of ATS, with skill training being cut and preference given to low-quality YTS-type courses.

Tripartite CBI, TUC and government. As in membership of the MSC.

Tripartite the division of secondary (and nowadays also tertiary) education into segregated academic, technical and 'non-academic' tracks or sectors.

TSP Training for Skills Programme. MSC's first-year apprenticeship support programme; ended when YTS started.

TUC Trades Union Congress.

TURC Trade Union Resources Centre. Centres funded by LEAs or TUC, offering advice and resources to local people at work or unemployed.

TVEI Technical and Vocational Educational Initiative. Course introduced by MSC into selected schools in 1983 without prior consultation; initially, lavishly funded five-year pilot experiment; MSC evaluating it with view to replicate it; majority of LEAs taking part (to get the funding). TVEI aims to hive off significant bloc of 14–18 age group for narrow, vocationally based education and work experience; an important aspect of the drive to undermine comprehensive education, but being used in a few schools for significant comprehensive-compatible innovation.

21 hours courses Return to Learn courses in schools and colleges requiring less than 21 hours study time a week (to observe DHSS rule removing supplementary benefit from those studying longer hours); effectively disbars the poor from certain key areas of general education after 16.

/ Ultravox

UCATT Union of Construction, Allied Trades and Technicians.

UCW Union of Communications Workers.

UGC University Grants Committee. Unaccountable, unelected body which doles out (relatively) generous funds to universities; used by Conservatives to reshape university sector and make it more 'relevant' to employers' needs.

USDAW Union of Shop, Distributive and Allied Workers.

UVP Unified Vocational Preparation.

Vocational education and training defined by the MSC as 'preparing people for work in a particular occupation', but generally not applied to education or training for the professions or management; often applied only to those not staying on in full-time or 'academic' education after 16.

Voluntary sector organizations run by voluntary groups or charities; some co-operate with the MSC, others do not.

VPP Voluntary Projects Programme. Small MSC work programmes of short duration (often no more than a few weeks) for volunteers. No training allowances are paid.

WAMT Women and Manual Trades. Independent campaigning and support organization in the manual, male-dominated trades.
WE Work Experience. Component of traditional skills training; frequently used in MSC schemes as substitute for real work which employers get for nothing.
WEP Work Experience Programme. Started by Labour government in 1975, replaced by YOP and STEP in 1978.
WEEP Work Experience on Employers Premises. Part of YOP which Labour government started in 1979; accounted for three-quarters of YOP expenditure; often used to replace proper jobs by trainee labour; ended 1983 when YTS work experience replaced it.
Women in YTS research and campaigning organization concerned to protect the interests of young women on YTS.
Work Introduction Courses run by MSC for young people in FE colleges; part of now-dead YOP.
WOW Wider Opportunities for Women. Tiny MSC-funded programme, equal opportunities figleaf.

YOP Youth Opportunities Programme. Started in 1978 at request of TUC by a Labour government; widely disliked for its poor quality and widespread job substitution (in at least a third of places). By 1981 was processing some half a million young people every year, 90 per cent of them school leavers without a GCE O level; replaced by (an often little different) YTS in 1983.
Youthaid pressure group concerned with all issues affecting young people, including training; critical of YTS and other MSC programmes.
Youth Services National public service assisting young people in personal and social and recreational development; increasingly expected to pick up the casualties from MSC schemes.
Youth Skills Project MSC-commissioned project at University of Sussex to develop training for under-18s.
Youth Task Group set up by Minister of Employment (then Norman Tebbit) to push through YTS proposals and diffuse widespread criticism of NTI's youth training; published a report in 1982 suggesting improvements, most of which never materialized.

YTB Youth Training Board. Tripartite board appointed by the Employment Minister; advises MSC on YTS and helps to shape the new consensus. It supposedly also oversees the activities of the LCU.

YTS Youth Training Scheme. Launched nationally in 1983 as the main element of the NTI; initially a 12-month scheme for school leavers, now has a second year (supposedly more job-related); pays low allowances; offers as yet little real training during off-the-job portion in most schemes; quality education minimal; contains widespread discrimination and leaves most trainees with few rights and little choice. Some schemes are breaking new ground, but most serve employers with cheap labour. A significant number of young people 'refuse' or drop out; vast majority fail to get work with employer who 'trained' them; nearly half go back on dole at the end; those who get jobs would have got them anyway.

YTURC Youth Trade Union Rights Campaign. Started by Labour Party Young Socialists to organize youth against exploitation by MSC; labour movement leadership rarely co-operates with it, although it is one of the few attempts to organize young people.

YWS Young Workers Scheme. Wage-cutting scheme for young workers, started in 1982 and opposed by TUC; ended in 1986 when it impeded extension of YTS to a two-year programme.

Bibliography

T. Addy, 'The MSC and the Management of Unemployment', in *Christian Social Concern: Two Contemporary Issues*, The William Temple Foundation, Occasional Paper 12, Manchester Business School, Manchester, 1984.

M. Anderson and J. Fairley (eds.), *The Politics of Industrial Training Policy*, University of Edinburgh Centre for European Governmental Studies, Conference Papers, Edinburgh, 1982.

M. Apple (ed.), *Cultural and Economic Reproduction in Education*, Routledge & Kegan Paul, London, 1982.

P. Atkinson *et al.*, *Social and Life Skills: The Latest Case of Compensatory Education*, Cardiff University Sociological Research Unit, Cardiff, 1980.

AUEW-TASS, *TASS on Training*, London, 1982.

J. R. Austen, 'Black Girls on the Youth Training Scheme', unpublished M.Sc. thesis, Research Unit on Ethnic Relations (RUER), University of Aston, Birmingham, 1984.

Action for Youth Rights and Opportunities (AYRO) *Conference Reports*, London, 1985.

I. Bake (ed.) *Schooling for the Dole? The New Vocationalism*, Macmillan, London, 1984.

B. Barker, 'The Myth of Technology: the MSC and the Comprehensive School', in *Head Teachers' Review*, Winter 1983.

J. Barnes, *Unemployed Centres: a Critical View*, Newcastle Trades Council, 1984.

G. Barr, 'Further Education and the YTS: Time to Pull Out', *NATFHE Journal*, London, October 1984.

G. Barr and P. Aspinall, 'FE and the YTS: Thoughts on Year One', *NATFHE Journal*, London, October 1984.

L. Barton *et al.*, *Race, Class and Education*, Croom Helm, London 1983.

A. Benavot, 'The Rise and Decline of Vocational Education', *Sociology of Education*, Vol. 56, No. 2, 1983.

C. Benn and B. Simon, *Half Way There: The Comprehensive School Reform*, Penguin, London, 1972.

C. Benn, 'A Comprehensive World: Education and Training in Japan, Norway and the USSR', in H. Pluckrose and I. Wilby (eds.), *The Condition of English Schooling*, Penguin, London, 1979.

C. Benn, 'A Good Idea in a Bad Cause?' *Annual Guide*, National Association of Careers and Guidance Teachers, 1986.

C. Benn, 'Independence and Accountability for All: The Private Sector', in A. M. Wolpe and J. Donald (eds.), *Is There Anyone Here From Education*?, Pluto Press, London, 1983.

C. Benn *et al.*, 'The Education of Girls and Women: An Equality Policy for Labour', *Socialism and Education*, Vol. 9, No. 2, 1983.

C. Benn *etal.*, 'Equality Control in the Classroom – Discrimination against Girls and Women in Education', *New Socialist*, No. 17, June 1984.

C. Benn, 'TVEI – Time to Speak Up', *The Careers and Guidance Teacher*, Spring 1984.

C. Benn, 'CPVE: Learning Your Place', *Teaching London Kids*, No. 22, 1984.

Birmingham Careers Service, *Facing Decline and Change: A Study of the Destinations of Birmingham School and College Leavers in 1983*, Birmingham, 1984.

Birmingham Trades Council, *Review of TVEI*, Birmingham, 1984.

R. Boffey, 'Further Education and the YTS', *NATFHE Journal*, October 1984.

R. Boffey, 'Further Education and the YTS Core', *NATFHE Journal*, March 1985.

R. Boudon, *Education, Opportunity and Social Inequality*, John Wiley, New York (USA), Chichester (UK), 1974.

F. Bourdieu, 'The School as a Conservative Force', in R. Dale *et al*, (eds.), *Schooling and Capitalism*, Open University, Milton Keynes, 1976.

C. Boyle and J. Grassby, 'The MSC: What Next?' *NATFHE Journal*, December 1984.

I. Breugel, 'Women as a Reserve Army of Labour: A Note on Recent British Experience', *Feminist Review*, No. 3, 1979.

P. Broadfoot (ed.), *Selection, Certification and Control, Issues in Educational Assessment*, Falmer Press, Lewes, 1984.

H. Brown *et al.*, *Class of '84*, Report of Girls on YTS by the Fawcett Society and the National Joint Committee of Working Women's Organizations, London, January 1985.

J. Bruner, *Towards a Theory of Instruction*, (USA), 1961.

Careers Workers Action Group (CWAG), *Better Training, Real Jobs*, London, 1982.

Central Policy Review Staff, *Education, Training and Industrial Performance*, HMSO, 1980.

Centre for Contemporary Cultural Studies, Birmingham, *Unpopular Education: Schooling and Social Democracy Since 1944*, Hutchinson, London, 1981.

Centre for the Study of Comprehensive Schools (CSCS), feature on TVEI in *Contributions*, York, Winter 1984.

J. Chambers, 'The YTS and the Education Service', *Secondary Education*, NUT, London, March 1985.

Child Poverty Action Group, 'YTS and Welfare', *Welfare Rights Bulletin*, No. 56.

J. Clarke and P. Willis, Introduction to I. Bake (ed.), *Schooling for the Dole?*, Macmillan, London, 1984.

F. Coffield, 'Is There Work After the MSC?' *New Society*, 26 January 1984.

P. Cohen, 'Against the New Vocationalism', in I. Bake (ed.), *Schooling for the Dole?*, Macmillan, London, 1984.

P. Cohen, 'School for the Dole', *New Socialist*, January 1984.

M. Cole and B. Skelton, *Blind Alley: Youth in a Crisis of Capital*, Hesketh Publishers, Ormskirk, 1980.

Commission for Racial Equality (CRE), including:

D. Brooks and K. Singh, *Aspirations vs. Opportunities, Asian and White School Leavers in the Midlands*, 1978.

Look for Work: Black and White School Leavers in Lewisham, 1978.

Response to the New Training Initiative, 1981.

G. Lee and L. Wrench, *In Search of Skill: Ethnic Minority Youth and Apprenticeship*, 1981.

YTS Study: Southwark, 1984.

Equal Opportunities and the YTS, 1984.

Racial Equality and the YTS, 1984.

Communist Party, 'The New Training Initiative', a statement, 1982. *Comprehensive Education*, special issue No. 48, 1984: *TVEI and YTS: Are They Compatible With Comprehensive Education?*, including Anne Jones, 'TVEI and YTS in Comprehensive Education'; Morris Kaufman, 'YTS: Hopes or Threats?'; Peter Hamilton, 'Some Reflections on the YTS'; Dan Finn, 'The MSC and the YTS – First Year'; Tom Dodd 'TVEI'; Bernard Barker, 'Is TVEI Compatible With Comprehensive Principles?'; P. Green and D. Poat, 'TVEI in One School (Countesthorpe)'; Beryl Fawcett, 'TVEI and Comprehensive Education'.

Confederation of British Industry, *YTS: An Information Guide*, 1982.

Confederation of Health Service Employees (COHSE), 'Discussion Paper on the MSC and Related Special Programmes', H. Barnard, July 1983.

Conference of Socialist Economists (CSE), 'Critique of the Youth Training Scheme', *Journal*, Winter 1983.

Conservative Party, *A Time for Youth*, Central Office, 1978.

G. Courtenay, 'Analysis of Data from the Survey of YOP Entrants 1980–81', unpublished paper, SCPR, London, 1983.

M. Cross, *Training Opportunities for Ethnic Minorities in the UK*, ESRC, Research Unit for Ethnic Relations, University of Aston, 1982.

M. Cross, *Equality of Opportunity and Inequality of Outcome: The MSC, Ethnic Minorities and Training Policy*. Centre for Research in Ethnic Relations, Warwick University, 1985.

M. Cross, *The Training Situation of Ethnic Minority Young People in Britain*, CEDEFOP, Berlin, 1985.

D. Cumming, 'Qualifications, Jobs and Unemployment', unpublished paper, Nottingham, 1983.

R. Dale *et al.* (eds.), *Schooling and Capitalism*, Open University, Milton Keynes, 1976.

G. Daniel, 'Training in Crisis Conference', introduction to GLC Conference on Training, London, 10 May 1984.

B. Davies, 'Thatcherite Visions and the Role of the MSC', *Youth and Policy*, Spring 1984.

R. Deem, *Schooling for Women's Work*, Routledge & Kegan Paul, London 1980.

S. Delamont, 'The Sociology of Women', *Studies in Sociology*, George Allen & Unwin, London, 1980.

Department of Education and Science (DES), including:

Half Our Future (Newsom Report), HMSO, 1963.

Curriculum 11–16, HMI, 1977.

16–19 Education (MacFarlane Report), 1979.

A Framework For the School Curriculum, 1980.

The School Curriculum, 1981.

School Education in England: Problems and Initiatives, unpublished, 'yellow-book', July, 1976.

Mapping 16–19 Education, jointly with the Schools Council, 1982.

Costing Education 16–19, 1982.

Report on the Youth Training Scheme in Further Education, HMI, 1984.

17-Plus, A New Qualification, 1982.

Better Schools, Cmnd 9469, 1985.

Education and Training for Young People, Cmnd 9482, 1985.

Further Education Unit:

Unified Vocational Preparation: A Pilot Approach, 1976.

A Basis for Choice, first edition, 1979.

Day Release – Desk Study, 1980.

Curriculum Control, A Review of Major Styles of Curriculum Design in FE, 1981.

Vocational Preparation, 1981.

Progressing From Vocational Preparation: The Issues, 1982.

Profiles: A Review of Issues and Practice in the Use and Development of Student Profiles, 1982.

A Basis for Choice, A Report of a Study Group on Post-16 Pre-employment Courses, second edition, 1982.

Teaching Skills: Towards a Strategy of Staff Development and Support for Vocational Preparation, 1982.

Supporting YTS: Guidance for Colleges and Others Involved in YTS, 1982.

B. Emery *et al. Evaluation of FE Contribution to the YTS 1983–1984*, 1984.

Department of Employment (DE), including:

Unqualified, Untrained and Unemployed, 1974.

A New Training Initiative: A Programme for Action, Cmnd 8455, 1981.

(With Cabinet Office), *Vocational Training and New Information Technologies: New Community Initiatives 1983–1987*, HMSO, 1982.

The Role of the Careers Service in the Youth Training Scheme, 1983.

Training For Jobs, Cmnd 9135, 1984.

'First Employment of Young People', *Department of Employment Gazette*, October 1984.

Employment the Challenge for the Nation, Cmnd 9474, 1985.

Devon County Council and the Institute of Local Government Studies, Conference on the Management of Change in the 14–19 Sector, *Report*, 1984.

P. A. Dutton, 'The New Training Initiative: What are its Chances?', *Managerial Law*, Vol. 23, No. 4, 1981.

P. A. Dutton, 'YTS – Training for the Future', *Public Administration*, Vol. 62, Winter 1984.

P. A. Dutton, 'The Development of Training Policy 1979–82', in M. Anderson and J. Fairley (eds.), *The Politics of Industrial Training Policy*, University of Edinburgh, Edinburgh, 1982.

Edinburgh and District Trades Council, Youth Committee, *What is YTS?*, 1983.

Education, Science and Arts Committee of the House of Commons, including: *Education and Training 16–19-Year-Olds*, Session 82/3, HMSO, 1983.

T. Edwards, *The Youth Training Scheme: A New Curriculum*, Falmer Press, Lewes, 1984.

Employment Committee of the House of Commons, including:
The Work of the Department of Employment Group, HC 594 iv, v and vi, Session 1979–80.
The Manpower Services Commission's Corporate Plan 1980–84, HC 444, Session 1979–80.
The Manpower Services Commission's Corporate Plan 1981–1985, HC 101, Session 1980–81.
The Manpower Services Commission's Corporate Plan, 1983–87, HC 262-i, Session 1982–3.
The Youth Training Scheme, HC 335-i, Session 1982–3.
Youth Unemployment and Training: New Training Initiative, HC 221-i and iii, Session 1981–2.

Engineering Industry Training Board, *Economic and Industry Monitor*, March 1985.

H. Entwhistle, *Antonio Gramsci, Conservative Schooling for Radical Politics*, Routledge & Kegan Paul, London, 1979.

Equal Opportunities Commission, *Sidetracked? A Look at Careers Advice Given to Fifth-Form Girls*, 1981.

Estimates Committee of the House of Commons, including: *Manpower Training for Industry*, HC 548, 1966–67.

European Economic Community, First Action Programme: *Transition of Young People from Education to Adult Working Life* and *Girls and Transition*; Second Action Programme, *Thirty Pilot Projects*, Brussels, 1984.

T. Evans, 'YTS: More Questions than Answers', *Socialism and Education*, Vol. 10, No. 1, 1984.

Expenditure Committee of the House of Commons, *People and Work, Prospects for Jobs and Training*, HC 105, Session 1977–8.

Fabian Society.
'On To A Comprehensive Employment Service', B. Showler, No. 309, 1973.
Education Beyond School, Young Fabians, 1974.
The Rise of the MSC, C. St John Brooks, 1985.

J. Fairley, 'The YTS and Democracy', *Youth and Policy*, Winter 1984.

J. Fairley, 'The Great Training Robbery', *Marxism Today*, November 1982.

J. Fairley and A. Gordon, 'The Skillcentre Closures,' *Radical Scotland*, April/May 1985.

M. Fairley, 'Foundation Training for All', *NATFHE Journal*, May 1982.

J. Farley and J. Grahl, 'Conservative Training Policy and the Alternatives', *Socialist Economic Review*, Merlin Press, London, 1983.

R. Fiddy, *In Place of Work*, Falmer Press, Lewes, 1983.

D. Finn, 'A New Deal for the Young Unemployed', *Youth and Society*, Spring 1983.

D. Finn, 'Britain's Misspent Youth', *Marxism Today*, February 1983.

D. Finn, 'Leaving School and Growing Up: Work Experience in the Juvenile Labour Market', in I. Bake (ed.), *Schooling For the Dole?*, Macmillan, London, 1984.

D. Finn *et al.*, 'Social Democracy, Education and the Crisis', in G. MacLennan *et al.* (eds.), *On Ideology*, Hutchinson, London, 1978.

D. Finn and G. Markall, *Young People and the Labour Market: A Case Study*, Department on the Environment, 1981.

Forum For New Trends in Education, special issue: *A Comprehensive Approach to the Education and the Training of the 16–19 Age Range*, Vol. 25, No. 1, 1982. Joan Simon, 'Agenda for Action'; Maurice Plaskow, 'The Three Nations'; Clyde Chitty, '16–19: Learning for Life'; Hilary Steedman, 'Training Provision in Europe'; John Fairley, 'The Decline of Industrial Training'; Valerie Glauert, 'Schools and the 16–18s'; Ian Morgan, 'The Tertiary Connection: Curriculum in Action'; Michael Austin, 'The Tertiary College Solution'.

Further Education Staff College, Coombe Lodge:
MSC: Securing a Future for Young People, 1978.
Further Education and Industrial Training in England and Wales, 1984.
Coombe Lodge Reports, including:
'New Patterns of Initial Skill Training: a Trade Union Response', Vol. 16, No. 6, 1983.
'YTS and the Education Service', Vol. 16, No. 7, 1983.

A. Gamble, 'Thatcherism and Conservative Politics', in S. Hall and M. Jacques (eds.), *The Politics of Thatcherism*, Lawrence & Wishart, London, 1983.

General, Municipal, Boilermakers and Allied Trade Union, *YTS Handbook and Agreements*, 1983.

B. Gibson, 'Employers' Selective Criteria in YTS Schemes', *MSC Forum Report*, Newcastle-on-Tyne Trades Council, 1984.

D. Gleeson, 'Tripartitism and the Labour Market', in D. Gleeson, (ed.), *Youth Training and the Search for Work*, Routledge & Kegan Paul, London, 1983.

N. Goldstein, 'The New Training Initiative: A Great Leap Backward', *Capital and Class*, June 1984.

A. Gramsci, *Selections From Prison Notebooks*, in Q. Hoare and G. N. Smith (eds.), Laurence & Wishart, 1983.

W. Grant and H. Rainbird, *Employers' Associations and Training Policy*,

Institute for Employment Research, Warwick University, 1985.

J. Grassby, 'Responding to Radical Change', *NATFHE Journal*, December 1983.

Greater London Training Board, Discussion Papers, including: 'The YTS in London', 1983; 'Adult Training Strategy', 1983; 'Review of the NTI', 1981–4; 'Training in Crisis', 1984; 'Training and Disability', 1985; 'The London Labour Plan', 1985.

Greater London Training Board Reports, inluding: *'Comments on the MSC Corporate Plan 1983–4*, (TB96); *Comments on the MSC Corporate Plan 1984–8* (TB234); *Training for Women in London* (TB50); *Promoting Equal Opportunities for Women*, (TB304); *MSC Proposals to Close Skillcentres*, (TB317); *The Skillcentre Training Agency and Adult Training* (TB332); *YTS and Compulsion*, (TB334); *The Community Programme*, (TB338)

A. Green, 'Under New Masters', in A. M. Wolpe and J. Donald (eds.) *Is There Anyone Here from Education?*, Pluto Press, London, 1983.

D. Gregory and C. Edgar, 'Youth Unemployment and MSC Special Programmes', *Trade Union Responses from Wales and the North West of England*, William Temple Foundation, Manchester, 1980.

W. N. Grubb and M. Laverson, 'Vocational Solutions to Youth Problems: The Persistent Problems of the American Experience', *Education Analysis*, Vol. 3, No. 2, Summer 1981.

Hackney Trade Union Support Unit, *Training for Recovery*, 1983.

G. Hainsworth, '16–19: The Need for a Comprehensive Appraisal', *Secondary Education*, NUT, London, March 1983.

S. Hall, 'Education in Crisis', in A. M. Wolpe and J. Donald, *Is There Anyone Here From Education?* Pluto Press, London, 1983.

S. Hall and M. Jacques (eds.), *The Politics of Thatcherism*, Lawrence & Wishart, London 1983.

A. Harvey, 'MSC (Social Engineers) Ltd', *NATFHE Journal*, April 1985.

C. Hayes, *Foundation Training Studies, A Report for MSC*, Institute of Manpower Studies, 1982.

Health and Safety Executive, *Proposals for Regulations Extending the Coverage Under Health and Safety Legislation of Trainees on the Youth Training Scheme*, HMSO, London, 1983.

D. Hirsch and C. Short, 'Young and Tebbit Strike', *Liberal Education*, No. 48, Spring 1983.

D. Hofkins, 'A Pattern for the Future', *Education*, 31 August 1984.

G. Holland, 'The Challenge of Long-Term Unemployment', address to the Stock Exchange, 18 June 1984.

M. Holt, 'Vocationalism, the New Threat to Universal Education', *Forum*, Vol. 25, No. 3, Summer 1983.

Home Office Research Unit, *Ethnic Minorities in Britain: A Study of Trends in Their Position Since 1961*, Fields *et al.*, Report No. 68, 1981.

S. Iliffe, 'Dismantling the Health Service', in S. Hall and M. Jacques (eds.), *The Politics of Thatcherism*, Lawrence & Wishart, London 1983.

Income Data Services:

Young Workers Pay, June 1983. *The Youth Training Scheme*, Study 293, July 1983, *YTS: A Review*, 311, April 1984.

Independent Labour Party (ILP):

Labour Leader, Supplement on YTS, 1982.

NTI: An Exposure, 1982.

YTS: The Tories Poisoned Apple: A Critique of YTS, P. Scoffield *et al*, 1983.

Industrial Relations Services, *Guide to the Youth Training Scheme*, Industrial Relations Review and Report, 1983.

Industrial Society, *A Survey of Training Costs*, 1985.

Industrial Training Research Unit, *A–Z Study*, 1981.

International Labour Organization (ILO), *Youth Unemployment: Social Aspects and Attitudes*, G. Schneider, 1977.

I. Jamieson, *Schools and Industry: Some Organizational Considerations*, Schools Council Industry Project, Part 2, 1982.

R. Jenkins, 'Managers, Recruitment Procedures and Black Workers', Working Papers on Ethnic Relations, No. 18, Research Unit on Ethnic Relations, University of Aston, 1982.

K. Jones, *Beyond Progressive Education*, MacMillan, London, 1983.

M. Kaufman, 'Is There a Future for Training?', *NATFHE Journal*, May 1981.

D. Knox and S. Castles, 'Education with Production: Learning from the Third World', *International Journal of Educational Development*, Vol. 2, No. 1, 1982.

M. Kogan, *The Politics of Educational Change*, Fontana, London, 1978.

Labour Movement National Inquiry into Youth Unemployment and Training, 'Critique of the TUC/Labour Party's "Plan for Training" ', *Bulletin*, No. 2, September 1984.

Labour Party:

16–19 Learning for Life, 1982.

YTS: Attack on Young Workers, Labour Party Young Socialists (LPYS), 1982.

A Charter for Young Workers, LPYS.

Youth, The Tory Record, 1983.

Give Us a Future: Jobs for Youth Campaign, 1983, (with TUC).

Proposals for YTS, LPYS, 1984.

A Plan for Training, 1984, (with TUC).

Education 5–16: Parents' Charter, 1985.

'A Socialist Policy for Education and Training', study group paper, 1986.

Labour Research Department:

Youth Training: A Negotiator's Guide, 1983.

'Join Your Union', leaflet for YTS trainees.

Bargaining Report, No. 30, (YTS), December 1983.

'Young Workers Scheme', October 1981.

Bulletin:

'Decline of Apprenticeship', August 1982 and January 1983.

'YTS in Practice', December 1983.

'Growth of Private Training Agencies', March 1984.

G. Lander, 'Further Education and Corporatism: The Significance of the Business Education Council', in D. Gleeson (ed.), *Youth Training and the Search for Work*, Routledge & Kegan Paul, London, 1983.

D. Lawton, 'The Curriculum and Curriculum Change', in B. Simon and W. Taylor (eds.), *Education in the Eighties*, Batsford Academic, London, 1981.

C. Lea, 'TVEI Report', *Forum*, Vol. 26, No. 2, Leicester, 1984.

G. Lee and J. Wrench, *In Search of a Skill: Ethnic Minority Youth and Apprenticeships, A Summary with Recommendations*, CRE, 1981.

Lewisham Women's Employment Project, *Women and Training: Who said Opportunities?*, 1981.

D. Lisle, 'Training of Women and Girls', *Training and Development*, September 1984.

S. MaClure, 'The Educational Consequences of Mr Norman Tebbit', *Oxford Review of Education*, Vol. 8, No. 2, 1982.

A. McMurray, 'Comprehensive Schools: Threatened or Challenged?', *Forum*, Vol. 26, No. 1, Leicester, 1984.

A. McRobbie and T. McCabe, (eds.), *Feminism For Girls*, Routledge & Kegan Paul, London, 1982.

Manpower Services Commission

Annual Reports:

Corporate Plan, updated annually and published each year since 1982: 1982–6; 1983–7; 1984–8.

Vocational Preparation for Young People, 1975.

Young People and Work, G. Holland, 1977.

Training For Skills: A Programme for Action, 1977.

TOPs Review, 1978.

Ethnic Minorities and the Special Programmes for the Unemployed, Special Programmes, Special Needs, 1979.

Give Us A Break: Widening Opportunities for Young Women, 1979.

Outlook on Training, A Review of the 1973 Employment and Training Act, 1980.

National Training Survey, 1975–6, *Employment Gazette*, November 1980.

Young Workers and the Labour Market, A Case Study (with Department of Environment), G. Markall and D. Finn, 1981.

A New Training Initiative, A Consultative Document, May 1981.

A Framework for the Future, Sector by Sector Review of Industrial and Commercial Training, 1981.

Review of the Third Year of Special Programmes, 1981.

Off-the Job-Training on YOP: a Summary of Research Findings in Work Experience Schemes, 1979–82, K. Greaves, P. Gostyn and C. Bonsall, 1982.

Youth Task Group Report, 1982.

Long-term Unemployment, Manpower Paper, 1982.

Voluntary Organizations and Special Programmes, September, 1982.

Information for Sponsors, Community Programme, 1982.

Open-Tech Task Group Report, 1982.

Job Training: YOP and YTS, by K. Greaves *et al.*, 1983.

School and Community Planning Research Report, Survey of Community

Programme Participants, 1983.

Towards an Adult Training Strategy, 1983.

'Youth Training Scheme – A Sign of Quality' (three sheets), 1983.

Training and Ethnic Minorities: Case Studies in Three Areas, B. Sheppard, Manpower Intelligence and Planning, 1983.

Women in Skillcentres, M. Nicod, 1984.

Managing 'gents Direciory, Mode A Schemes (3,500 entries), 1984.

Equal Opportunities in the Youth Training Scheme, February 1984.

Standards and Controls, The Key to YTS Quality, G. Tolley, 1984.

Ethnic Minorities and the Youth Training Scheme, Youth Training Directorate, 1985.

Reports to the Youth Training Board, 1984–1985.

Survey of YTS Providers, Youth Training Board, March 1985.

Review of the Area Manpower Boards, 1984.

MSC Research and Development Series:

'Youth Unemployment and Special Measures', No. 1, 1981.

'Trainee-Centred Reviewing', No. 2, 1981.

'Young People on YOP', No. 3, 1981.

'Trainees Come First', No. 4, 1981.

'Guidance and Support Within the Youth Opportunities Programme', No. 5, 1982.

R. Stares *et al.*, 'Ethnic Minorities and Their Involvement in MSC Special Programmes', No. 6, 1982.

'CEP is Working', No. 6, 1982.

'Training Workshops', No. 8, 1982.

'Learning at Work', No. 9, 1982 '10'.

'Work Introduction Courses', No. 10, 1982.

'Off-the-Job Training on YOP', No. 11, 1982.

M. Cross *et al.*, 'Ethnic Minorities – Their Experience on YOP', 1983.

T. Bedemann and G. Courtenay, 'One in Three – The Second National Survey of YOP', No. 13, 1983.

'Youth Opportunities in a Rural Area', No. 14, 1983.

'Voluntary Work and Unemployment', No. 15, 1983.

'YOP In Contrasting Local Areas', No. 16, 1983.

S. Fenton *et al.*, 'Ethnic Minorites and the Youth Training Scheme', No. 20, 1984.

V. Millman *The New Vocationalism in Schools*, Coventry LEA, 1984.

V. Millman *Teaching Technology to Girls*, Elm Bank Teachers Centre, Coventry, 1984.

J. E. Monk 'School Pupils' Opinions of the New Youth Training Scheme', *Links*, Vol. 8, No. 3, 1983.

M. Moos, 'The Training Myth: A Critique of the Government's Response to Youth Unemployment and its Impact on FE', in D. Gleeson (ed.), *Youth Training and the Search for Work*, Routledge & Kegan Paul, London, 1983.

M. Moos, 'A Critique of YTS', *Liberal Education*, No. 48, Spring 1983.

R. Murray, 'New Directions in Municipal Socialism' in B. Pimlott (ed.), *Fabian*

Essays in Socialist Thought, Gower, London, 1984.

National Association of Multicultural Education (NAME), *Black Youth, YTS and Choice*, 1983.

National Council for Voluntary Organizations, *Reporter*, February 1985.

NATFHE:

The Education, Training and Employment of the 16–19 Age Group, 1977.

The Great Training Robbery: An Interim Report on the Role of Private Training Agencies within the YTS in the Birmingham and Solihull Area, Birmingham Liaison Committee, 1984.

National Association of Youth Clubs, *Working With Girls Newsletter*, issues 20 and 21 ('Women, Unemployment and the YTS).

National Economic Development Council and MSC *Competence And Competition*, 1984.

National Foundation for Educational Research (NFER): *Learning and Earning: Aspects of Day Release in Further Education*, W. Van Der Eyken and S. M. K. Barry, 1975. *Employer Involvement in Schemes of UVP*, 1982.

National Joint Council of Working Women's Organizations, *Report on Youth Training Scheme*, 1982.

National Youth Bureau

B. Davies, *From Social Education to Social and Life Skills: In Whose Interests?*, 1979.

B. Davies, *The State We're In: Restructuring Youth Policies in Britain*, 1981. *Social Education in YOP*, 1981.

The Youth Worker As Educator and Trainer

B. Troyna and D. Smith, *Racism, School and the Labour Market*.

G. Lee and J. Wrench, *Skill Seekers: Black Youth, Apprenticeships and Disadvantage*, 1983.

Trainee Participation in YTS: Principles and Practice, 1984.

YTS and Racial Minorities: Equality or Inequality, 1985.

Network Training Group, *Training and the State: Responses to the Manpower Services Commission*, Manchester, 1983.

NUS, *A YTS Pack* (for students in FE colleges).

NUT, *Guide to Careers Work*, H. Dowson, 'My Fears for TVEI', 1985.

T. O'Brien, 'Enough to Make you WEEP', *Leveller*, No. 6, 1981.

Office of Population Census and Surveys: *Labour Force Survey*, 1981; *Country of Births and Ethnic Origin*, 1983.

Organization for Economic Co-operation and Development (OECD), *Education and Working Life*, 1977.

P. J. C. Perry, *Sand in the Sandwich*, British Association for Commercial and Industrial Education (BACIE), London, 1984.

P. J. C. Perry, *The Evolution of British Manpower Policy*, BACIE, London, 1976.

J. Pilger, A critique of YTS, *Daily Mirror*, 15 February 1985.

A. Pollert, *Racial Discrimination and the Youth Training Scheme*, West Midlands YTS Research Project, Birmingham, 1984.

A. Pollert, *Unequal Opportunities: Racial Discrimination and the Youth Training*

Scheme, TURC Publishing, Birmingham, 1985.

C. Pond, 'The Generation Gap', *New Statesman*, 1984.

Public Accounts Committee, House of Commons (Department of Employment and MSC), *Special Employment Measures, Fourth Report*, Session 1983/4, HMSO, London, 1984.

D. Raffe, 'The End of the Alternative Route? The Changing Relation of Part-time Education to Work-Life Mobility among Young Male Workers', in D. Gleeson (ed.), *Youth Training and the Search for Work*, Routledge & Kegan Paul, London, 1983.

J. Randall, 'NTI: How the MSC Benefits Education', *Socialism and Education*, Vol. 10, No. 1, 1984.

Rank and File, College Issue, 1982: 'MSC and the YTS, Critique from FE'.

S. Ransom, 'Towards a Tertiary Tripartism: New Modes of Social Control and the 17-plus', in P. Broadfoot (ed.), *Selection, Certification, and Control*, Falmer Press, Lewes, 1984.

T. L. Rees and F. Atkinson, *Youth Unemployment and State Intervention*, Routledge & Kegan Paul, London, 1983.

A. Richardson, 'Construction Training and the State in Britain', Bartlett School Paper, University College, London, 1984.

K. Roberts *et al.*, 'Racial Disadvantage in Youth Labour Markets', in L. Barton *et al.*, *Race, Class and Education*, Croom Helm, London, 1983.

Rubber and Plastics Processing Industry Training Board:
  The Education/Training of 16–18-Year-Olds, 1975.
  Work and Learning: Proposals for a National Scheme for 16–18-Year-Olds at Work, 1978.

P. Ryan, 'The New Training Initiative After Two Years', *Lloyds Bank Review*, April 1984.

Harry Salmon, *Unemployment: Government Alternatives and the MSC, A Radical Look at Government Policy*, Association of Community Workers, 1982.

B. Salter and T. Tapper, *Education, Politics and the State*, Grant McIntyre, 1981.

Scottish Committee, House of Commons, *Youth Unemployment and Training*, Vol. 2, HC 96ii, Session 1980–81, HMSO.

Scottish Council for Development and Industry, *Youth Training and Beyond: An Appraisal*, Edinburgh, 1985.

Scottish Council for Research in Education, 'Modules for All?', discussion paper by C. E. Spencer on new proposals for the education of 16–18s, 1984.

Scottish Education Department, *Action Plan, New Courses for 16–18*, HMSO, 1983.

Scottish Vocational Preparation Unit (SCVOP), Jordanhill College: *Crossing the Threshold, 1983*; *Assessment in Youth Training: Made to Measure?*, 1984.

C. Seale, 'FEU and MSC: Two Curricula Philosophies and their Implications for the Youth Training Scheme', *Vocational Aspects of Education*, Vol. xxxvi, No. 9, May 1984.

P. Sharp, 'The Lessons of YOP', *Liberal Education*, No. 49, Summer 1983.

Clare Short, 'Time to Quit the MSC', *Labour Herald*, 7 January 1983.

B. Simon, *Does Education Matter?*, Lawrence & Wishart, London, 1985.

B. Simon and W. Taylor (eds.), *Education in the Eighties: The Central Issues*, Batsford Academic, London, 1981, including 'The Curriculum and Curriculum Change' by Denis Lawton.

Socialist Educational Association (SEA): *A Review of YTS*, 1985; *16–19*, 1985.

Socialism and Education:

Vol. 8, No. 2, 1981, YOP issue (Clare Short, Mick Farley, Neil Kinnock, Roy Jackson).

Vol. 8, No. 3, Youth and Community issue (David Smith, Judith Young, Barbara Bleiman, The Community Challenge Group).

Vol. 10. No. 1, 1983, Education and Training Issue (J. Hamilton, J. Randall, V. Stern and C. Waugh).

Vol 1, No 2, 1985, 16–19 Education issue: Going Tertiary.

Socialist Society, *The Youth Training Scheme: A Strategy for the Labour Movement*, (C. Benn, M. Moos, A. Green and C. Waugh), 1983.

Society of Civil and Public Servants, *Back to Work: An Alternative Strategy for the MSC*, October 1982.

J. Solomon, *The Politics of Black Youth Unemployment*, Aston University, May 1983.

South East Region TUC (SERTUC), *Comments on the New Training Initiative*, 1981.

D. Spender, *Invisible Women*, WPRC, 1982.

D. Spender and J. Sarah (eds.), *Learning to Lose*, Women's Press, 1980.

V. Stern, 'YTS: The Doubts of the Voluntary Agencies', *Socialism and Education*, Vol. 10, No. 1, 1984.

Trade Union Resources Centre, Birmingham (TURC): YTS Trainees' Rights Card; Video Library of TV coverage of MSC and Training Issues; *Rights? Wot Rights?*, video profile of the YTS.

Training Research Group, *Training on Trial: Government Policy and the Building Industry*, Conference of Socialist Economists, London, October 1981.

Transport and General Workers Union

Manchester Region, Youth Training and the MSC: The Need for a Trade Union Response', Manchester, March 1983.

Guide to YTS, London, 1983.

The Youth Training Scheme, London, 1984.

TUC:

Industrial Training Consultative Conference, Discussion Document, March 1981.

Youth Training: a Guide for Trade Union Negotiators, 1982.

MSC's Youth Training Scheme: TUC Handbook, 1983.

Women in the Labour Market, March 1983.

Plan For Training, (with the Labour Party), 1984.

Unemployment Unit:

Youth Wages and Unemployment, 1983.

'Critique of Community Programme', Paper No. 4, September 1982.

'Myth of Public Spending', Paper No. 6, February 1983.

'How Britain Compares' (to other countries), Paper No. 7, May 1983.

UNESCO, *Educational Planning and Unemployed Youth*, A. Callaway.

T. Warren, 'What will "Training for Jobs" Mean for the Colleges?', *NATFHE Journal*, February 1985.

K. Watson *et al.*, *Youth, Education and Employment*, Croom Helm, London, 1983.

A. G. Watts, *Education, Unemployment and the Future of Work*, Open University Press, 1983.

A. G. Watts, 'Political Education in YTS', *Liberal Education*, No. 49, Summer 1983.

A. G. Watts, 'Skill Transfer and Post-YTS Realities', *Lifeskills Teaching Magazine*, April 1983.

C. Waugh (ed.), *Fighting for Further Education: A Collection of Papers from the NATFHE General Studies Group*, 1985.

C. Waugh, 'Guidelines for YTS', *Liberal Education*, No. 48, Spring 1983.

C. Waugh, 'YTS: In Whose Interests? The Coming Struggle for the Left', *Socialism and Education*, 10, No. 1, 1984.

R. White *et al.*, *Tales Out Of School*, Routledge & Kegan Paul, London, 1983.

J. White, *The Areas of Education Restated*, Routledge & Kegan Paul, 1982.

J. Williams, 'Abergale – Trailblazers in TVEI', *The Careers and Guidance Teacher*, Spring 1984.

R. Williams, *Culture and Society*, Penguin, Harmondsworth, 1958.

R. Williams, *The Long Revolution*, Penguin, Harmondsworth, 1961.

N. Williamson, 'YOPs: Taiwan Wages', *Tribune*, 1982.

P. E. Willis, *Learning to Labour – How Working-Class Kids Get Working-Class Jobs*, Saxon House, 1977.

W. Wilms, 'The Dubious Promise of Post-Secondary Vocational Education', *International Journal of Educational Development*, Vol. 2, No. 1, 1982.

A. M. Wolpe and J. Donald, *Is There Anyone Here From Education?*, Pluto Press, London, 1983.

Women and Manual Trades (WAMT), *Women in the Trades*, Report on a USA conference, London, 1983.

Women's Action Group (WASSAG), 'Critique of Community Programme', September 1982.

J. Wrench, 'Ethnic Minorities and the Youth Training Scheme', unpublished paper, Research Unit for Ethnic Relations, Aston University, 1983.

M. F. D. Young, 'Taking Sides Against the Probable', *Education Review*, Vol. 25, No. 3, 1973.

Youthaid:

'Education and Training for 14–19-Year-Olds', 1978.

'YOP and UVP: the New FE or a Tertiary Modern System?', G. Holland, M. Kaufman and G. Melling, 1981.

Annual Reports, 1983, 1984, 1985.

'Quality or Collapse? Review of YOP', 1981.

'Unemployment and YOP in the Inner City', A. Sawdon *et al.*, 1982.
'Cheap Labour?', G. Markall, 1983.
'Youth Unemployment, A Background Paper', D. Hirsch, 1983.
'What Opportunities for Youth?', P. Jones, 1984.
YTS Briefing Paper, 1984.
'The Vanishing Youth Labour Market', D. Ashton and M. Maguire, 1984.
'Studying on the Dole: An Investigation of Part-time Study by Unemployed
    Claimants under the 21 Hour Rules', John Pelican, 1984. 'Nothing Like a
Job', C. Horten, 1985. 'Report of a Study of the First Year of the YTS in
London', 1986.
Bulletin:
'The Failure of YOP', No. 1, December 1983.
'Health and Safety: The New Evidence about YTS', No. 18, October 1984.
'The Price of a Job', P. Lewis, December 1984.
YTS Workers Bulletin, London: 'Critique of YTS', Issues 1, 1983; Critique of
the 2 and 3, Community Programme, Issues 8 and 9, 1983.